The Economics and Management
of System Construction

Management Studies Series

under the editorship of E. F. L. Brech, B.A., B.Sc. (Econ.), F.B.I.M.

The Economics and Management of System Construction

by George Leon,
M. Phil., F.R.I.C.S., F.I.O.B., F.I.Arb.

Longman

LONGMAN GROUP LIMITED
London

Associated companies, branches and representatives throughout the world

© Longman Group Limited 1971

First published 1971

ISBN 0 582 44580 9

Printed in Great Britain by
William Clowes & Sons Limited,
London, Colchester and Beccles

Contents

List of Illustrations

ix

List of Plates

The plates appear between pages 13 and 14.

Preface

The large number required of all types of building, and the shortage of available skilled labour for their construction has led to the development of mechanised methods of factory production and site erection for the manufacture, assembly, and rapid construction of standardised buildings and component parts in order to achieve greater productivity, minimise site labour requirements, and reduce total construction costs.

The prefabrication of building components can reduce material costs by standardising high outputs, minimise site labour costs by finishing and assembling in the factory components which incorporate services and fittings, replace manual labour by machinery, and substitute semiskilled or unskilled factory workers for skilled craftsmen on site.

Industrialised system building subordinates the costs of enclosing large spaces to a minimum of standardised components manipulated to achieve a variety of buildings with diversity of shape, height and appearance. Economic construction depends upon efficient design, programming and control of all operations; coordination of design, manufacturing and erection processes; and adequate volume of sustained demand.

Selected ranges of standardised components available on the open market and suited to the requirements of each particular building type could provide a flexible architecture of interchangeable parts of buildings with adaptability to improved space and living standards. Ultimate economy is obtained when the design factor determined all the processes involved. Present diverse and uncoordinated industrialised building techniques obviate the possibility of merely assembling 'open' components selected from Catalogues of British Standard Component parts for all types of buildings. Until Government policy provides for a planned long-term sustained demand for a vast programme of new buildings geared to the building and allied manufacturing industries' capacities to undertake it, system building will tend to achieve faster construction and increased outputs rather than economy of cost when compared with techniques based on traditional methods of construction which employ more site labour and less prefabrication.

Acknowledgements

The author wishes to express his appreciation and acknowledgement of the help and courtesies afforded to him by Professor Z. S. Makowski (Head of Faculty) and Mr. R. L. Wajda (late Reader) of the Department of Civil Engineering, University of Surrey, Mr. E. F. L. Brech (former Chief Executive of the Construction Industry Training Board) and the following Government Departments, Local Authorities, Organisations, Industrial Firms and Professional Institutes by their permission to undertake research on building sites and in factories under their control, and use their libraries: The Greater London Council, The Ministry of Public Building and Works, The Ministry of Health, The Ministry of Education, The Ministry of Housing and Local Government, The Building Research Station, Garston, The National Building Agency, The Cement and Concrete Association, The British Iron and Steel Federation, The Association of Industrialised Component Manufacturers Ltd., The Aluminium Federation, The Hampshire County Council, The Royal Institution of British Architects, The Royal Institution of Chartered Surveyors, The Institution of Building, The Institution of Quantity Surveyors, The Institution of Arbitrators, The Institution of Civil Engineers, The British Museum, and the many individuals, trade and professional journals, development associations, foreign Research Institutions, and firms of Building and Civil Engineering Contractors and Component Manufacturers who have afforded him assistance in undertaking research, and wish to remain anonymous.

One of the author's greatest pleasures in undertaking this research was to meet with so much kindness and help from the Construction Industry and Allied Trades and Professions. He received much assistance from so many sources, that it is possible there have been some ommissions in these acknowledgements. The author therefore asks anyone who has not wished to remain anonymous, but has been overlooked, to accept his sincere apologies and most grateful thanks.

The publishers wish to thank the Ministry of Public Building and Works for supplying the detail from which figure 3.13 was drawn, and also for Plate 2 (Crown copyright). Wates Construction Ltd. kindly supplied the illustrations of Panel Systems in Chapter 3, and Plates 1 and 3.

1

Review of Existing Systems

Industrialised system building comprises methods of planning and organising the increased production and rapid assembly of standardised buildings and their component parts integrated into a complete building by coordinating design requirements with industrialised production techniques and machinery in order to speed erection and save manpower. These results are achieved by various methods which involve: the factory production of standardised complete buildings; the integration into a building system of standardised structural steel sections, or prefabricated precast concrete structural elements and mass produced non-structural components of various materials incorporating services or parts of services; rationalised methods of poured in-situ concrete construction for structures, and prefabricated components for finishings; and rationalised brick load-bearing structural elements, with prefabricated secondary elements such as front and rear timber clad infill panels, floors, and roofs, which are handled to position and fixed by crane in one operation.

The sequences of traditional building constitute well defined boundaries as between structural work, cladding, carcassing, finishing trades, and decorations. Such divisions are less clearly defined in system building, where a structural element may contain service pipes and electrical conduits, be faced externally, and finished sufficiently smooth and true internally as to require only decoration on exposed room surfaces.

Industrialised building systems are designed to minimise site labour and the adverse effects of bad weather on erection operations, avoid chance happenings, eliminate cutting, fitting and wastage of materials, and determine the economic mass production of a minimum number of standardised components and the methods and sequence of their rapid and simple assembly.

One example of the substantial cost reductions that can be achieved by efficient standardisation is evidenced by the savings obtained through standardising 35 to 55 ft bridge sections in 1957. At current prices, these cost approximately 30 per cent less than similar non-standard sections, despite the great increases in costs that have taken place since that date.

Building systems are suited to the standardisation of complete single unit buildings on individual sites, such as small factories, sub-stations, rural schools and the component parts of most types of buildings which can be standardised. They are not appropriate for special purpose buildings, such as museums and churches.

The economic standardisation of industrially manufactured components needs to be based on a more developed application to selected building types than at present in order to provide a wider range of design within limited component ranges. In theory, the economics of enclosing large spaces with standardised frames and cladding units is mainly influenced by the number of components designed to achieve aesthetic effect. There is no fundamental difference between the requirements of a four-person dwelling type or a hundred-person maternity ward type hospital, whether to be built in London or Reading, except for variations in the substructure due to differing site conditions—the same basic standards apply within the buildings. But at present components are being designed and manufactured in relation to an excessively large number of different types of systems for too limited a variety of building types on the basis of non-integrated and uncoordinated conceptions. This complexity prevents the full advantages of system building being obtained, which include optimum replacement of manpower by machinery; rapid speed of construction; improved standards of finish due to more controlled and accurate factory processes; reduction of temporary ancillary works such as scaffolding and shuttering; reduction of non-productive time due to bad weather, drying out wet trades, and one trade waiting on another; economic factory production costs derived from large serial runs; obviating by accuracy of manufacture time required for cleaning down, cutting and fitting, and making good; reduction of design costs; good psychological effects in the operatives due to their witnessing the rapid results of their work.

Centralised management of the whole building process is essential from design stage to completion of construction works. This includes the coordination and design of modular planning, tolerances and jointing techniques; weathering details, thermal and acoustical insulation, cladding finishes, standardised structural elements based on strength and cost economy; dry finishings; mechanical, plumbing, and electrical services design and installation, crane layouts, erection sequences, the economical balance of site labour and mechanical plant, and the coordination of factory production and delivery sequences.

Climatic conditions and available local sources of materials strongly influence the types of building systems most economically suited to a particular country. In the U.S.S.R. which has long and extended cold winter months when site work is difficult, housing systems are based on the indoor factory production of large dense pre-cast concrete panels or boxes for the rapid construction of high rise blocks of dwellings during the comparatively short summer months. In the U.S.A. domestic building is mostly based on low-rise timber construction, because machinery is cheap compared with labour, and timber is readily available and suited to factory mass production methods for components. In Great Britain timber construction is expensive compared with concrete and brickwork, and is mainly used for fittings and secondary elements such as infill cladding units, floors and roofs.

The main disadvantages of industrialised system building relate to design disciplines required for standardisation, which impose certain restrictions on freedom of design, and dependence upon adequate volume demand for economic factory component production.

'CLOSED' AND 'OPEN' SYSTEMS

At present, two different categories of systems are used in Great Britain for industrialised building: 'closed' and 'open' systems. This distinction does not exist in countries with a planned and controlled economy.

'Closed' systems are operated by sponsoring contractors on the basis of proprietary and often continental designs, subject to the payment of royalties for production under licence in relation to a limited range of building types based on the sponsors' assessment of market conditions. A severely limited number of structural elements, which are not interchangeable with other systems, are individually designed and manufactured by each separate sponsor of a 'closed' system, and supplemented with standardised non-proprietary components obtainable in the open market from outside manufacturers.

Sponsors have fairly complete control over these firms, as they are usually specially selected to accord with their own particular expertise.

As a consequence, they are able to ensure that deliveries of these components are geared to suit site assembly requirements in order to avoid any delays to the cycle of erection operations.

'Open' systems are not subject to the payment of royalties, and are based on components designed by government departments, local authorities, and other clients for buildings with similar basic requirements and performance standards, with sufficient flexibility to comprehend other types of building. A system of standardised structural elements is dimensionally coordinated with a sub-system of standard non-proprietary components which are designed and selected for assembly in different ways. Examples of such systems include:

The 'Public Building Frame', designed by the Ministry of Public Building and Works in conjunction with the Cement and Concrete Association. This is an open system not tied to any commercial interests, which incorporates standardised profiles of precast concrete framing suited to most types of multistorey buildings. The basic elements comprise storey height columns, edge beams with end cantilevers, and a minimum of other components which can be readily assembled and jointed with simple grouted dowel connections.

The Compendium of Hospital Building Assemblies is published by the Ministry of Health for the Industrialised Hospital Building Programme in order to ensure that components and assemblies presented in the Compendium have the widest possible use in the Hospital, Health and Welfare programmes. This procedure saves designers' time in producing a system; and eliminates separate tendering for individual projects by selecting three or four component manufacturers in national competition. It enables designers to select standardised components from the Compendium which are suited to the hospital programme, and schedule those selected for pricing at the most competitive rates offered.

The C.L.A.S.P. and S.C.O.L.A. systems[1] are suited to schools, and developed and controlled by consortia composed of various educational authorities who have pooled their potential resources and building programmes in order to obtain a sufficient volume of demand for economic industrialised production. These types of systems are complicated, and provide contractors with less control over site deliveries of manufactured components.

[1] Consortium of Local Authorities (C.L.A.S.P.); Second Consortium of Local Authorities (S.C.O.L.A.)

Some component manufacturers have developed their products to form essential features of certain open systems. The liaison between main contractor and component manufacturer can be differently arranged in both open and closed systems. Thus the 'A.75' system for dwellings is based on a central coordinating group which arranges for the delivery of materials and components for site erection by a main contractor who is not made responsible for their specification and ordering.

METHODS OF SYSTEM PRODUCTION
Standardised complete buildings

The manufacture of complete buildings by flow-line production methods is suited best to small unit buildings with similar requirements on individual sites. Such buildings can be economic in cost, but are generally lacking in flexibility of design and aesthetic value, and are unadaptable to social changes. One current attempt to mass produce low cost standardised 'semi-permanent' dwellings with light new materials is based on glass reinforced polyester units lined with thermo-plastic, with a life of about thirty years. The units are of standardised exterior shape for connection on all sides, top and bottom. Self-contained living cells are designed which can be grouped together to form any type of house from a single-storey terrace design to a two-storey family dwelling with spiral staircase and courtyard. The minimum plan layout consists of three separate units, which contain an entrance hall with bathroom, a kitchen/dining unit, and a living/sleeping unit, and cost approximately £300.

In the U.S.A. ranges of standardised complete dwellings of timber frame construction are listed in catalogues and mass produced in vast quantities each year for delivery in packages and rapid erection on prepared foundations. Some factories producing these dwellings are based on automated methods, and provide a variety of twelve designs for low cost dwellings with areas ranging from 1100 to 3800 sq ft (102·19 to 353·03 m²).

In addition to this type of housing approximately 220,000 new mobile homes are prefabricated each year, and delivered to sites complete with all fixtures and fittings, including refrigerators, washing machines, and furniture. Site installation consists of manoeuvring the unit onto prepared foundations, and connecting up services in a matter of hours.

Complete rooms are prefabricated for insertion into existing blocks of dwellings to improve living standards in New York slum areas. Factory produced kitchen and bathroom units are hoisted by crane and inserted one on top of the other through specially prepared openings formed in existing roofs and floors. Each unit comprises a self-contained heating plant, kitchen and bathroom; with a refrigerator, sink, gas stove, fitted cupboard, bath, shower, toilet and medicine chest. The time required to instal one unit is six days of eight working hours each. Such construction would normally take five to six months with traditional methods.

In Great Britain, standardised complete bungalows and other building types are mass produced at low cost. Factory-made single-storey steel frame standardised buildings of various types are also available. They are designed on the basis of plastic theory, and programmed on a computer which can produce the optimum economic design to suit user requirements within one day. Portal frames ranging from 30 ft (9·144 m) to 150 ft (45·72 m) span and 16 ft (4·88 m) in height are mass produced in 15 ft (4·57 m) and 20 ft (6·10 m) lengths for delivery to site and completion of the structure within two weeks.

Standardised structural elements combined with non-structural components

Steel structural elements obtained from outside manufacturers. Most systems for multistorey buildings are based on reinforced concrete structural elements or rationalised composite steel and concrete construction rather than on steel frame skeletons, for reasons of fire protection and economy. Numerous steel based systems have been designed for schools, factories, low-rise dwellings, and other simpler building types, which incorporate light steel structural elements, and cladding units of timber, sheet metal, or various other materials.

The MAES system for dwellings is based on light steel foam-filled panels forming load-bearing curtain cavity walls, and shuttered steel frames with poured in-situ concrete casings.

The PREFRAME system for hospital construction is based on standard steel sections for columns, and standardised joist, castellated, and open-web lattice beams.

Some systems suited to two-storey dwelling types are based on light steel joist or tubular sections, with sheet metal or other type of cladding.

The S.C.O.L.A. system for schools up to four storeys in height is based on a light steel frame with lattice type beams, 3 ft 4 in (1·02 m) planning grid, and a range of components for which bulk purchase tenders can be obtained for Consortia requirements.

The N.E.N.K.[1] system developed by the Ministry of Public Building and Works for all types of services buildings is based on a 4 ft × 4 ft (1·22 m × 1·22 m) grid, with $2\frac{3}{4}$ in (69·85 mm) and 4 in (101·60 mm) square steel columns, 2 ft (0·61 m) deep double layer flat grid space decks formed from 4 ft × 4 ft (1·22 m × 1·22 m) (on plan) pyramids constructed with mild steel angles, and steel rod or tube diagonals.

This complicated system is supplemented with the Ministry's precast concrete frame or panel systems.

Precast concrete structural elements. Precast concrete structural elements for closed panel, frame, or composite precast and poured in situ concrete systems are manufactured to suit individual sponsors' required productions. Permanent factories are installed away from the site for the production of vast continuous outputs of units to serve many different projects, or alternatively temporary factories are set up on individual sites for the limited requirements of each particular project, and subsequently dismantled for use on other sites.

The elements required for open systems may be similarly produced, or else obtained by contractors from outside specialist manufacturers of precast concretework.

Precast concrete panel systems are used extensively in Great Britain, Europe, the U.S.S.R., Japan and elsewhere abroad for housing developments, and comprise wall and floor panel units with jointed connections for box-shell construction. A minimum number of structural elements are standardised for economic production and simple, rapid site erection. Factory production of the elements achieves close control of the concrete to obtain improvement in quality, savings in materials costs, satisfactory finishes to exposed concrete surfaces and incorporation of service pipes and electrical conduits in the moulds. Maturing of the concrete takes place before units are built into the structure, thus eliminating shrinkage of fresh concrete.

Panel systems require an adequate volume of sustained demand for economic factory production. In the U.K. outputs of units for 1800 dwellings per annum can be obtained with a speed of site erection averaging nine hours crane time and 120 man-hours per dwelling.

[1] N.E.N.K. is the name given to an open and modular method of building developed by a team working under Sir Donald Gibson, Director-General of Research and Development, Ministry of Public Buildings and Works.

Greater outputs are obtained in some countries which have a controlled economy and less stringent building regulations.

Frame systems. Frame systems permit extensive unification of the structural frame based on a modular system suited to building types with relatively large areas and spans. Their main disadvantage is that too many other structural elements cannot be standardised so readily for economic factory production and coordination into a complete system. As a result, floors, staircases and stability walls are often constructed with poured in-situ concrete, thus involving two erection teams and reducing crane productivity.

Some systems suited to high-rise structures incorporate an increased standardisation and coordination of structural elements. By standardising T-shape spine frames and L-shape traverse frames stabilised by precast concrete floor slabs and perimeter beams, panel units for party walls and gable ends can be incorporated to complete the basic structure.

In the U.S.A. prestressed precast concrete structural elements have been developed to provide very large open spans. Units of 110 lb per cu ft (1762·03 kg per m³) density with strength of 5000 lb per sq in 351·54 kgf/cm²) at twenty-eight days are cast with large ducts for service pipes and pre-finished smooth on top surfaces and soffits to form wall, floor and roof elements up to 100 ft (30·48 m) long × 8 ft (2·44) wide and 20, 21 and 22 in (508·00, 533·40 and 558·80 mm) deep. Permissible loading on floor units varies from 62 lb to 108 lb per sq ft (302·52 to 527·28 kgf/m²) for spans up to 70 ft (21·34 m) and 283 to 400 lb per sq ft (1381·72 to 1952·97 kgf/m²) for spans up to 40 ft (12·19 m).

The precast concrete structure of a two-storey school in California with 59,000 sq ft (5481·28 m²) of classroom area incorporating such units was recently constructed on prepared foundations in fifteen days at a cost of £4 10s per sq ft (£48·80 per m²).

Composite precast and poured in-situ concrete systems. Systems for dwellings based on the factory production of load-bearing precast concrete wall units and poured in-situ concrete floor construction compensate tolerances in the erection of walls and other vertical units, and obviate the complex jointing of fully precast concrete systems.

Site factory production of units for 1500 dwellings a year can be achieved with rapid erection by comparatively few operatives. A tower block with forty-eight dwellings can be erected in forty working days of 9½ hours each with one erection crane and associated teams of twenty-two men.

Rationalised methods of poured in-situ concrete construction

Systems utilising these methods are based on designs of prefabricated shuttering or proprietary steel shutters, steel reinforcement, methods of accelerated concrete curing, and available sources of aggregates.

For limited volumes of production insufficient to justify the economic installation of a site factory, carefully designed systems based on poured in-situ concrete construction can approach the productivity, speed, and accuracy of precast concrete panel construction. Such methods are unsuited to vast-scale production because of the larger number of site man-hours required, and the limitations of batching plant and equipment.

Fast construction is obtained by prefabricating standardised shutter elements of steel or timber for handling by cranes in large accurate units to form both wall and floor shutters. The concrete is formed with surfaces capable of spray painting or wall papering. Accelerated concrete curing reduces the striking time of shutters so that floor slabs poured during an afternoon can be self-supporting the following morning. Cracking in slabs is reduced by introducing limestone or light-weight aggregates, such as pulverised fuel ash. Reinforcing units are designed of maximum size for handling by cranes. The units can be wired together with electrical and other services at ground level and hoisted to position in one operation. Site labour can be reduced by prefabricating partitions and cladding panels which incorporate plumbing and electrical services, and help to achieve accuracy of the structure.

Rationalised methods of brick construction

These methods are used mainly for low-rise dwellings and include construction based on prefabricated storey height brick panels and mechanised methods of handling bricks, and traditional brick load bearing structural elements dimensionally coordinated to brick sizes so that bricklayers can complete their work independently of other operations. Secondary elements such as infill panels, floors and roofs are handled to position and fixed complete in one operation by crane. When combined with a suitable mechanical handling system for off-loading palletised brick deliveries, conveyers for transporting the pallets to required positions, and platform hoists to speed the handling of bricks to higher levels, systems based on these methods can achieve high productivity with comparatively low site manhours.

Patented methods of precasting standard bricks into 12 ft × 5 ft (3·66 m × 1·52 m) units with a similar potential to precast concrete panel construction are suited to most building types up to about thirteen storeys in height.

External wall panels are prefabricated with a brick outer skin, and a light-weight inner concrete skin which varies in thickness according to building height. The brick panels can be used for cladding steel or concrete frames.

Inner skins and internal load-bearing walls are based on similar size panels of gravel, no-fines, or light-weight aggregate concrete. Provision is made at the time of casting for ducts, switch points, fixings, and holes.

Floors and roofs are of standard concrete, steel or timber construction. One crane and associated team, including the crane driver, can erect the panel units to form the equivalent of a two-storey dwelling in one day.

COMPONENT PRODUCTION

Traditional building is mainly an assembly industry, which is already industrialised to some extent. Many conventional materials and building components are produced in factories to satisfy a vast and continuous volume of demand, thus tending to increase productivity and reduce costs through specialisation of production and long series runs. But for greater economy, traditional separate item production for a variety of uniquely designed parts should be replaced gradually by the efficient use of suitable mass production methods to achieve vast outputs of selected, standardised, dimensionally coordinated and interchangeable components suited to each particular building type.

Optimum standardisation is essential so that component manufacturers can obtain larger series runs to balance turnover against capital, minimise time taken in changing over machines, reduce production costs by the bulk purchase of materials, and attain better quality production of fewer component types with fast operating cycles related to a large and sustained volume of demand. Ranges of standardised units for staircases, refuse chutes, wall units and similar type components could be greatly extended merely by standardising storey heights.

Modern industrial production methods normally operate with short cycle times and/or continuously in shift operations to achieve high serial runs, the production line moving from one station to the next with varying frequency in time. These methods involve high capital and operating costs, and are suited to a limited variety of components with a large and maintained volume of demand. The completely automated production of simple components such as baths or doors, standardised to comparatively few types and sizes would achieve an enormous increase of productivity. If limited to five sizes and types, annual outputs of approximately half a million severely standardised units could be obtained, so great is the increase within a given production method with the same kind of machine.

Such a limited variety and vast output is not suited to many types of components. Even a comparatively simple component such as a flush door would require standardising runs at say, 3 ft (0·91 m) widths, and eliminating w.c. doors 2 ft 6 in (0·76 m) wide for completely automated productions, as any complexity of size and type obviates the economic use of the method. Most types of components are better suited to less sophisticated assembly-line and semi-automated methods for effective production and economy.

Factory production of pre-cast concrete structural elements

Permanent off-site factory production. This type of production is based on mechanised handling methods and semi-automated production line principles under controlled conditions for a high output ratio of accurately prefinished units. Economy largely depends on the maintenance of an adequate and sustained volume of demand, often unknown, in order to justify the highly intensive capitalisation required for production. Some sponsors have become bankrupt through their failure to secure a sufficient continuity of orders for economic production.

Off-site production replaces labour costs by capital costs, minimises all forms of wastage by regular production and control, and avoids the 'learning curve' and falling off in efficiency that may arise each time a temporary site factory is installed and dismantled. High volume production of standardised modular coordinated components can be achieved with minimum variation and maximum interchangeability to satisfy a high, constant and long-term volume of demand.

Several disadvantages are involved. Long production series geared to a vast predetermined programme are essential for economy. Insufficient volume of continuous demand results in decreased utilisation of expensive machinery and plant, with consequent increase of production costs. Factory overheads are heavy. The cost of transporting large and cumbersome units to distant sites is high, and it is difficult to predict accurately delivery times in congested traffic areas. Moreover, double handling in transport, with consequent increased risk of damaging units tends to delay erection operations.

Temporary site factory production. Transportation problems around city areas, combined with uncertainty of adequately sustained volume of demand in relation to capital expenditure and high running costs, have led some sponsors to produce their precast concrete structural elements in temporary factories installed on sites for individual projects where adequate space is available. Factories can be set up readily, dismantled, and transferred to other sites without additional overheads.

Capital costs are within contractors' normal financial resources, and relate to a known volume of demand. Moulds can be acquired to suit individual projects; timber moulds for small outputs, and steel moulds when there is continuity of production for other sites. Capital investments can be amortised within three years on the basis of outputs of 10,000 cu ft (283·17 m³) of concrete units per week. Any number of production lines can be set up as suited to a particular project, whereas with off-site production, outputs are limited to the same standardised units.

Factory production and site assembly can be integrated under one control to coordinate output with assembly requirements, reduce double handling and transportation costs, and minimise delays to the erection cycle due to late deliveries, or damage to units in transit.

Successful construction is based on uncomplicated component design to reduce site jointing, highly prefinished units geared to site cranage, tolerances which facilitate erection, and the maintenance of production targets to balance stock piling with demand.

SITE ASSEMBLY AND ERECTION

In addition to economic design and factory production, the success of a system also depends upon effective programming, timing, and the control of all activities. Labour must be integrated with mechanical plant facilities, and supplies of materials and components phased with transportation and erection requirements to ensure a smooth flow in the movement and cycle of all site operations.

Detailed day-to-day planning and site supervision is essential to achieve coordination of the overall programming and continuity of the erection cycle. Individual items of mechanical plant should be positioned for interactivity, and movement of materials controlled to maintain continuous operation at maximum capacity, with regular servicing of all plant and equipment to minimise repairs and breakdowns. Plant should be served by site power circuits and pick-up points which increase mobility, and extend the use of portable power tools. All site activities should be timed and planned to assist one another. The overall programme should relate the timed construction sequences to relevant unloading areas, labour, materials, components, plant and transportation facilities.

The advantages of industrialised system building can only be realised when good management obtains in all its aspects, as mechanised methods of the prefabrication and handling of components are highly sensitive to delays and interference of productivity.

CLASSIFICATION OF EXISTING SYSTEMS

Building systems may be classified according to: type of sponsorship, method of production, degree of prefabrication and site mechanisation utilised, structural type, materials, weight and methods of assembling structural elements, application to different building types, flexibility of design, and their varying permutations.

In general, load-bearing wall construction is more suited economically to building types with small spans, such as dwellings, and frame construction to other types. Systems for buildings up to five storeys in height generally can be designed economically as column and beam structures, with cladding panels and non-structural components selected from the wide variety of components available on the open market to provide flexibility of design and appearance. Structures over five storeys in height, where vertical loading increases, and supporting columns become larger, are suited to panel construction, which takes these heavier loads over a larger area, but requires additional structural stability against wind forces by bracing with cross walls.

The use of different materials for walls, floors and facades increases costs. The fewer different kinds of materials utilised for structural elements, the greater the economy of construction.

The most significant differences between different building systems relate to their structural types. These include cross wall construction, storey height plank construction, framed structures, box-shell construction, composite systems, and box construction.

Precast concrete frame system

The National Building Frame system has been used on single-storey and multistorey buildings up to ten storeys high. The Barvis N.B.F. 1 system is an adaptation of the N.B.F. system with a basically dry construction and small range of precast concrete units joined by semi-mechanical techniques. There are usually no cross beams as the system

1. Site factory and erection cranes for multi-storey precast panel systems

2. Frame system: fixing props to temporary support mullions in position whilst being held by the erection crane

3. Panel system: lowering floor slab into position before 'stitching' joints with in-situ reinforced concrete

is based on the use of large-span standard double tee floors spanning between 20 in (508 mm) deep edge and spine beams only. Precast concrete staircases and staircase or lift enclosure units complete the system.

Conventional load-bearing cross wall construction may utilise concrete, brickwork, concrete blocks, or timber framing, concrete, timber or steel framed floors and roofs; cladding of pre-cast concrete, brickwork, pre-fabricated timber infill panels with glazed windows and boarded finish, or curtain walling of aluminium, steel, or other materials.

Insulated timber infill panels with a variety of finishes are lighter and quicker to erect than faced and insulated pre-cast concrete facade units, but are not so durable, and require more maintenance. Timber frames can involve difficulties in erection due to fitting the more accurately manufactured frame units into an in-situ constructed frame with coarse tolerances, and high maintenance costs due to the timber shrinking and twisting under climatic conditions.

Curtain walling tends to be used less frequently than formerly due to problems of water penetration, heat insulation, jointing, aesthetics, and the difficulty of obtaining site tolerances which enable factory precision made units to be fixed easily.

Storey height plank construction in 16 to 24 in (406 to 510 mm) widths of aerated precast concrete units is designed to form load bearing walls, floors and roofs for a variety of low-rise dwelling types.

Framed structures of steel, concrete, or timber beams and columns are able to support all live and dead loads, and are integrated with pre-fabricated floors and roofs, and cladding of conventional materials. Such systems are suited to isolated low and medium-rise building types with large room sizes and comparatively few partition walls such as schools, fire stations and factories.

Load-bearing panels for the box-shell construction of low, medium and high-rise dwellings are formed with medium weight (2½ tons) (2·54 tonnes) or heavy weight 6 tons (6·10 tonnes) and over precast concrete panels for parts of, or full room size wall and floor units based on pin jointed box-shell construction. Panels are designed so that all walls under wind loading remain in compression throughout their length, and have no continuity of bending moment through the joints. Panel systems can be modified to form composite precast and poured in-situ concrete structures, with in-situ concrete staircase walls or lift shafts that provide structural rigidity, and cladding formed with timber, brick, prestressed skins, or other materials.

Composite systems with steel or concrete frames are designed with load bearing precast or in-situ concrete external walls, floors and cross walls. Cladding units are prefabricated of precast concrete, brickwork, sheet metal, aluminium, or other materials.

In-situ concrete systems. Some in-situ concrete systems are based on precision made steel shuttering for pouring concrete in rectilinear tunnel sections of room height and width, the shuttering being heated to accelerate concrete curing and enable striking operations to proceed within approximately thirteen hours. Other systems are based on pre-fabricated timber moulds which climb up the building from floor to floor, and are struck after the top floor has been poured; or other types of pre-fabricated and standardised shuttering.

Box construction of monolithic or composite three-dimensional units for housing developments are prefabricated with various degrees of finish and equipment to form completed dwellings. Some systems are based on monolithic room-size boxes which form bathroom or kitchen units of concrete or plastics integrated with plumbing and electrical services, doors, windows and all fittings, and decorated and completed in the factory. A small number of room elements (three or four maximum) restricts design flexibility, as the cost of more rooms greatly increases production costs.

The concrete elements are heavy ($12\frac{1}{2}$ tons) (12·74 tonnes) and over but provide good insulation and finish, satisfactory rigidity to stabilise the building, reduce site labour requirements, and speed erection. Manufacture involves a comparatively small production series, so that a very high volume of demand is required to justify the capital investment needed for economic factory production, and the heavy trailers and mechanical plant for transport, handling, and erection.

Similar boxes, but assembled from panels of concrete, timber or plastics, are also manufactured to reduce transport and handling costs.

Precast concrete box components have been used for vast scale re-housing projects in the U.S.S.R., and for some hotel projects in the U.S.A. One 21-storey hotel with 496 rooms was built in Texas and opened to the public nine months after work commenced on site. The four lower

3

floors were constructed with conventional poured in-situ reinforced concrete while room-size boxes were being precast off the site. These boxes were delivered to site on special trailers, and hoisted to position within a few minutes.

A box component for dwellings recently developed in the U.K. is prefabricated with storey height precision-made steel boxes and lightweight concrete infilling, and incorporates doors and windows.

Properly selected building box systems create instant space for dwellings and hotels, and enable a relatively large choice of bigger and more prefinished components to be assembled in smaller series from an assortment of relatively fewer unified simple products mass produced in large series, but require heavy and costly mechanised equipment for rapid site erection.

2

Principles of Economic Architectural Design

GENERAL

The design of standardised factory-made components for high serial runs of mass produced parts of buildings need not lead to a monotonous form of architecture. Many of the finest buildings known to us in the West are based on the aesthetic standardisation of component parts, as for example, classical Greek temples, medieval Gothic cathedrals, or the best of the Italian Renaissance buildings.

The design of an industrialised building system should aim to combine aesthetic value and satisfaction of user requirements with economy of materials, production methods, and erection techniques. The fundamental similarities of each building type can be comprehended by standardising plan forms and structural components to provide an economic basis for a variety of appearance by using different materials for cladding and finishings of façades. Economy of construction depends on standardising components suited to the simple assembly of standardised building types.

Economic design should avoid over-specification, and take into account methods of factory production in order to limit the number of components and their essential variations for each particular building type, in order to minimise alterations to moulds and shuttering, and standardise methods of factory production. Industrial operations can be reduced by sizing units as large as possible in order to minimise handling, cutting and fitting, jointing, and control accuracy of component dimensions within required tolerances. Units can be incorporated in a more prefinished state and combined with services and other components in order to eliminate wet trades, reduce the installation of services on site, and speed erection operations by carefully planned and controlled production processes geared to site assembly requirements.

An efficient design enables all site plant and equipment to be operated

17

for continuous periods at full capacity. Erection operations can be simplified by minimising variations in foundation depths and widths in order to reduce changes in mechanical excavating equipment, and maintaining finished floor levels at a constant and uniform level. Any necessary variations can be taken up where possible in thickness of screeds for pavings. Modular dimensioning and maximum standardisation of units should be related to crane capacity. Breaks and returns in walls can be reduced by keeping straight runs to simplify shuttering, brickwork, and excavations for foundations.

In order to avoid non-productive time caused by one trade waiting for another to finish, or by more than one team working on one operation at the same time, flow-line site production can be aimed at by designing brick walls as storey-height panels without openings, and doors and windows as storey-height units in order to confine the work of finishing trades to plain surfaces. Detailing should avoid division of trades and differences of materials in order to minimise jointing, and obtain optimum utilisation of mechanical plant for erection operations.

Other general factors that influence economic design relate to the percentage of public circulation space to total floor area; the ratio of external wall in ft run to total area enclosed in square feet; the ratio of load-bearing walls to non-load bearing cladding; the ratios of wall perimeter to height, floor slabs to cross walls, cross walls to cladding, cladding to floor slabs; the percentage of internal circulation area to total area within the building; the total ft run of non-load bearing partitions; the number of different plan types required; the location and nature of the site, and its environment; performance, specifications, materials and required finishes; required indoor climate; the effects on appearance of colour, shape, height, vertical or horizontal stream lining, curtain walling or open frame; the effects on design of design codes, building regulations, local byelaws, and any requirements of the Fine Arts Commission; density ratios in relation to building heights; the requisite structural type: dimensional disciplines determining the joints and tolerances of components; the use and life of the building; maintenance requirements; and any future planning requirements.

EFFECTS OF SITE CONDITIONS ON DESIGN

The location and nature of a site influences design and affects costs in several ways.

Buildings in remote areas may not be within reach of adequate power for working tower cranes, and involve additional costs of temporary cables and sub-stations. Substantial increased costs may be incurred for travelling time and transport of operatives to and from the site, or the provision of a hutted camp for the men's accommodation. Long haulage distances for deliveries of materials to site may be required, which substantially increase costs.

Buildings in crowded city areas may involve deliveries of materials and components being held up in traffic jams that seriously delay erection operations. Police regulations may restrict the off-loading of materials to within certain hours, and necessitate the extra cost of overtime work. The size of the site may restrict manoeuvrability of mechanical plant, or the installation of a site factory and stacking yard. The costs of underpinning adjoining buildings, or special requirements for protecting the public may be incurred.

Few sites are level, and at best usually require the increased costs of stepped foundations, or variations in finished floor levels. The nature of the strata and amount of hard material to be excavated greatly affects the costs of excavations. The softness of the ground determines the type of planking and strutting required, as well as methods of stacking bricks and storing bulk materials. When ground water level is near the surface of the site, pumping operations may be continually involved during excavations. A wet site may necessitate raising temporary sheds and offices on brick bases, and involve more costly temporary roads for lorries making deliveries to the site.

If the site has no load bearing strata near the surface, additional costs for piling or deep foundations may be incurred. A site near the sea may require additional tarpaulins to protect men working on scaffolding from strong winds, which restrict crane working.

A site located near schools or large housing estates may involve additional costs for expensive hoardings, or the provision of warning patrols for additional site protection against wilful damage.

Building layouts should be considered in relation to the environmental area of the site as a whole, and be determined by ground contours in relation to earthworks, and crane layouts, as well as aesthetics. It is more economical to plan layouts so that one crane moving on rails can serve several buildings, instead of using two tower cranes, or one crane that has to be dismantled and set up again in other positions.

All spaces around and between buildings should be designed to fit into an environment planned so that more costly elements capable of resisting intensive use can reduce wear on less durable areas.

Extensive site developments may cause problems of water conservation by altering the surface porosity of the soil. One successful concept for a pedestrian town has been planned on a vast site in the form of a huge mound, with an office and shopping centre located at the crest. Low- and medium-rise dwellings are grouped around on the sloping sides in order to minimise cut and fill, and walking distances from the town's periphery to its centre. All traffic proceeds at natural ground level to central car parks, pedestrian access to the higher groundfloor level of the shopping centre being provided by means of escalators.

PLAN SHAPE AND FUNCTION OF BUILDING

The use of a building influences its plan shape, floor areas, and arrangement of space and services. Building types tend to produce their own especial characteristics, and one plan form will tend to utilise ground area more effectively than another.

In general, optimum economy is based on a simple open design which harmonises architectural and structural requirements, provides uninterrupted internal spaces, minimises planning restrictions, eliminates unessential internal columns, and reduces complicated structural connections. Where site conditions permit, the most economical plan shape for any building type will be based normally on a rectangular form and modular planning grid, with maximum planning at each floor level to minimise double handling, reduce crane traverses, provide the maximum use of shuttering, and afford direct access to the various parts of the building.

Some building types such as offices achieve planning economy by limiting floor spans to reduce beam sizes according to a column grid which maximises flexible planning within the building.

The provision of central heating in low cost dwellings conserves space by enabling the front door and staircase to lead straight into the living room, and bedrooms to be used during the daytime as bed-sitting rooms. As comparatively small changes of floor areas have little effect on areas of walls and roofs and quantities of materials and labour for structural frames, floor areas should not be too restricted, because future conversions to improved living standards tend to be more difficult when space is tight.

The cost of dwellings are directly related to areas planned as bathrooms, kitchens and toilets, as these rooms have the highest costs per square foot of floor space. Consequently, dwellings of similar finish and construction cost more per square foot of total dwelling space the smaller the floor plan.

The shape of a factory is influenced by the amount of coordination of manufacturing processes, size and weight of machinery for production, and type of product to be manufactured.

The plan shape of a school depends on educational methods and type of instruction to be provided, and on lighting. Increase of building depth may necessitate taller windows and higher rooms which reduce the enclosing wall perimeters, or uncomplicated roofing in order to obtain adequate natural daylight.

The exteriors of building types such as offices, which require an easily maintained façade without excessive deterioration, and incorporate large areas of glass to lighten deep rooms, can be designed economically with 'mullion construction' by means of which window mullions are load-bearing and coincide with the locations of partitions. Greater flexibility of their use can be obtained with open planning when the weight of partitions is treated as part of the superimposed loading. Areas with office equipment and stores require few partitions, and can be designed with light construction in order to increase the allocation of loading for stores and equipment. Areas planned as small private offices can have the floor loading reduced to 50 lb per sq ft (244·12 kgf/ m²) thus leaving available 50 lb per sq ft (244·12 kgf/m²) for partitions of heavy sound-resisting construction.

DIMENSIONAL DISCIPLINES DETERMINING JOINTS AND TOLERANCES

The early Greek temples were proportioned by a measure (*modulus*) which linked together all the separate parts of the building into an ordered whole and was applied to the standardisation of plain rectangular buildings and their component parts. These buildings achieve an elegance and beauty that far surpasses their simple austerity due to a relation of dimensions with fixed ratios based on 'proportion', 'rhythm', 'symmetry' and a perfection of optical illusion.

Proportion was considered as a problem of correctly dimensioning a building and its component parts in order to achieve symmetry. Symmetry was obtained by means of a common standard measure for the whole building. The interconnection of proportion and rhythm (periodicity) leads to harmoniously proportioned shapes with periodical recurrence analogous to the interplay of proportions in the successive notes or chords of a melody. By this means harmoniously arranged and rhythmetrically repeated geometrical proportions can introduce symmetry into an architect's plans to correlate measurements between all the various components of a building, and between each component of the whole plan.

When all the components were ordered in proportion by the correct relationship between width and height, and width and depth, and these dimensions were also correctly proportioned in the symmetry of the building, 'eurhythmy' was said to have been achieved.

The early Greek thinkers were attempting to discover intellectual laws in the universe, and for a brief period in their history obtained a clear understanding of law and order. Their architects were trying to express these concepts by basing their designs on eternally valid rules of form and proportion related to a human scale. Their mastery of optical illusion enabled them mathematically to adjust proportions in order to improve the 'rhythm' and perspective of colonnades and obviate the optical and psychological influences affecting bare architectural forms. Their success in so doing is indicated in the remains of the Parthenon, for example, which has strongly influenced architects through the ages, including some of our most eminent modern architects, for instance Le Corbusier and his 'modular' system.

Industrial techniques and building construction are related by coordinating component sizes with a basic module, specifying a system of tolerances, and establishing a grid to enable a complex variety of units for different building types to be assembled dry with maximum flexibility of design. At present there is no national module, but work on modular coordination has been proceeding in the British Standards Institute, the International Modular Group, the component coordination group of the Ministry of Public Building and Works, and in meetings organised by E.E.C. in the attempt to apply component standardisation to building types other than housing, and achieve construction with acceptable standard ranges and conventions for jointing, and a realistic understanding of tolerances.

The Ministry of Public Building and Works publication D.C.10, *Dimensional Coordination for Building*, provides recommended dimensions of basic spaces for selected building components and assemblies used in educational, health, housing and office buildings. However, at present, various systems are based on different grids and modules. Some precast concrete panel systems for high rise dwellings are based on modules which determine the size of moulds in relation to cranage; other types of systems use other grids.

All modular techniques are limited by joints and tolerances due to the degree of accuracy achieved in setting out the building, manufacturing processes and varying thicknesses of components as determined by physical and chemical properties.

A typical example of a commonly used grid, the 'tartan grid', is based on a constant wall thickness, 1 ft (0·304 m) planning grid lines, and a

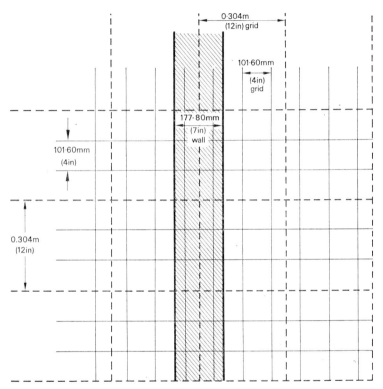

FIG. 2.1   Tartan grid with 1 ft 0 in (0·304 m) planning grid, 4 in (101·60 mm) component grid and 7 in (177·80 mm) wall thickness

4 in (101·60 mm) internal grid. So long as the tolerances specified relate to the design of the building and are compatible with production processes and methods of erection and completion, unavoidable inaccuracies can be accommodated by design and will not obstruct the success of the system. Thus irregularities up to 1 in (25·4 mm) on the shells of rational-ised in-situ concrete systems are masked by external rendering and

internal wall board linings, and in systems based on the tartan grid, by make-up pieces. Figure 2.2 indicates how tolerances in the assembly of partition components can be taken up.

The amount of information required to be shown on standardised drawings for building systems can be substantially reduced by providing: Site key plan. Location drawings. Assembly drawings which detail the methods and sequence of assembly, and all necessary holes and fixings

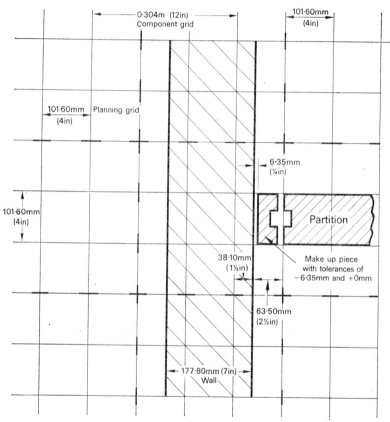

FIG. 2.2   Method of determining tolerances in partition components

required to ensure safety, ease of rapid erection, and adjustment of joints between units. Schedules of components. Separate detail drawings for each component type or unit.

Such types of drawings can effect savings in design costs, because once a system has been detailed, all further buildings can be produced from the existing design sources, and also establish guides to maintenance requirements and running costs.

PRECAST CONCRETE PANEL SYSTEMS FOR HOUSING

The current urgent demand for more dwellings capable of rapid construction has resulted in a majority of large housing development projects being based on systems utilising factory produced precast concrete panel units for box-shell construction. Such systems require early cooperation between the architect and structural engineer in order to determine the following factors: size, number and maximum weight of units, which influence the number and type of vehicles required for transport from off-site factories to the site, or the number and type of cranes required for handling and stacking units produced in factories on site; size, number and type of cranes required for the hoisting and erection of units, and size and composition of teams for site erection cycle. Detailing of joints and prefabricated cages of reinforcement for precast units, and maximum permissible stresses on components during erection need determining early, as those involved in stacking and lifting precast units may be greater than the stresses exercised by the normal building loads. Provision must be made in the components for extra reinforcement where necessary. Columns which are lifted on end need extra stirrups at lifting sockets; wall units with door openings require struts or ties to prevent the beam over from breaking.

The closeness of tolerances affects manufacturing costs, as well as the costs of steel moulds for precast units. Extreme care is required for the determination of tolerances, $\frac{1}{8}$ in (3·2 mm) oversize on a unit 10 ft (3·05 m) wide may reduce a joint width from $\frac{3}{8}$ in (9·52 mm) to $\frac{1}{4}$ in (6·35 mm).

The programme of site erection should minimise double handling of units delivered to site wherever possible by their being lifted direct from lorries to required positions.

Design considerations should take into account safety aspects of the erection processes, especially where no external scaffolding will be required. By utilising a minimum number of precast structural units an open plan can provide an economic basis for the mass production of units for single developments of about 300 dwellings without the need for very costly factory plant and equipment to achieve rapid site erection. Where the design permits floors to be supported at only external bearings, site erection is further simplified.

DENSITY RATIO AND HEIGHT OF BUILDING

Density ratios strongly influence the construction costs of dwellings. The higher the density ratio per acre, the greater the cost per dwelling. The fewer persons per dwelling, the greater the cost per person in a dwelling. The more persons per dwelling, the lower the cost per person, but the greater the cost per dwelling.

Subject to land values and site conditions, it is generally more economical to build at the maximum density ratio with low-rise blocks of two-storey buildings for density ratios up to eighty to ninety persons per acre and three to five-storey buildings designed without passenger lifts (where sloping site conditions permit), for density ratios up to 120 persons per acre. With higher density ratios, greater economy can be achieved usually by constructing fifteen-storey or taller buildings.

The effect on total construction costs of tall blocks as compared with low- and medium-rise buildings is complex, and relates to effective design, type of structure and foundations, volume of demand, and improvements which reduce maintenance and running costs.

High-rise construction tends to increase work to structural frames, suspended floors, ratios of wall/floor areas, circulation areas with staircase and passenger lifts, and foundations. In some conditions the costs of foundations for high-rise point blocks can be substantially reduced by utilising large diameter bored piles without pile caps. These compare favourably with the foundation costs of low-rise dwellings, which require a relatively large area of pile caps and ground beams for a small load the approximate cost of load carried by tower block is 88p per ton compared with £12·5 to £15·0 per ton of load for low-rise dwellings on normal strata.

Tall dwellings have greatly reduced roof areas, and can achieve economies for services in point blocks over thirty storeys high, as they serve the same number of dwellings when planned in low-rise blocks, but with less runs of pipework and conduit. However, these savings may be substantially reduced by the need for costly pumping installations.

In general, blocks of multistorey dwellings up to about ten storeys cost more per dwelling than those from ten to twenty storeys. There are several reasons for the increased cost. One roof does not cover so many dwellings, and less uses can be obtained from the shuttering of in-situ concrete standardised concrete beams and slabs. The expensive tower cranes used for handling materials and components to position cannot operate so economically. Time required for hoisting units to the higher floors of taller buildings can be reduced by quickening the speed of the crane's lift. Increased labour output attainable by the effects of repetitive operations is less on lower buildings, as there are fewer floors in relation to the learning time required for the various tasks. The cost of lift installations, required in buildings over four storeys high, cannot be so economically apportioned to each dwelling. However, the cost of lift installations for blocks over twenty storeys high are substantially increased due to the need for operating high speed lifts.

SPECIAL PROBLEMS OF TALL BUILDINGS

Tall buildings present several problems which do not affect low- and medium-rise buildings.

Compression of foundations is frequently not completed until about twenty years after completion of the building, although the most significant effects usually arise within five years. Moreover, concrete shrinkage does not occur consistently, the main vertical shrinkage of columns is not complete until a similar period has elapsed.

Structural movement. High buildings which sway in the wind can cause joints to open and shut and enable water to percolate into the building. All such joints, sealing materials and methods of application require detailing to form an integrated and watertight system early in design stage.

Climatic conditions. Wind velocities increase with height and can delay cranes working, cause problems of oscillation, rain penetration, heat loss, air filtration, and natural air ventilation, and impair chimney efficiency.

The rain catch on roofs of tall buildings is much greater than on lower façades, and requires adequately sized outlets and rainwater pipes.

Thermal movement may occur due to differential movement between the north and south sides of a building. The expansion and contraction of slabs and major beams with larger spans may deflect and cause cracks in walls and partitions.

Noise and vibration. The control and virtual elimination of noise from occupants inside buildings, and noise and vibration from traffic and aircraft outside is becoming a matter of increasing importance.

One effective method of insulating tall buildings from underground railway and road traffic is based on synthetic and natural rubber steel reinforced pads prefabricated with alternate layers of rubber and fibrous material placed underneath the foundations, at a cost of approximately 1 per cent of total construction costs.

INDOOR CLIMATE

Condensation caused by the sudden cooling of atmospheric water vapor inside a building, or by interstitial condensation within its structural elements can be avoided by carefully designing walls, roofs and ground floors to provide a high resistance to thermal transmittance with a low 'U'-value; maintaining a background of warmth throughout the building, with some form of mechanical ventilation to assist airflow; and selecting materials for wall and ceiling finishings which provide an adequate degree of permeability to avoid cold bridges.

Considerable problems of virulent condensation have arisen in many recently constructed dwellings based on precast concrete panel construction. The vast expanses of concrete surfaces finished with wall paper, lino tiles, spray painting and other materials contribute very little to minimising heat loss in rooms supported by inadequate heat distribution and spasmodic periods of occupation.

When such buildings are not continuously heated these problems may be avoided at design stage by including sandwich façade panels designed with insulation near outside surfaces, when no vapour barrier has been included on the inside surfaces of external walls. Where this barrier has been provided, the arrangement of the panels is immaterial so long as the overall level of insulation is adequate to prevent surface condensation. Additional insulation should be installed in corners behind inside wall surfaces and wherever the insulation is bridged by structural members.

Buildings constructed with precast concrete panel units and provided with a high temperature background from a costly heating system require good insulation to reduce the capital and running costs of the installations. Buildings provided with only intermittent heating require wall insulation located near inside surfaces to ensure rapid warming when the heating is turned on, and provision of a vapour barrier to prevent condensation within wall panel units.

The economic value of a building's thermal insulation requires assessment on its individual merits by comparing the costs of the heating system and insulation provided on the basis of: insulation costs, heating installation costs, areas of windows and exposed surfaces, and standard of heating to be maintained.

More open planning can assist air circulation to dispel dampness. Where cost limits permit, the design of a system should provide for the removal of all sources of hot humid air and sufficient moisture liberated inside the building to prevent humidity rising to a level when it will condense on wall surfaces, the replacement of exhausted air with fresh air from outside the building, and the selection of materials for room finishings which minimise heat losses, and avoid critical water pressure by ensuring that sufficient water vapour is dissipated to the outside air by effective ventilation.

Problems of controlling heat supply according to outdoor temperature, and adequately ventilating air inside a building in order to maintain a constant temperature for warming incoming air are complicated by designs which provide large areas of glass which permit a degree of solar radiation which affects room temperatures to an extent requiring counteraction, light insulated cladding units which do not even out adequately daily temperature variations, increased use of materials such as plastics and prefinished concrete panels, and rooms with low ceiling heights and restricted floor space; these include a comparatively small volume of air per person, with more claims on fresh air supply.

User requirements and habits may also tend to induce condensation, such as tenants decreasing day temperatures at night for reasons of comfort or economy.

Effective ventilation, air conditioning, and controlled heating are essential for the improvement of indoor climates, noise reduction, and increased comfort and health. High-rise dwellings in urban areas necessitate more effective procedures of replacing traditional individual heating systems by the provision of heat from a central source, with mechanical ventilation to assist natural air flow. This would enable substantial economies to be obtained from low grade fuels, which can be burnt at uniformly high efficiency, reduced maintenance costs (which would be low compared with the maintenance of large numbers of the smaller heating installations required to provide heating to the same standards), less air pollution, and economy of labour. Large heating stations can be operated with a minimum of labour, and controlled and supervised by a conventional electronic computer system. The use of alternative fuels, and modifications at low capital cost would enable the most economic fuel to be utilised at a particular period, such as North Sea gas, or atomic energy for electricity generation, and savings could be achieved by the incorporation of refuse incineration, and the recovery of waste heat.

SOUND INSULATION

All possible paths by which noise might enter a building should be considered at design stage in order to provide effective methods of sound insulation. These are influenced by weight of walls, airtightness of construction, pitch of sound, indirect transmission, and structural discontinuity.

Precast concrete panel systems for high-rise dwellings can achieve a measure of sound insulation with dense concrete wall units and compressed polystyrene insulation on floor units. Other types of construction for systems applicable to low-rise dwellings reduce the weight of party walls to 12 lb per sq ft (58·6 kgf/m²) (instead of 85 lb per sq ft (415·0 kgf/m²) as required by the Building Regulations when a solid wall is used) by incorporating light-weight insulated units to form cavity walls which achieve the same acoustic performance.

WATER PENETRATION

Modern materials such as concrete, steel, glass, aluminium and plastics have widely different coefficients of expansion. As surface temperatures in Great Britain on relatively large components vary from above boiling point of water to many degrees of frost, the thermal expansion and contraction of joints between large panel units pre-fabricated of these materials is much greater than those of traditional materials. Their impervious weathering skins increase the risk of water penetration due to water collecting to form an unbroken sheet which may be sucked in at any gap in the cladding of tall buildings as a result of differences of pressure, or else blown upwards through openings left in façades.

The joints of metallic façades may corrode due to discontinuity of the surface, which encourages the retention of water or dirt; the use of potentially aggressive sealants; contact between the metal and surrounding material; or bimetallic action at the junction of two different materials.

DESIGN AND OBSOLESCENCE

Precast concrete panel systems for dwellings are not readily adaptable to future changes in user requirements and improved standards of living. They may well become the slums of the future, when every householder may be able to enjoy the increased comforts provided by more living space, artificial ventilation, improved sound insulation, and many other advantages provided by the use of new materials and techniques being rapidly developed all over the world.

Similarly, many new office buildings of recent construction are likely to become obsolete in the future through lack of requisite floor space, and improved standards of living.

We build at present for a forty to sixty years unchanged environment, but should base our thinking on designs that will provide structural stability to take increased loading from future user requirements; provide bigger spans to enable removable non-structural units forming rooms to be utilised for increasing living and working space within a building; and enable curtain walling and other forms of cladding to be readily altered to suit changed user requirements.

The increase of population that is expected to take place within the century will inevitably affect design requirements so that the present scarcity of land will tend to increase, necessitating higher buildings, despite recent panic over the partial collapse of a multistorey block of dwellings; and sewage problems may arise.

Advances in building technology will affect design solutions in view of improved living standards such as artificial ventilation, improved sound insulation, larger living and working areas. The utilisation of North Sea gas which may render uneconomic the use of electricity for domestic purposes, and the more general use of new materials such as structural plastics for non-load bearing walls in place of brickwork and concrete, may also influence design considerations.

Current tendencies to seek quantity and speed of erection while passing over the improved living standards that must inevitably result from the advances of technology, and the need for higher buildings to provide increased population density may well lead to the creation of more slums. These could involve the unnecessary and costly demolition of dense reinforced concrete structures capable of lasting hundreds of years, yet too confined in area and lacking in current living standards to justify their continued existence on valuable land.

Design requirements should attempt the provision of solutions to such problems by providing multipurpose buildings with sufficient foundation to take future additional loading for increased storey heights and changes in user requirements. Some form of frame construction is required that will achieve more open planning to provide for change of building type, the future incorporation of new and lighter materials to facilitate replanning of internal rooms and alterations to façades to accord

4

with changed user requirements; provision of pipework in service ducts for future installations utilising cheap gas, and some form of ducting in substructures to accommodate future sewers.

Good design alone is not sufficient to solve these problems and attain the undoubted advantages that could be gained from industrialised building and more sophisticated techniques of construction. Efficient preplanning and good management is decisive for economic system building. Present unnecessary and artificial factors inflating building costs need to be swept away, including unnecessarily stringent fire grading regulations, uneconomical design codes, the separation of the various professions with watertight compartments, and obsolete methods of measurement and tendering procedures suited to another age.

3

Principles of Economic Structural Design

CHOICE OF MATERIALS FOR STRUCTURES

Structural stability and aesthetic value should not be considered separately; they should be integrated and based on the groundfloor plan of a building. This requires a complete understanding of a valid method of statistically integrating all components, and the logical and organic behaviour of all load-bearing structural elements.

Systems are limited by the range of materials available for standardised structural units and their jointing techniques, but principally by volume of demand.

The two most readily available materials at present suited to meet the structural requirements of multistorey buildings are steel and reinforced concrete. The unreliability of concrete in tension, and its dependence on good workmanship can be overcome by adding steel reinforcement, strict quality control, and mechanisation of production. The tendency of steel to rust, and to weaken under fire can be overcome by encasing it in concrete. This provides a composite material with great strength that can be varied and concentrated exactly where needed.

Prestressed concrete enables the full strength of the constituent materials to be utilised, it is comparatively costly but provides economic advantages for composite designs when its weight is an appreciable part of the load to be carried, and structures subject to impact forces or fatigue. The processes of prestressing and precasting fit into the trend of system construction by replacing quantity by quality, labour by machinery, and craftsmanship by automatic control. By prestressing together a number of precast units to form a continuous structure, a greater control over the stresses induced in the structure can be introduced in its design.

The use of the particular material selected imposes strict disciplines on design owing to its strength, and may affect available supplies, as well as transportation and handling costs, and the amount of protection or treatment of the material needed to ensure minimum maintenance.

The economic advantages of steel and concrete relate to the effective use of their properties with high quality materials. High yield steel, which has the same elastic modulus as mild steel, is more flexible for sections of equal carrying capacity, and can be used to a greater limit of permissible stresses than mild steel. It also permits an increase in working stress of 40 per cent with a smaller section, thus achieving a net saving in costs.

In elastic design, the ratio of the elastic modulus for steel and concrete is usually limited to 15, the complementary compressive stress in the concrete being from one-fifteenth to one-thirtieth of the working tensile stress in the steel, according to the grade of steel used. Lower concrete stresses tend to increase floor thicknesses, and increase their dead weights. No advantage is gained from the use of high quality materials unless full utilisation can be made of their working stresses.

Costs of materials must be balanced against labour costs, and the availability of skilled labour. If concrete has been selected as the more suitable material for a system, available labour is of poor quality, and batch control not readily available under sufficiently stringent conditions, design stresses need to be related to an agreed mix by volume, rather than to a designed mix.

Other general factors which influence the choice of materials relate to current price levels in the steel and cement industries, user requirements for the building, nature and size of site, standardisation of structural sections, and fire resistance requirements.

Fire protection is one of the main factors which at present prevents steel from being economically competitive with concrete. Unprotected steel beams which would compare in cost with reinforced concrete beams, when bearing on load-bearing brickwork can cause wall collapse in fires due to expansion in the length of the beam pushing out the walls, and require the additional cost of fire protection.

In general, economies can be achieved by the use of high tensile steel framing to lower storeys and ordinary mild steel for the upper framing of multi-rise steel framed structures. Higher strength concrete structural units to lower storeys, and lower strength concrete for the units above can be designed for reinforced concrete structures, with light-weight materials for cladding and non-structural partitions. Structural partitions can be located in positions that minimise loading.

Design codes have tended to become increasingly irrational and successively modified by arbitrary decisions which prevent full advantage being obtained from potential structural economies. The development of new materials and techniques of construction increase the importance of imposed loads as compared with dead loads. Improved knowledge of loading for different types of purposes could increase economies obtainable from controlling materials strengths.

More rational design rules would relate to the consideration of a set of limit states with suitable margins of safety, so that design could be on a semi-probable basis due to the difficulty of assessing many of the factors which influence the likelihood of failure or defects in a structure. Digital computers make the use of 'limit state design' practical by allowing more accurate structural analysis and statistical analysis of concrete strengths which lead to economies in cement. Such refinements of design can provide increased flexibility and reduce costs, particularly where fire resistance is required, although the design approach may induce added structural movement in reinforced concrete structures.

Present research into the possible use of fibrous and nylon reinforcement of concrete, better cements and light-weight aggregates, improved mix designs, higher crushing strengths, the increased use of more reliable light-weight aggregates for reinforced and prestressed concrete, the development of special steels, epoxy resins and other jointing and weather proofing materials, and the methodical study of the behaviour of concrete during maturing, should lead to greater economies in the costs of reinforced concrete as a structural material.

Steel

The manufacture of steel involves standardised processes which make mass production easily possible on a huge scale, far beyond the capacity of other current mediums. High annual outputs are achieved of extensive ranges of standardised structural sections manufactured with fine tolerances for various purposes, with strengths controlled and established during manufacture.

The universal steel sections and joists manufactured in accordance with B.S. 4 (1) Section 5 and 4 (2) Section 3 have entirely changed the design and functions of steel structures due to their extensive ranges and sections, which are proportioned to minimise the need for compounding with plates. Developments in cutting and automatic welding now enable welded box and other sections to be used for structural units. Circular, square and rectangular hollow sections produced to comply with the requirements of B.S. 4 (2) provide great potential advantages for use as structures. These sections enable structures of all types to be rapidly erected and sealed in so that other trades can follow on continuously. In congested city areas transport delays in delivery of steelwork and precast concrete units from off-site factories may hold up site operations. Such delays can be avoided by manufacturing the precast concrete units on site when space is available for setting up a site factory and stacking yard.

High tensile steel to B.S. 4232 (4) with a yield stress of 23 tons per sq in (36·22 Kgf/mm²) provides a higher strength/weight ratio and higher working stresses than mild steel, but requires the accommodation of deflections. It can achieve savings in structural and foundation costs by reducing the cross-sectional area of columns required to carry principal vertical loads.

The strength to weight ratio of steel and the variety of shapes and forms in which it is manufactured provide many ways for use as rapidly erected load-bearing structural units. But as the basic cost of steel is approximately £45 per ton before going through a steelworks, it is essential to reduce the weight of a steel structure for economy of costs. Savings may be achieved by carefully spacing columns to reduce their weight by as much as 35 per cent by reducing a span in order to substitute a lighter girder section and economise through savings in smaller section stanchions and reduced foundation bases.

The economic advantages of structural steel frames for multi-storey buildings include overall reduction in size of structure, as the columns are smaller in section and obstruct less floor space; precision of erection; lower foundation costs due to reduction in dead weight of the structure; flexibility in planning; and adaptability to the requirements of future user changes and improved standards of living. A complete change of cladding to façades and alterations to the layout of internal planning can readily be made to suit changes of user requirements.

Design techniques for structural steel frames should not limit the stiffness required to stabilise a building to the framework, but take into account the potential for composite action between the various components of the structure, and the ability of floors, lift shafts and staircase walls to resist lateral loads in order to minimise permanent bracing systems and specially designed fixed end joints. Economic design can be achieved by transferring the disturbing forces through walls to the ground planning floors to act as horizontal girders between strong points, and designing stair well enclosures, service areas and permanent partition walls to act as vertical cantilever girders anchored to the foundations.

Structural steelwork can be closely and rapidly integrated with other materials and forms of construction such as in-situ and precast concrete, light preformed steel floor decking, dry-jointed plastic and steel façades fabricated in three-storey lifts complete with factory inserted window components, and with fabricated false ceiling and partitions. For large spans and light loading, open web beams are suited to economic mass production techniques.

Steel framing in composite construction of simply supported light steel beams, designed either with or without shear connectors acting as integral units with in-situ concrete floors according to design approach enables materials to be used economically so that the concrete takes the compression, and the steelwork is fairly uniformly stressed in tension.

Where user requirements and site conditions permit, multi-storey buildings may be rapidly erected by means of hull-core construction achieved with steel perimeter stanchions and an efficiently planned reinforced concrete core structure, with the lift shafts, staircases, service ducts and lavatory blocks built with sliding shuttering, and continuously poured in-situ concrete and composite floors. Alternatively, hull construction can be designed so that the whole perimeter of a building is stiffened by the steelwork, which becomes a huge tubular section.

Where wind resistance is provided by a concrete core, economies can be achieved by designing perimeter stanchions to support vertical loading only, with conventional steel beams linked to the stanchions, and tied to the core.

Fire protection

Lack of structural fire protection can result in small fires developing into large destructive fires. Good design can help to control and limit a fire to small proportions. Present local authority regulations concerning the protection of steel structures against fires are based on unrealistic assessments of fire hazards, and do not satisfactorily take into account the efficiency of modern fire brigades and fire-fighting techniques and the properties of steel. Such regulations constitute one of the factors which at present unnecessarily add to the cost of building.

There are considerable discrepancies between actual fire loads and assumed fire grading. Some structural elements which have been shown by actual fire tests at the Fire Research Station to comply with all the requirements of B.S. 476 (1, 3) are disallowed for use in actual buildings. Fire grading is arbitrarily based on classification of usage, instead of on the actual fire load present, although a higher degree of fire protection may well be necessary for different classes of building occupants.

Numerous fire tests have shown that for columns carrying their design load, the critical temperature at which failure occurs is reached when the mean steel temperature rises approximately 450-550°C. The temperature to which a heated, unprotected steel section is raised at the end of a given time depends on the weight of the section, or its thermal capacity, and the shape of the section and the area over which the heat is applied. Thus lighter sections reach critical temperature more rapidly than heavier sections. In multi-storey structures, sections used at lower levels would normally provide more than one hour fire resistance without any fire protection.

The Post-war Building Study No. 20 (*Fire Grading of Buildings*) establishes the relationship between the fire load and furnace test period (e.g. 12·5 lb/ft² (58·60 kgf/m²) = 1 hour), but research undertaken by the Joint Fire Research Organisation indicates that the better method of assessing potential fire severity is achieved by taking into account the ventilation of the building, and expressing the fire load per unit window area. A more balanced assessment of the appropriate fire resistance to a building has been established by the Fire Research Committee at Rotterdam in 1966.

The essentials of fire resistance require adequate construction which enables occupants to leave a building safely in the event of fire, and permits firemen to deal with the fire without undue risk. The degree of protection to be afforded should be related to the fire load, which is the average amount of fuel in the contents and construction of the building expressed in terms of equivalent weight of timber per unit floor area. Consideration should be given to the isolation of areas of high risk and fire load, sprinkler installations, and roof ventilation, and the position and exposure of the various protected elements.

Reinforced concrete provides much greater heat resistance than steelwork, as the steel bar reinforcement is protected to some extent against temperature rise by the concrete cover. Where suspended ceilings form a part of the construction, the design of steelwork can ensure economical fire protection by concealing steel beams in the overall thickness of floors. In order to reduce the weight of a structure to a minimum, the steel work may be protected by asbestos spraying or light prefabricated dry casings.

The economics of fire protection depend on more realistic regulations; designing the steel frame to act compositely with structural concrete casing to support the final loading; utilising light-weight casings to beams and columns to reduce foundation loading and achieve savings of concrete and excavation in each stanchion base, and improved fire detection systems. Recent developments include infrared detectors. Current research is investigating the possible application of lasers which produce coherent monochromatic radiation.

Concrete

Concrete is a flexible material which can take the forms of plain mass, reinforced or prestressed concrete as suited to structural requirements due to its relatively low cost, high compressive strength, good resistance to fire and corrosion, and constructional simplicity suited to unskilled labour. It can be precast to special requirements, or used to bring production line methods to the site for the mass production of standardised structural units where a sufficiently large and continuous volume of demand justifies requisite capital investment.

The disadvantages of concrete relate to hidden deficiencies and specific characteristics which make its structural behaviour impossible to forecast accurately because of its variability of strength where good site control is not maintained, high thermal sensitivity, shrinkage, and plasticity. The elastic modulus of concrete varies according to the problems inherent in mixing, placing and curing, and changes due to plastic stresses and viscosity. These problems can cause defects when the mixing leads to differences in the elastic modulus of the concrete in two collaborating members of the same structure, or when structural importance is related to decrease of the modulus with stress, or increase under repeated loading, or plastic flow under load. Nevertheless, reinforced concrete provides the possibility of designing structures in conformity with aesthetic and structural needs. It is the optimum structural solution where conditions necessitate either raft or pile foundations, lends itself to standardisation and easy formation of shapes, and permits the design of a reduced number of structural sections to standardise components with a minimum of variations and increased use of shuttering on account of high compressive strength.

The cost of any extra concrete thickness due to over design is comparatively negligible, as it is the labour content of any ordinary portland cement concrete item which is critical and needs to be minimised.

Precast reinforced concrete panels for internal walls and floor slabs with domestic loading can be economically cast as standardised units in steel or concrete battery moulds. With box-shell construction for multi-storey dwellings, walls can be standardised at 7 in (178 mm) thickness to provide good sound insulation at any height, as no savings in costs are achieved by reducing their thickness. Thus the thickness of floor panels can be standardised even in corridors and narrow bedrooms where their thickness could be reduced, because it is cheaper to use the same steel moulds, with the insertion of a stop to reduce the width of the slab.

Concrete can be produced economically on site by the use of controlled batching plant, and aesthetically developed by the use of colouring or white aggregates and cement, facing with exposed aggregates to imitate varieties of natural stone, or embellishment by profile treatment. Unlike steelwork, concrete utilises a high proportion of unskilled labour for rapid site construction.

On jobs where only intermittent supplies are required, or the nature of the site would otherwise preclude in-situ construction, or towards the end of the job when space becomes strictly limited, ready-mixed concrete can be used to maintain production requirements.

No-fines concrete in which all sand and fine stones are omitted from the aggregate, and the coarse aggregate is cement coated together provides a better heat and water resisting concrete than dense concrete. As the hydrostatic pressure is greatly reduced, comparatively light shuttering for large prefabricated two-storey box shutters can be used many times for no-fines infill built integrally with dense reinforced concrete frames. However, the potentialities of no-fines techniques are affected by the increasing shortage of natural aggregates for concrete, and research into the development of artificial aggregates is being undertaken on a vast scale.

Aerated concrete is virtually a weak strength grout, and contains no coarse aggregate, being composed of cement and lime putty with finely divided silica. Satisfactory results to obtain compressive strengths of 300 to 600 lb per sq. in (21·09 to 42·18 kgf/cm^2) require high pressure steam curing, so that the material is best suited to precasting.

The use of light-weight aggregate concrete can expand design possibilities. It is economical where the least density and greatest porosity are required for a given strength, and industrial waste products such as pulverised fuel ash and expanded clay or shale are readily available. By reducing the weight and thickness of walls, substantial savings can be made in foundations with large precast concrete components of lightweight aggregate.

The insulation of concrete by an expanded plastic either internally as a sandwich, or externally as an applied layer is expensive. The use of light-weight concrete can reduce haulage and handling costs, but requires a space wasting thickness of 14 in (356 mm) to obtain a U value of 0·2. By massive air-entrainment, light-weight aggregate concrete can be reduced to 80 lb per sq ft (391 kgf/m²) with reduced K and U values.

Reinforced light-weight concrete, which comprises aggregate and aerated concrete, has the disadvantage of being subject to damage in site erection, and the advantages of reduced weight, easier transportation and handling, and improved thermal insulation.

On one site in the U.S.A. light-weight aggregate was used for pre-casting concrete units to save prestressing and reinforcing steel, and achieve greater use of the erection crane's working capacity. Beams and floor slabs were pre-tensioned in timber moulds, and wall panels cast in steel moulds to permit the design of extremely thin rib sections.

The development of techniques for spraying concrete into place by pneumatic pressure ('gunite') has been used in Sweden for dwellings. Portland cement and sand (1 : 3) with a foaming agent are used to produce a light-weight 'concrete' (50 lb per cu ft; 800·92 kg/m³) which is sprayed on hessian fixed to scaffolding or a light steel framework. The technique has been used in the U.K. for the airduct to the Dartmouth tunnel, and developed in the U.S.A. for certain types of space structures.

COMPARATIVE ECONOMIES OF POURED IN-SITU AND PRECAST CONCRETE

Factors influencing decisions as to whether or not it will be more economical to precast or to pour concrete in-situ for structural members relate to type of units required, amount of standardisation possible, volume of production, and type of building. Dwellings, which have small rooms and spans suited to panel construction, and building types with regular plan shapes suited to modular grids and standardisation are suited to precast construction, as opposed to one-off buildings of individual intricate design. These are more economically constructed with in-situ concrete. The finalisation of all details and services, and the availability of completed working drawings and specifications before commencing work on site is essential for economic construction. If full details are not available until work has commenced on site, resulting variations can be more readily incorporated into in-situ construction without the excessive costs and delays entailed with precast construction. Lack of detailed information regarding holes and chases for service installations makes it difficult to coordinate pipe runs, etc. and substantially increases costs.

Precast concrete units can incorporate finishings and services in the moulds to reduce site finishing time by approximately two-thirds, and save time by obviating the shuttering and fixing of steel reinforcement required for pouring concrete in situ.

Where several buildings are to be erected on a site, the faster erection achieved by precasting can be maintained, whereas by in-situ pouring, speed of erection is considerably slowed down by the additional time required for finishings trades and service installations.

Precast systems require cranes to handle and position structural units weighing from 2 to 10 tons (2·03 to 10·16 tonnes) according to design, yet may also be required to hoist skips of concrete weighing only $1\frac{1}{2}$ tons (1·51 tonnes) for stitching the in-situ joints between units. Such uneconomic cranage can be avoided on structures up to four storeys high by utilising a second and smaller mobile crane for hoisting the skips. The cost of cranes to handle units weighing 10 tons (10·16 tonnes) is more than double the cost of cranes with a hoisting capacity of 5 tons (5·08 tonnes). Differences in the cost of cranes with hoisting capacities of between 5 tons and 2 tons (5·08 and 2·93 tonnes) is not so excessive.

Poured in-situ concrete structures up to ten storeys high generally require a crane with a hoisting capacity for $\frac{1}{2}$ cu yd (0·38 m³) skips weighing $1\frac{1}{2}$ tons (1·51 tonnes) filled with concrete. This is usually the heavier element, unless the design of shuttering for stability walls greatly exceeds this weight, and therefore enables lighter and much less costly cranes to be utilised.

Rates for in-situ concrete contain a high labour element; for ordinary in-situ work, approximately 40 per cent materials, 40 per cent labour, and 20 per cent plant. These ratios differ for precast concrete work, which are approximately 20 per cent labour, 40 per cent materials and 40 per cent plant, the higher plant costs replacing labour.

Moulds for precast concrete units are more costly than the formwork required for similar poured in-situ concrete members because the materials for the moulds required in precast concrete factory production are of very costly precision made steel, instead of timber or other much less expensive materials. A mould for a precast concrete unit such as a beam has to stand in isolation to produce the unit. If constructed of timber, substantial side supports and ties across the top are required. Formwork for similar poured in-situ concrete members do not require so many stiffeners and side supports, as the beam and slab are complementary, and support one another.

Work in foundations and the floor to floor erection cycle for either precast or poured in-situ concrete operations for multistorey dwellings, takes approximately the same time. But the finishing trades of precast concrete structures twenty storeys high can start during the fourth week at fourth-floor level, thus enabling the whole building to be handed over 8 weeks after the twentieth storey has been roofed over. This is achieved by the finishing trades having progressed to the sixteenth floor by the time the roof is completed.

With poured in-situ concrete construction, when the twentieth storey has been roofed over the finishing trades will only be proceeding at about the tenth floor, consequently it will take approximately sixteen weeks to hand over the building on account of the considerable extra time required for finishing trades and service installations.

A stronger mix can be obtained with precast concrete able to work economically with any steel reinforcement. Systems based on precast concrete construction avoid the need for external scaffolding to façades, and employ a minimum of site labour for the rapid erection of large and continuous outputs of mass-produced units. An initial stock pile of precast units should be assembled before erection operations commence, as twenty-one days must elapse before 80 per cent of the shrinkage in beams and wall panels will have taken place. Columns can be erected after seven to ten days of casting, because any further shrinkage tends to be counteracted when taking up their loading.

Concrete production on site, irrespective of whether for precast or poured in-situ concrete, normally averages out at approximately 40 to 50 cu yd (30·58 to 38·23 m³) per day, based on a $\frac{1}{2}$ cu yd (0·38 m³) skip and a mixing cycle of two to three minutes. Under these conditions, one tower crane would be utilised and suited to a $\frac{1}{2}$ cu yd (0·38 m³) mixer producing ten batches of concrete per hour for a daily output of approximately 40 cu yd (30·58 m³). It would not be economical to use a mixer of 1 cu yd (0·76 m³) capacity, as it would produce all the concrete required for one day's operations in five hours, leaving the mixer standing idle for the remainder of the day, and the crane under-utilised.

The economic gang strength for producing either precast or poured in-situ concrete averages eight men for mixing and placing approximately 40 to 50 cu yd (30·58 to 38·23 m³) of concrete per day. The gang normally comprises two men on the mixer, one crane operator, one banksman, and four men placing, vibrating, and screeding the concrete.

If the size of the building required two cranes for its construction, each placing the same amount of concrete per day, greater economy would be obtained by using a larger mixer and heavier cranes, one crane pouring the concrete, while the second crane carried out other handling operations. The advantage of using a 1 cu yd (0·76 m³) mixer for greater outputs enables handling costs to be reduced by approximately 50 per cent. This saving is offset by increased capital or hire charges for more expensive plant and cranes, and is only justifiable on sites requiring considerably increased daily outputs of concrete.

CHOICE OF STRUCTURAL TYPE

Structural design aims to provide requisite strength, stiffness, lightness and rapid erection of a structure on foundations which obtain full advantage of subsoil properties, and is founded on construction techniques.

Economy of design is influenced by the optimum use of the characteristics of available materials for maximum standardisation of sections, and a minimum of simple repetitive assembly operations with the concentrated use of suitable mechanical plant to speed erection and reduce total construction costs.

The trend towards lighter structures has aggravated problems of noise in buildings, for although higher working stresses for structural materials can achieve slender sections when designed solely for strength, particular attention should be taken at design stage in order to avoid vibration problems arising due to insufficient stiffening of the structure.

Although there are a number of alternative forms of construction which may be used to satisfy the functional requirements of a given structural problem, many of these become unexpectedly uneconomical when not used to the best advantage. Selection of structural type may be complicated by foundation problems, the availability of materials and labour, and the need to balance relative costs with time required for completion. In 1946, when there was a general shortage of steel following the war period, government legislation provided for public buildings to be designed in reinforced concrete rather than in structural steelwork, and initiated a tendency which still generally persists today.

Different forms of construction usually require fundamental differences of planning. Multirise dwellings, which have comparatively small room spans, are generally more economically constructed in concrete of box-shell construction, rather than with structural steel framework.

With other building types, the designer is faced with a wider choice of many complex factors.

Under normal conditions, length variations with prismatic components such as beams and columns are less costly than with panels. Wing panels cast integrally with columns at one or both ends help to stabilise loading. With buildings up to five storeys in height it is usually more economical to design a frame structure and select cladding panels which give flexibility of design and appearance from the present wide variety of components obtainable on the open market, unless they form part of a large development with tower blocks. With structures over five storeys high, the vertical loading becomes much heavier, and consequently the supporting columns are greatly increased in section. Panel construction takes these loads over a much greater area, but requires additional structural stability against wind forces by bracing with cross walls.

The economic principles of planning steel and reinforced concrete frames have changed. With light loading, floors are more economically composed of units spanning in one direction, but with change of direction in adjacent bays to ensure even loading on beams. With heavier loading, the units are more economically designed to span in two directions. Economic multistorey construction requires the combination of the maximum utilisation of the best characteristics of steel and concrete

Steel frames

Steel structural frame systems are suited economically to building types requiring horizontal and vertical repetitive units. Such systems can reduce dead weight by transmitting all loads by stanchions bolted at their feet to foundations, save floor space, and provide large areas for flexible planning by allocating load bearing and space enclosing functions to the structural frame, and light cladding. Suitably positioned solid walls required for functional purposes can be designed to withstand wind pressure on the structure, and thus achieve economy in the steel frame.

Where planning requirements permit, standardisation and economy of sections may be achieved by equalising the loading in different parts of the frame on the basis of a regular grid layout, with stanchions spaced as closely as possible, because short span beams cost less per linear foot than long span beams.

For normal loading, the deepest available standard joist section with the required strength provides the greatest economy. Even where excessive, it may cost less than a shallower but heavier section. For heavy loading and spans exceeding 50 ft (15·24 m) the weight of steel increases in relation to the volume of the building, with consequent extra costs.

High tensile steel sections may offset local reductions in size and weight of sections to save height or floor space which offset the extra cost of the more expensive material. However, such savings may be obviated by packings required to obtain uniform overall finished sizes in accordance with architectural requirements.

In a multistorey building, the floors and amount of beamwork per storey is identical; only the stanchions increase in section to take the extra loading. Traditional design assumed that the skeleton of beams and columns supported the concrete floor slabs and wall cladding in isolation. Any fire protection of concrete casing was assumed to make a very small contribution to support imposed loading, and normally provided for variation in section every second storey, because steel sections were bought in 20 ft (6·10 m) lengths. A stanchion size was determined at the top of the structure, and proceeding downwards the stanchions were compounded by additional plates.

The introduction of universal steel columns has enabled the compounding stanchions to be largely superseded, as there are several different weights of U.C. available for every size section, which simplifies connections. These are made more economically by internal cover plates, instead of division plates and external cover plates.

The most important single factor that influences the cost of steel-framed structures relates to the selection of the column module. The cheapest frame is that with the least dead weight, and consequently the closest column grid, which transmits the supported load to the foundations in the most direct way. As the number of columns in a steel-framed structure decreases, the total weight of steel remains more or less constant, irrespective of the grid module. But the weight of the beamwork, which costs less per ton than stanchions, increases as the number of columns decrease when the grid is widened. This increases the costs of mass concrete foundations to isolated stanchions, which on a normal site is approximately 5 per cent of the total cost of the structure.

Advanced steel framework design has introduced changes in fabrication techniques so that it is generally more economical for details and connections to be shop welded, and bolted at site with friction grip bolts. Where confined space makes these bolts difficult to fix, high tensile R type bolts form a suitable alternative.

Structural steelwork can be very readily and quickly erected, and provides a more flexible layout than a concrete frame, but cannot be shaped to profile as concrete. A standardised light steel section sufficient to carry shuttering without props in combination with concrete designed to take all loading achieves greater economy than sections of steelwork designed only to support the loading, with concrete casing to the steel for fire protection. The shuttering for beams and columns can be standardised and reused floor by floor commencing at ground level.

Steel frames can also be designed economically by minimising the number of stages by which the load is carried. Thus where user requirements permit, the grid can be closed to obviate secondary beams so that fewer sections need handling. Columns can be arranged in serial sizes based on the different weights of the same section. For example, on the basis of a 20 ft × 15 ft (6·10 × 4·57 m) grid, a thirty-storey frame could be standardised at the top with 6 in × 6 in (152 mm × 152 mm) stanchions, which would serve six storeys; 8 in × 8 in (203 mm × 203 mm) stanchions for ten lower storeys; 10 in × 10 in (254 mm × 254 mm) stanchions for ten storeys below, and 12 in × 12 in (305 mm × 305 mm) stanchions for the lower floors and basements. The effect of increasing the size of the grid is to increase column sizes, the cost of which is offset to some extent by the fewer bases required for their foundations.

Steel frames for multistorey dwellings should be designed with a relatively low perimeter-plan ratio, and effective integration of the plan to the structural system, rigidly standardised spans, light-weight prefabricated cladding units which provide adequate weather, fire and insulation protection; standardised light weight fireproof casings, and full utilisation of all repetitive factors. Cladding must be efficiently jointed, and for rapid erection may be secured to the frame in units of three storeys in height.

An economic plan form for multistorey dwellings twenty storeys high based on wall cladding of not more than 25 lb per sq ft (122 kgf/m²) and a maximum wind loading (Exposure B) of 18 lb per sq ft (88 kgf/m²) would provide for four three-apartment flats without balconies, two lifts in one shaft, and one staircase per floor. Construction would consist of a simple steel frame with dry casings, standard 5 in (127 mm) precast floor beams of 9 ft (2·74 m) and 11 ft (3·35 m) spans resting on the top flanges of the steel, and precast floors for light cranage. Costs of such construction would compare with a normal in-situ concrete frame with brick infilling, or a precast concrete system based on rigid standardisation of spans and a limited output of severely standardised units.

Factors which tend to narrow the differences in costs between steel and concrete structures for dwellings, offices, and other types of multi-

5

storey structures relate to the use of light-weight fireproof cladding, high tensile steel, torque bolting, composite action between steel and concrete, and ultimate load basis of design.

Disadvantages of steel skeleton frame structures are that tower cranes cannot be utilised to maximum efficiency due to the extra lifting, slewing, trolleying and dropping required to handle concrete skips or components to positions between the steel frame; restrictions of working at wind velocities of 15–20 m.p.h. (6·70 to 8·94 metres per second) as compared with wind velocities of up to approximately 35 m.p.h. (15·64 metres per second) that prevent crane movements handling concrete skips and components; and the additional labour required to pack and vibrate in-situ concrete between steel sections and shuttering compared with normally reinforced concrete sections.

REINFORCED CONCRETE CONSTRUCTION

Many more systems for multistorey buildings are being developed in reinforced concrete rather than steel because reinforced concrete structural sections can be precast to combine weather resistance, fire protection, sound and heat insulation, and finished appearance in one operation, and enable more rapid completion of the building. Structural sections can be economically formed by standardised shutters or moulds for beam and column sizes, extra steel reinforcement being incorporated to take heavier loads. Buildings based on steel frame construction generally cost approximately 10 to 20 per cent more than similar buildings based on reinforced concrete frames.

In general, buildings with short spans are more economically constructed with reinforced concrete, and are particularly suited to precast concrete construction. For large spans, the weight of the concrete structure is high in relation to the load carried, the dead weight/imposed load ratio being approximately unity. With steel structures, this ratio is only about one-fifth. This indicates that on sites for large-scale developments, economies could be achieved in tower blocks by planning larger buildings with maximum column grids.

For reasons of economy and fire protection, the forms of structure most frequently used for multistorey building types are in-situ reinforced concrete frames; combination of in-situ precast concrete frames with panel infillings; and precast concrete box-shell construction. Comparatively few structures of steel frame skeletons or composite steel and concrete construction are being constructed for such buildings at present.

In-situ monolithic concrete construction. In-situ monolithic construction has the advantages of reducing deflection in structural members; and distributing reduced bending moments more uniformly throughout the structure than in discontinuous precast concrete structures. This achieves light members of uniform section which can be sized to the maximum bending moment, thus minimising wastage of material at less highly stressed points. Less rapid increase in the dead weight of beams is required with increase of span, as stress distribution requires extra material over the supports to take up the weight directly without increasing the bending moment, which it would do if placed in the centre of the span. Mainly unskilled labour can be employed for erecting the structure, and a variety of light infilling used for façades. Alternatively, white cement and coloured aggregates can be used to combine architectural finish with structural sections.

Changes of reinforcement, beam and column sizes, slab and wall thicknesses, size and shape of foundations, and adjustment of formwork can be minimised by standardisation of design. It is generally more economical to design poured in-situ suspended concrete slabs with a higher percentage of steel rather than with a thicker slab and less steel, because a heavier slab necessitates larger beams with a higher percentage of steel, with increased loading on foundations.

Taller buildings require higher strength concrete. Where the slenderness of designed columns in a tall building requires a concrete strength of 7500 lb per sq in (527·80 kgf/cm^2) which is better obtained under factory conditions rather than on site, the slump test should be 5 lb per sq in to avoid the concrete losing some of its workability before hoisting to the top of the structure.

The main disadvantages of in-situ reinforced concrete construction relate to the adverse effects of differential foundation settlement causing secondary shearing forces and bending moments in the beams and columns due to the distortion of the frame caused by rigid joints; temperature movement similar to foundation movement; and the time lag between pouring concrete and striking of shuttering. Concrete curing impedes the reuse of shuttering, and obstructs working areas for long periods. These delays can be shortened by using methods of accelerated curing.

Steel reinforcement should be designed to form a stable structure capable by itself of sustaining the load, so that the added concrete can implement the equilibrium by connecting the steel bars and absorbing compressive stresses.

Composite construction with poured in-situ concrete walls or stability core and a precast concrete frame has the disadvantages of the in-situ concrete rising at a slower rate than the precast concrete frame. As a result, the site becomes obstructed by formwork, unless sliding shutters are utilised for the in-situ core. Moreover, the distribution of stress in members composed of in-situ and precast concrete may be uncertain and need testing. Where precast concrete sides are not continuous throughout the height of a building but are jointed at floor levels, the in-situ core is continuous, and the whole of the composite section is required to be load bearing due to loading conditions, some form of bonding is required to prevent the precast concrete sides buckling away from the core. The effects of differential shrinkage in lateral and longitudinal directions between the core and the sides need careful determination. Steel links will be required which project into the core from the precast concrete sections. Shrinkage can be reduced by designing a fairly dry mix in the core to achieve the same ultimate loads as for the poured in-situ concrete. Fire resistance requirements can be obtained by utilising sintered pulverised fuel ash light-weight aggregate in both the precast units and the core.

Economic monolithic in-situ concrete box-shell construction for multi-rise dwellings over eleven storeys high requires formwork designed in as large units as possible with props attached, and loose parts minimised for crane utilisation and rapid erection.

Walls and floor slabs act together as beams because of the total monolithic character of the in-situ construction, which provides full continuity throughout beams, columns and slabs. The particular distribution of stresses and consequent variation in disposition of material enables almost any shape to be formed. But the high cost of formwork, which amounts to approximately one-fifth of the total cost, necessitates simple structural shapes so that economical shutters can be designed for repeated use.

Basic construction consists of pouring the in-situ monolithic box-shell structure within a rigid module. Formwork is prefabricated in storey height panels weighing about 3 tons (2·03 tonnes), with concrete batches arranged so that the skips plus the contents are of about the same weight in order to achieve efficient crane utilisation.

Internal cross walls are poured before the floor shuttering is erected. Unskilled labour can be employed for placing welded mesh panel floor reinforcement. After the floors have been poured, the shuttering panels can be jacked down and wheeled towards the outside of the building for handling by crane into their subsequent positions. This method speeds the erection cycle by enabling finishing trades to proceed simultaneously with the main construction. Walls and ceilings can be papered or sprayed with paint, and floors screeded and finished before the next wall lift proceeds. Staircases, and any projecting balconies are usually more economically constructed with precast concrete

An economic method of monolithic in-situ box-shell construction of multistorey structures for dwellings up to eleven storeys high can be obtained by traditional methods utilising 6 in (152 mm) reinforced concrete load bearing walls and 6 in (152 mm) in-situ hollow pot floors for spans of 9 ft (2·74 m) 10 ft (3·05 m) and 17 ft (5·18 m). Economies are achieved by avoiding intensive capital investment for factory equipment and tower cranes, using light shutters, and limiting mechanical plant utilisation to 12/18 weigh batch mixers with four-minute cycles, and hoist towers with skips. Concrete is hoisted to required floor levels and stored in containers for barrow delivery to placing points. The wall shutters are formed with 8 ft × 4 ft (2·43 m × 1·21 m) plywood sheets $\frac{3}{4}$ in (19 mm) thick on 4 in × 2 in (102 mm × 51 mm) studs spaced at 16 in (1·22 m) centres and stiffened with three rows of 6 in × 3 in (152 mm × 76 mm) whalings for handling by two operatives. These shutters are bolted together with 3 in × 3 in (76 mm × 76 mm) concrete blocks of wall thickness in length, perforated for a $\frac{3}{4}$ in (19 mm) bolt with nut and 3 in × 3 in × $\frac{1}{4}$ in (76 mm × 76 mm × 6 mm) plate washers for easy assembly and striking.

The seven-day erection cycle comprises:

1st day—Erect wall shuttering, place steel reinforcement and pour 3000 lb (1360 kg) concrete to walls (50 cu yd) (38·22 m³)
2nd day—strike shuttering to walls.
3rd day—erect bearers, centres and plywood shutters for floors and staircases.
4th day—lay floor pots, place steel reinforcement and electrical conduits.
5th day—pour concrete to floors and stairs.

Concrete to the floors and stairs is left to cure over the weekend, and the cycle commences on the next floor above on the following Monday, the shuttering being struck at the end of the week. Site labour for erection comprises a carpenter team of ten men for the erection of 500 sq yd (418 m²) of shuttering, and a team of twelve men for the in-situ concreting. The building needs an external scaffolding for the cladding, and incorporates wet trades for floor, wall and ceiling finishes. The average time taken to erect one eleven-storey block of forty-two flats is about eighteen months, but the cost per dwelling is extremely competitive.

Lift slab technique used for multistorey buildings of regular shape is alleged to provide economies by avoiding complicated formwork and cranage for floor and roof slabs, but this is uncertain. The slabs are cast at ground level one on top of the other, with holes left in so that the slabs can freely slide up the columns, and be kept separated. After the in-situ concrete columns and stabilising walls have been cured, the slabs are lifted to their respective levels in the building by hydraulic jacks, and supported on brackets fixed to the columns.

Shuttering. Good shuttering is of vital importance for economic poured in-situ concrete construction. Its successive removal subjects the structure to temporary strains and irregular conditions of loading. Designs for in-situ work should provide adequate strength to take the dead and live loads imposed by the wet concrete, operatives and plant; avoid excessive deflections; ensure tight joints which prevent loss of moisture which reduces the ultimate strength of the wet concrete; enable shutters to be readily constructed, erected and struck, and provide an optimum number of uses.

Economy is related to the costs of labour (which is the major factor), materials, type of construction, required finish to face of concrete, ease of handling, and number of uses obtainable. Shuttering costs are greatly influenced by degree of repetition, and the correct phasing of erection and striking with the curing time of concrete and progress of the works.

For optimum economy, shuttering and scaffolding should be minimised to enable the structure to be self-supporting during course of construction, and obstruction to floors reduced due to propping of shutters which slows down the erection cycle.

Reinforced concrete design may reduce the sectional dimensions of structural members to a minimum, so that the cost of shuttering required greatly exceeds the cost of the structural members themselves. Concrete should be designed to achieve economic shuttering compatible with minimal section sizes by standardising column sizes to obtain more uses from the forms; standardising beam depths, so that their projections below slabs are uniform in depth and optimum use of the forms can be made to the sides of beams; spacing beams to maximise standardised shuttering to soffits of slabs; and utilising kickers for walls and columns.

Sliding shutters. Economies in shuttering to structures over 60 ft (18·28 m) high may sometimes be obtained by using sliding shutters which continuously rise at a rate of 6 in (152 mm) per hour, or more. They are suited to buildings of simple, regular plan form and cross section throughout their length and height, or for the walls of service cores and lift shafts built in advance of the main structure. These cores often provide the main stability of the building, and their early construction supports the following structure against wind loads. A very high degree of detailed pre-planning is required to avoid stoppages. Efficient concrete control, supervision, and constant checking are needed to ensure that the forms are kept level and in alignment, and prevent the continuously moving forms from jamming. Any faults that may occur must be corrected immediately.

The design of the core should be as simple as possible with a minimum of cross walls and boxings for services. To reduce the loading in foundations, thin core walls can be designed with heavy compressive reinforcement, although this may result in difficult placing of an excessive amount and weight of reinforcement in the short construction time available.

The 2 in (51 mm) diameter climbing tubes pass through hydraulic jacks bolted to steel vertical frames spaced at 6 to 10 ft (1·82 to 3·04 m) centres around the perimeter of the core walls. The tubes are 16 ft (4·87 m) to 18 ft (5·48 m) long, and are jointed together with sleeved couplings as the work proceeds. Each jack has two internal clutch mechanisms, with a screw, turning head, and threaded collar fixed to the shutters. As the screw is turned it obtains purchase from the clutch, which engages the tube under load and raises the collar with the attached shutters. When the piston has reached its full extension, one clutch holds the shutters, while the other clutch and piston are returned by a spring to the original position.

The hydraulic system has a central control so that the whole of the shutters to the perimeter walls can be raised as a single unit. The jacks operate from a ring coupled to a power unit and booster, with a working load of 2 to 3 tons (2·03 to 3·04 tonnes) and an operating rate of approximately 1 in (25 mm) to 10 minutes, based on the time for maturing of concrete. The height of the shutters for this speed of lift would be 4 ft (1·22 m).

The core can be erected in the form of a tower so that the carpenter gang can be fully employed, and non-productive time of precast concrete erectors minimised.

When sliding shuttering is used for the central service and lift core of a building twenty storeys high of composite precast and in-situ

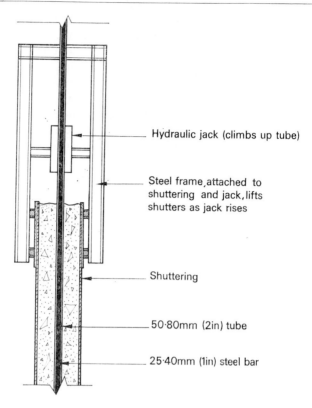

Hydraulic jack (climbs up tube)

Steel frame, attached to
shuttering and jack, lifts
shutters as jack rises

Shuttering

50·80mm (2in) tube

25·40mm (1in) steel bar

FIG. 3.1   Sliding forms with hydraulic jacks and steel vertical frames and
braces

construction, pouring of the in-situ concrete walls commences from the
bottom, and the walls rise about 90 ft (27·43 m) in height by the middle of
the second week of operations. As the structure does not achieve wind
stability above 120 ft (36·58 m) to 130 ft (39·62 m), the building would
become unstable through the walls having advanced far beyond the
rate of casting the floors, unless provision were made for a floor to be
rapidly cast at the tenth floor to act as a diaphragm. The shuttering for
one floor soffit is set up at ground level within the structure and hoisted
to the tenth floor level so that concrete can be poured as quickly as
possible to avoid delaying the rapidly rising walls. Holes of 1½ in (38 mm)
diameter are cast in for threading steel wire ropes through in order to
lower the further soffit for casting the floors below, commencing with the

ninth floor and proceeding down to first floor level. To speed erection, a second shutter soffit can be placed on the tenth floor and hoisted to roof level for subsequently pouring the remaining floor slabs, commencing at twentieth floor level and proceeding downwards to the eleventh floor level.

This method of using dropping shutters can achieve very rapid construction time. It is more costly than slower, traditional methods of construction, which require careful integration of the precast concrete erection cycle with the slower in-situ concrete pouring cycle to avoid non-productive time caused by delays in curing concrete and shuttering operations.

Various other mechanised methods of shuttering enable whole floors to be speedily decked out, and are easily dismantled after the concrete has been poured.

With composite construction of this type, wind forces are restricted by the in-situ concrete core, and the precast perimeter frame can be tied to the floor by the precast units. Optimum economy is achieved by three or four precast perimeter columns being hoisted together in a metal jig and positioned over precast concrete edge beams supporting the floor slabs, the perimeter columns being designed to carry only central axial forces.

One system for high-rise housing up to thirty storeys high is based on in-situ concrete cross wall construction using sliding shuttering. The plastic concrete is placed in a slip-formwork assembly and moulded to the structural plan shape. The sliding shutters move upwards at a rate of two and a half storeys a week, and the average labour content, including erecting off-site prefabricated components, averages 800 to 900 manhours per dwelling.

The economic use of sliding shuttering depends on the correct integration of shuttering, reinforcement, and concreting operations into interdependent coordinated processes; utilisation of cranes and mixing plant to achieve outputs of 6 to 12 cu yd (4·59 to 9·17 m³) of concrete to be placed per hour; and overtime and night work to be undertaken during the construction of the in-situ tower.

In general, the higher the structure, the greater the economy attained due to the high cost of setting up and making the sliding shutters.

The main advantages of this form of shuttering include high speed of construction, with a centralised mixing plant; reduced costs of shutters because only one complete lift of shutters is made for the whole structure, and the cost of handling heavy shutters by tower crane and fixed scaffolding is avoided; comparatively low man hours are required on site; and a jointless structure is obtained with a good finish.

Disadvantages comprise; high rates of labour due to the need for skilled operatives, and shiftwork; high costs of installing and making the forms, and reserve plant and power must be available in case of breakdowns.

Hydraulic telescopic shutter systems are manufactured for supporting poured in-situ concrete soffits based on a standard component comprising adjustable wheeled towers with telescopic legs with bearing capacities of 5 or 10 tons (5·08 or 10·16 tonnes) per leg and soffit shutters. The legs are adjusted hydraulically by a small portable compressor. The whole structure can be moved as shuttering operations progress, and towed to other sites where required. The shuttering system can be dismantled and redesigned to form a new system for supporting concrete soffits of different kinds of structures. Less site labour is required for the repetitive erection and striking operations, and craft labour is eliminated.

Prefabricated steel tunnel shutters. Some systems are based on precision made steel interlocking shutters designed for transverse walls and plain floor slabs finished for direct spray painting or wall papering to reduce site labour. The room size shutters are in the form of tunnels, with sides of one piece steel panels full storey height, and soffit divided at the centre and extending the full span of the floor. Each half is jointed to the vertical member to make a right-angle bracket.

Location pins, clamps and dowels ensure a true surface; and screw jacks, removable props and quick release clamps with four-wheeled trolleys enable the tunnels to be withdrawn within reach of the erection crane for ease of striking, quick turn round, and minimum damage.

Concrete maturing is effected by means of steam pipes attached to the formwork, temperature being controlled to ensure that the concrete hardens overnight. By these means, a complete floor can be constructed in two days.

Setting out for subsequent floors is eliminated by means of a steel kicker incorporated in the shutter for the next wall above. Scaffolding is obviated, as the shutters provide a working platform which follows up the building, and is used for wheeling on the tunnels prior to handling by crane to the floor above. Fast erection times can be achieved with a small labour force. A complete two-storey house shell can be cast with four tunnel shutters.

PRECAST CONCRETE CONSTRUCTION

Panel systems.

Industrialised techniques based on the production of precast concrete structural units can speed construction with fewer operatives. However, the capital cost of factory plant and equipment necessitates a much higher volume of demand for economy than that normally provided by developments on individual sites. Additional disadvantages are that the precast units are heavy and cumbersome, and require costly cranes for handling to position. Where structural members are joined to others at beam and column intersections, the in-situ connections are complicated and expensive to construct. There is a delay while the in-situ work matures, tending to offset the time advantage of prefabrication. The structural units are heavier than steel sections and require more costly foundations and cranage; flexibility of design is restricted. Condensation problems are expensive to resolve, and other defects may arise which have not yet been fully discovered due to the comparative novelty of industrialised building techniques.

Precast concrete box-shell structures with jointed connections capable of resisting both tension and shear stresses approximate to thin wall spatial systems in which every element resists a local load which is transmitted to strong points in the system. Floors resist bending out of plane and transmit the load to walls. Transverse loaded walls resist compression and transmit loads to foundations and longitudinal walls. The structural components participate in the three-dimensional stressed state of the whole system, which may not always prevail under the local load. The rigidity of the structure depends on the plumbness of the walls and the stiffness of the joints to resist any rocking tendency (Plate 3).

Buildings constructed in this form comprise complex statically indeterminate systems with composite structures of load-bearing walls pierced with door and window openings, supported on ground foundations. The walls become elongated beams and columns forming an eggcrate, with the façade filled in with a variety of infilling.

Large concrete panels for floors, load-bearing wall units and partition walls can be standardised for economic factory production to achieve speed and simplicity of erection. A floating floor finish can be used to avoid the impact noise of rigid fixing.

The tendency of large panel techniques to increase panel sizes to dimensions of two or three rooms and minimise the number of component types and site joints requires a vast volume of demand for economic production.

An open plan which uses a minimum number of precast concrete structural units provides an economic basis for mass producing units without the need for very costly factory plant and equipment, and can achieve simple site erection. A design that permits floors to be supported only as external bearings further simplifies site erection.

Structural design criteria for panel systems is related to the total cubic feet of concrete per dwelling; the percentage ratio of concrete in cladding to structural units per dwelling; the percentage of floor to wall areas; and the total number of components per dwelling.

Provision for handling units should be detailed at design stage to ensure that permissible stresses are not exceeded during erection. Lifting devices should be inherently safe, easily inspected and operated, and ensure that the units hang correctly for placing in order to avoid double handling. The handling of units from the moulds may require different devices from those used for hoisting units to position, such as projecting or recessed loops to accommodate standard hooks or shackles, sleeved or plain holes formed in units, cast in projecting bolts, or vacuum pads.

Factory production with steel moulds enables the concrete to be closely controlled to reduce materials costs and improve quality. Where concrete surfaces are to be exposed, the production of a satisfactory finish and the installation of service pipes and electrical conduits is facilitated in the moulds.

Plan modules used to achieve maximum mould utilisation for high-rise dwellings should be related to a frontage module, determined by the maximum span; a second module for room widths related to the size of moulds used for casting, and a third module related to storey heights.

The optimum room size for most panel systems for high-rise structures requires units weighing not more than 8 tons; floor slabs about 22 ft × 9 ft 6 in (6·70 m × 2·90 m), and wall units about 22 ft × 8 ft 6 in (6·70 m × 2·59 m). Some systems are based on a limiting weight of 10 tons (10·16 tonnes) per unit, and require heavier and more costly cranes.

For maximum economy and fast erection cycles with tower cranes, basic room sizes should be developed to fit the productivity of the system. Designs should avoid the need for external scaffolding to façades, and utilise preglazed windows, cladding panels and curtain walling fixed from inside the building. Balcony units and staircases should be precast, and any work required to elevations executed off cradles.

One type of precast concrete system for low-rise housing up to four storeys in height is based on simple load-bearing structures which can be built up with floor slab panel units and L-shaped wall panel units. These provide considerable stability, and are equivalent to a wall buttressed by another at right angles, without need for structural joints between the wall panels. Joints at abutting wall units are formed with non-structural filling for sound insulation. Openings between walls can be of storey height, and where located externally are filled in with light infill units of timber framing incorporating doors and windows.

One of the main disadvantages of precast concrete construction is that continuity and rigidity are more difficult to attain than with in-situ concrete structures. The lowering of a precast concrete unit into its final position is a critical point. Centre lines of gravity must be calculated to ensure that the unit is dropped into position without any other movement than propping. Units must not be dropped on splay, and subsequently aligned vertically, because lateral movements of the crane are dangerous. Any plumbing up should be very small, and carried out on props. The erection crane has to hold and steady medium and heavy weight panel units, and handle them into position with a jib attachment based on stays, and bolted inserts cast into the unit, whose weight, shape and position varies the time of crane operations. Thus a wall unit requires a certain amount of staying, a floor unit has to be positioned and levelled, and a staircase unit more delicately so.

Unless there is a sufficient volume and continuity of demand, at least approximately 300 dwellings on one site, factory production is uneconomic.

Example of production and erection requirements for a panel system. Structural components suited to site factory manufacture of units for four twenty-storey blocks on one site, each block approximately 100 ft × 50 ft (30·48 m × 15·2 m) on plan, and comprising two 3-bedroom, two 2-bedroom, and one 1-bedroom dwelling per floor would be based on the following panel types (max. 6 tons) (6·10 tonnes) per floor:

Panel type	Size (approx.)	No. required
7 in (178 mm) wall panels		
A	15 ft × 8 ft	24
	(4·57 m × 2·44 m)	
C	13 ft 8 in × 8 ft	2
	(4·16 m × 2·44 m)	

Panel type	Size (approx.)	No. required
7 in (178 mm) wall panels—*cont.*		
G	8 ft 6 in × 8 ft	7
	(2·59 m × 2·44 m)	
H	5 ft 6 in × 8 ft	4
	(1·67 m × 2·44 m)	
J	7 ft 6 in × 8 ft	6
	(2·28 m × 2·44 m)	
7 in (178 mm) wall panel with beam		
K	7 ft 9 in × 8 ft	2
	(2·35 m × 2·44 m)	
12 in (305 mm) wall panels		
D	15 ft × 9 ft	4
	(4·57 m × 2·74 m)	
E	5 ft 6 in × 8 ft 3 in	4
	(1·67 m × 2·51 m)	
F	8 ft 6 in × 8 ft 3 in	1
	(2·59 m × 2·51 m)	
6½ in (165 mm) balcony panels	17 ft × 5 ft	4
	(5·18 m × 1·52 m)	
	11 ft × 3 ft	8
	(3·35 m × 0·91 m)	
	9 ft × 3 ft	4
	(2·74 m × 0·91 m)	
6½ in (165 mm) floor panels	15 ft 9 in × 8 ft 6 in	9
	(4·58 m × 2·54 m)	
	8 ft 9 in × 8 ft 6 in	5
	(2·64 m × 2·54 m)	
	9 ft × 3 ft 3 in	5
	(2·74 m × 0·98 m)	
	16 ft 6 in × 10 ft 9 in	7
	(5·02 m × 3·27 m)	

Unit type	Size (approx.)	No. required
8 in (203 mm) mullion (2 storeys high)	16 ft 9 in × 1 ft 4 in (5·10 m) × (0·42 m)	22
16 in (406 mm) corner (2-storeys high)	16 ft 9 in × 1 ft 4 in (5·10 m) × (0·92 m)	4
Dust chute unit 2 ft dia (610 m)	8 ft (2·44 m) long	1
Ditto floor ring 2 ft dia (610 m)	6 in (0·15 m) high	1
Single flight stair unit	—	2
Landing slab unit	—	2

Internal partition slabs would be cast $2\frac{3}{4}$ in (70 mm) thick. Approximately 100 cu ft (2·83 m³) of poured in-situ concrete and 16 cwt (0·81 tonnes) of steel reinforcement per floor would be required for 'stitching' joints between units.

Site factory production. The site factory would be sited to accord with erection requirements, and operate with a manager and team of about twenty-three operatives. The production cycle would be based on twenty-four hours for a weekly output of units for $1\frac{1}{2}$ floors, comprising approximately 9500 cu ft (269·41 m³) of precast concrete working ten hours per day for five and a half days. Steel moulds would be heated by steam to accelerate curing for the following daily production cycle:

The floor slabs would be cast and lifted horizontally; wall cladding units would be cast horizontally in tilting moulds; wall and partition slabs cast vertically in batteries with mild steel bars cast in and threaded top and bottom to provide vertical continuity during assembly. The excess bolt length would fit into purpose-made cones in a pocket formed at each end of a wall unit, above which a steel rod would run full height and project at the top to form a levelling bolt for the floor above. Threaded lifting sockets would be cast into all units together with the steel mesh reinforcement.

Erection operations. The sequence of erection operations would comprise:

positioning floor slabs on foundation walls with a gap between equal to the wall thickness less bearing, and steel reinforcement in loops projecting from edges of floor slab and top of foundations; reinforcing stitches between joints with lateral steel bars provided to tie the structure together;

Daily Factory Production Cycle for Panel System

Unit	Type	Size	Quantity per unit cu. ft	Mould type	Strike, clean and prepare mould (mins)	Fix electrics (mins)	Fix steel reinfct (mins)	Cast concrete (mins)	Total time (hours)
S.O.1	6½" (165 mm) floor slab	15'10" × 8'7" (4·82 m) × (2·61 m)	79	Horizontal	45	30	15	15	1¾
S.O.2	6½" (165 mm) floor slab	8'10" × 8'7" (2·68 m) × (2·61 m)	44	Horizontal	60	15	15	15	1¾
S.O.3	6½" (165 mm) floor slab	9' × 3'3" (2·74 m) × (0·99 m)	17	Horizontal	45	15	15	15	1½
S.O.4	6½" (165 mm) floor slab	16'7" × 10'10" (5·04 m) × (3·29 m)	90	Horizontal	45	15	15	15	1½
4 No.J	7" (178 mm) wall units in	7'7" × 7'11" (2·3 m) × (2·41 m)	4 No.=140	Vertical					
2 No. H. Battery A		5'7" × 7'11" (1·69 m) × (2·41 m)	2 No.= 52	Battery A					
3 No.G		8'6" × 7'11" (2·58 m) × (2·41 m)	3 No.=117		165	105		60	5½
1 No.K		7'10" × 7'11" (2·38 m) × (2·41 m)	1 No.= 36						
			Total 345						
3 No.A	7" (178 mm) wall units in	15'1" × 7'11" (4·59 m) × (2·41 m)	3 No.=210	Vertical					

1 No.C	Battery B	13′8″ × 7′11″ (4·16 m) × (2·41 m)	1 No.= 63	Battery B	120	90		45	$4\frac{1}{4}$
			Total 273						
1 No.E	12″ (305 mm) and 7″	5′7″ × 8′4″ (2·3 m) × (2·58 m)	1 No.= 47	Vertical Battery C					
1 No.F	(178 mm)	8′5″ × 8′4″ (3·06 m) × (2·93 m)	1 No.= 70		120	90		60	$4\frac{1}{2}$
4 No.A	wall units in Battery C	15′1″ × 7′11″ (4·59 m) × (2·41 m)	4 No.=220						
			Total 337						
	Half landing and stair flight		36		75		15	15	$1\frac{3}{4}$
	Mullions	16′8″ × 1′4″ × 8″ (5·08 m) × (·406 m) × (203 m)	15		75		15	15	$1\frac{3}{4}$
	$6\frac{1}{2}$″ (165 mm) Balcony slabs	17′ × 5′ (5·18 m) × (1·52 m)	46						
		11′ × 3′ (3·35 m) × (0·91 m)	18		75		15	15	$1\frac{3}{4}$
		9′ × 3′ (2·74 m) × (0·91 m)	15						
	$2\frac{3}{4}$″ (57 mm) partitions in vertical batteries B & C.								

6

pouring in-situ 'stitching' concrete into the gaps, and vibrating it to form a joint which ties the structure together,

lining and levelling the nuts on top of the levelling bolts projecting through the units from the wall below, and placing a steel washer over each nut,

laying a stiff mortar bed in the recess over the structural joint between the floor slabs where bearing on wall units,

lowering cross wall units onto the washers and levelling bolts,

propping and plumbing the walls, and

cleaning off the excess mortar from the base of wall units. About forty-eight hours later, the levelling nuts would be slightly unscrewed and the pockets filled in flush with mortar,

Vertical joints between wall units can be formed with in-situ concrete poured into opposing serrated grooves to avoid cold bridging effects through the cladding in which a polystyrene layer is cast. Horizontal waterproofing of the façade panels may be obtained by inserting compressible butyl foam strips and light weight flashings.

When all the wall units are in place, the floor slabs for the next storey above are positioned to tie the lower storey units together. After this has been done, the props would be removed, and finishing operations commence.

The table on page 65 indicates average crane times for placing wall units.

The lifting speeds of the erection crane would be varied to minimise the hoisting time of units positioned at upper floors, for example:

Crane rig	Lifting speed per minute ft
4-*fall*	
low gear	33
medium gear	85
high gear	164
2-*fall*	
low gear	66
medium gear	170
high gear	328

Average times of Crane Placing Wall Units—in Minutes and Seconds

Unit	Initial lift	Level bolts	Set out position	Strike props	Strike floor channel or bks	Fix channel	Slacken bolts	Load out mortar	Strike cramp or transfer levelling nut etc.	Crane rig	Total
12th to 15th floor											
A	40·64	3·20	6·94	6·44	2·76	2·40	2·14	2·37	—	4 falls low	66·89
C	41·84	3·20	6·94	3·11	1·50	1·88	2·14	2·37	0·30	4 falls low	63·82
D	33·44	3·20	6·94	7·02	2·88	3·08	2·14	1·18	2·45	2 falls medium	62·33
E	44·44	3·20	6·94	3·51	1·50	1·88	2·14	1·18	6·39	2 falls low	71·18
F	50·84	3·20	6·94	3·51	1·50	1·88	2·14	1·18	6·60	2 falls low	77·88
G	37·48	3·20	6·94	3·22	1·50	1·88	2·14	1·18	0·30	2 falls medium	57·84
H	31·42	3·20	6·94	3·11	—	—	2·14	1·18	0·30	2 falls medium	48·29
J	45·84	3·20	6·94	8·36	—	—	2·14	1·18	—	2 falls medium	67·66
K	44·76	3·20	6·94	—	0·75	—	2·14	1·18	0·42	2 falls medium	59·39
16th to 19th floor											
A	42·16	3·20	6·94	6·49	2·76	2·40	2·14	2·37	—	4 falls low	68·41
C	43·36	3·20	6·94	3·11	1·50	1·88	2·14	2·37	0·30	4 falls low	64·80
D	35·12	3·20	6·94	7·02	2·88	3·08	2·14	1·18	2·45	2 falls medium	64·01
E	45·64	3·20	6·94	3·51	1·50	1·88	2·14	1·18	6·39	2 falls low	72·98
F	52·04	3·20	6·94	3·51	1·50	1·88	2·14	1·18	6·89	2 falls low	79·78
G	39·16	3·20	6·94	3·22	1·50	1·88	2·14	1·18	0·30	2 falls medium	59·52
H	32·30	3·20	6·94	3·11	—	—	2·14	1·18	0·30	2 falls low	49·17
J	47·52	3·20	6·94	8·36	—	—	2·14	1·18	—	2 falls medium	69·34
K	46·44	3·20	6·94	—	0·75	—	2·14	1·18	0·42	2 falls medium	61·07

The following tables indicate the average total crane and associated team's times for erecting wall units, including placing, lining and plumbing:

Average crane and team times, lining and plumbing walls:

Unit	Weight in cwt	Weight in tonnes	Crane time placing unit (min.)	Manhours levelling etc.	Total time (min.)	Crane rig	Floor level
A	93	4·72	66·89	26·66	93·55	4 falls low	12–15th
A	93	4·72	68·41	26·66	95·07	4 falls low	16–19th
C	84	4·28	63·82	26·59	90·41	4 falls low	12–15th
C	84	4·28	64·80	26·59	91·39	4 falls low	16–19th
D	97	4·92	62·33	32·32	94·65	4 falls med.	12–15th
D	97	4·92	64·01	32·32	96·33	4 falls med.	16–19th
E	80	4·06	71·18	10·12	81·30	2 falls low	12–15th
E	80	4·06	72·98	10·12	83·10	2 falls low	16–19th
F	71	3·60	77·88	12·84	90·72	2 falls low	12–15th
F	71	3·60	79·78	12·84	92·62	2 falls low	16–19th
G	52	2·64	57·84	15·46	73·30	2 falls med.	12–15th
G	52	2·64	59·52	15·46	74·98	2 falls med.	16–19th
H	34	1·73	48·29	17·78	66·07	2 falls low	12–15th
H	34	1·73	49·17	17·78	66·95	2 falls low	16–19th
J	47	2·39	67·66	12·40	80·06	2 falls med.	12–15th
J	47	2·39	69·34	12·40	81·74	2 falls med.	16–19th
K	27	1·37	59·39	37·66	97·05	2 falls med.	12–15th
K	27	1·37	61·07	37·66	98·73	2 falls med.	16–19th

Average crane and team time, placing and plumbing balcony units:

Type	Weight	Floor level	Crane rig	Lifting time	Placing time	Line and plumb	Total time
Balcony	3 to 6 tons (3·04 to 6·10 tonnes)	12–15	2 falls low	8·06	24·18	8·83	41·07
		16–19	2 falls low	8·82	26·46	8·83	44·11
Balcony	25 cwt to 3 tons (1·27 to 3·04 tonnes)	12–15	2 falls med.	6·70	20·10	8·83	35·63
		16–19	2 falls med.	6·83	21·49	8·83	36·15
Double height mullion	ne 25 cwt (1·27 tonnes)	12–15	2 falls high	5·79	17·37	42·48	65·64
		16–19	2 falls high	6·21	18·63	42·48	67·32
Corner mullion	ne 25 cwt (1·27 tonnes)	12–15	2 falls high	7·34	22·02	32·29	61·65
		16–19	2 falls high	7·76	23·28	32·29	63·33

Average crane and team times, placing and plumbing dust chute and stair units

Type	Weight	No. Floor level	Crane rig	Lifting time	Placing time	Line and plumb	Total
Dust chute	ne 25 cwt (1·27 tonnes)	12–15	2 falls high	8·42	25·26	—	33·68
		16–19	2 falls high	8·80	26·40	—	35·20
Floor rings	ne 25 cwt (1·27 tonnes)	12–15	2 falls high	3·69	7·38	5·29	16·36
		16–19	2 falls high	4·07	8·14	5·29	17·50
Single flight stairs	25 cwt to 3 tons (1·27 to 3·04 tonnes)	12–15	2 falls med.	8·12	24·36	15·37	47·85
		16–19	2 falls med.	8·47	25·41	15·37	49·25
Landing slab	25 cwt to 3 tons (1·27 to 3·04 tonnes)	12–15	2 falls med.	6·88	20·64	—	27·52
		15–19	2 falls med.	7·23	21·69	—	28·92

Under normal conditions, a static tower crane on concrete beams with sleepers and track, and tied back to the structure at increased heights would be used for hoisting all precast units from the stacking areas to required placing positions, handling reinforcement and in-situ concrete mixed at ground level for stitching joints. Mortar for bedding wall units would be mixed at each erection floor level.

The following tables indicate the average total crane and associated team's times for erecting wall units, including placing, lining and plumbing:

Type	Size	No.	Crane rig	Lifting time	Placing time
801	15'10" × 8'7"	19	4 falls med.	9·12	30·36
	(4·82 m × 2·61 m)				
802	8'10" × 8'7"	5	4 falls med.	9·12	27·96
	(2·68 m × 2·61 m)				
803	9'0" × 3'3"	5	4 falls high	7·96	23·88
	(2·74 m × 0·99 m)				
804	16'7" × 10'10"	7	4 falls low	12·43	34·71
	(5·04 m × 3·29 m)				

The erection cycle for a typical floor (12th to 15th) would be based on the following sequence of operations shown in the the following table:

Erection cycle for a typical floor (12th to 15th):

Operation	Quantity per floor	Site labour team in hours	Crane time in hours
Place and plumb walls	54 units	$77\frac{1}{2}$	58
Ditto balconies	12 units	8	2
Ditto floor slabs	36 units	14	$5\frac{3}{4}$
Load out $2\frac{3}{4}$ in partitions and place and plumb	42 units	$6\frac{1}{4}$	$1\frac{3}{4}$
Place and plumb stair flights and landing slab	2 units	2	$1\frac{1}{2}$
Ditto dust chutes	1 unit	1	—
Stitching steel in joints	16 cwt	5	$\frac{1}{4}$
In-situ concrete in joints	97 cu ft	7	$1\frac{3}{4}$
Place and plumb mullions	4 units	$17\frac{3}{4}$	$10\frac{1}{4}$

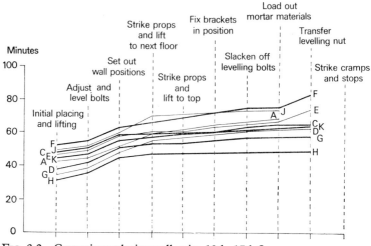

FIG. 3.2   Crane times placing wall units, 12th–15th floors

Metric Equivalents

	Tonnes	Cwt
A	4·27	93
C	4·28	84
D	4·92	97
E	4·06	80
F	3·60	71
G	2·64	52
H	1·73	34
J	2·39	47
K	1·37	27

Figures 3.2 to 3.7 summarise the associated crane times and sequences of erection operations, and indicate that differences in crane time hoisting units from tenth to twentieth floor do not vary by more than approximately 10 per cent increase from the time required for hoisting units to lower floor levels. This is due to quickening the speed of the crane's lift by changing to a faster gear, an advantage that may be obviated to some extent by more frequent high winds delaying crane working at increased heights.

All departures from standardised units involve a greatly increased time for placing. Wall units cast with a cantilever beam to form a corridor opening (unit K), and one levelling bolt instead of two, take longer to level because the beam rests on another seating and tends to pivot and skew when lined. Mullion units require two men working on different floor levels to balance their ends and line them horizontally and vertically.

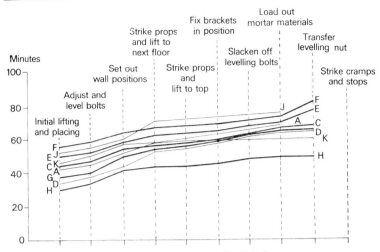

FIG. 3.3 Crane times placing wall units, 16th–19th floors

The heaviest floor slab units (127 cwt) (6·45 tonnes) bear on a greater number of wall units, and consequently require increased time for levelling and placing. Their extra weight necessitates more manhours pushing and pulling the units into position whilst still being held in position by the erection crane, but is of lesser significance because this type of unit can be dropped into position, and then propped.

Frame systems.

Designs for systems based on precast reinforced concrete structural frames should economise the high cost of the precision-made steel moulds required to produce standardised beam and column units with close tolerances by repeatedly using the same basic sections a sufficient number of times so that capital investment required for factory production can be recovered within a comparatively short period, and achieve savings in cost and time (Plate 2).

Standardised moulds for precast concrete frames can provide scope for the expression of individual designs in a variety of ways. Grids can be varied to provide any chosen module, e.g. 4 ft (1·22 m) or 5 ft (1·52 m) so that external mullions can be spaced at 4, 5, 8 or 10 ft (1·22, 1·52, 2·44 or 3·05 m) etc., centres. The structural frame can be exposed and manufactured with white cement and aggregates to obtain an acceptable architectural finish. External work can be brought off the grid by cantilevering the floor out to carry a curtain wall or other chosen elevation in any kind of materials and thus achieve variations in pattern, texture and colour.

Floors can be standardised, or patent types of construction utilised. Greater economy could be obtained, particularly in view of the coming change over to the metric system, if their dimensions were also to be

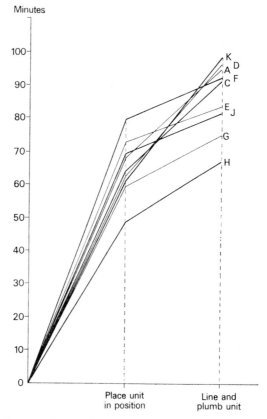

FIG. 3.4   Crane and team times placing, lining and plumbing wall units, 12th–15th floors

standardised. Columns, edge beams and spine beams can be cast to any length consistent with the span/load limitations. The whole framework can be tied together by a structural floor screed, which helps the floor to function as a horizontal diaphragm by transmitting wind loads through to shear walls.

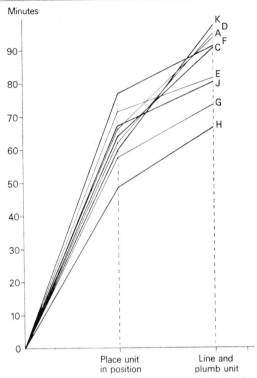

FIG. 3.5   Crane and team times placing, lining and plumbing wall units, 16th–19th floors

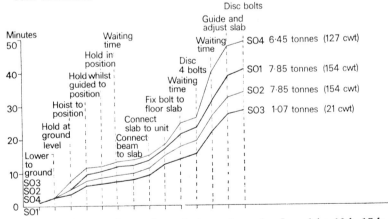

FIG. 3.6   Crane and team times placing and erecting floor slabs, 12th–15th floors

Erecting precast concrete frame units

Factors which affect the economy of precast concrete frame systems relate to maximum number of repetitive units; minimum amount of times each unit can be handled; availability of site facilities for production and stacking of units without impeding erection operations; the gearing of factory output to erection requirements, with efficient stacking to minimise damage and cranage; methods of yoking groups of units together to facilitate hoisting to position; efficient cranage for handling units; type of factory production and moulds, and jointing techniques.

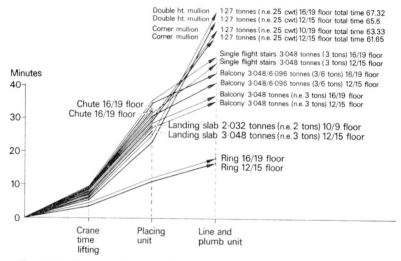

FIG. 3.7   Crane and team times placing and plumbing dust chutes, balconies, mullion and stair units, 12th–15th and 16th–19th floors

Precast frames are about 20 to 30 per cent cheaper than steel frames encased in concrete and comparable in cost with uncased steel frames, which require the additional expense of fire protection with other materials, thus reducing speed of erection operations. Precast frames avoid most of the disadvantages of in-situ work, benefit from some of the advantages of steelwork, and permit extensive unification of structural units for building types with relatively large areas and spans on the basis of a modular system. High tensile reinforcing steel, high strength concrete, prestressing techniques, and improved ratio of height to span enables dimensions to be increased for the economic factory production of standardised precast beam, column and curtain wall panel units, which can be rapidly erected by cranes. Improved moulding methods provide façade surfacing of units with smooth or textured weather proofed finish externally, and smooth inner surfaces ready for direct spray painting.

Five main component types are required to carry superimposed floor loads and provide for the stability of the structure:

exposed external, and internal columns;
beams—which may be visually absent, as in flush slab construction;
floors—solid, hollow and T-section;
stairs—flights and landings; and
stability walls—which may be independent, or form part of lift or staircase walls.

As the stability of the frame depends largely on the stability walls, so the loading of vertical components can be isolated to form racking forces by using internal walls. Joints between the frame are extremely vital, so visible signs of any movement in the structure should be controlled to occur only at these points.

The weight of the structure can be reduced by lowered strength characteristics and close control of materials to improve quality of concrete, standardising a minimum number of beam and column sizes, with varying loads taken up by alternative reinforcement, the joints between beams and columns being load-transferring; light cladding of maximum size for efficient cranage; and prefinishing units in the factory to reduce the work of other trades.

A pre-casting technique developed in the U.S.A. enabled the 7000 lb p.s.i. lightweight precast and prestressed structure for a ten storey building 115 ft (35 m) square on plan to be erected in 29 *working days*.

Columns and central core units were cast in forms the same length as the height of the building, with headers to separate units into one or two storey lengths.

Inverted T-beams with double-tee floor slabs resting on them span to the central core.

The building was framed so that all double tees spanned east and west on odd floors and north and south on even floors in order to keep loads evenly distributed to core walls and exterior columns, and avoid high stresses in any load-bearing walls. The dead load of the building compresses all joints so that wind loading is negligible.

JOINTING TOLERANCES

The design of precast concrete units for factory production should ensure that variations in dimensions after manufacture will be taken up in site jointing. This influences the systems' success and speed of erection due to problems affecting the handling, weight limitation, and ready assembly of structural elements, and the durability and ease of joint repair.

The most critical parts of precast concrete structures occur at the joints between units, which must be capable of transferring forces without undue deflection or deformation, with a minimum of support.

The physical limitations of concrete restrict precise connections to the interaction of concrete with other suitable media. Any in-situ mass concrete filling that may be required at the joints should be easily handled to position, poured, and compacted. Joints with steel reinforcement, bolts, and plates are difficult to make effective, much more costly, and delay the speed of erection operations. All joints designed to transmit tensile stresses must have the steel bar reinforcement lapped at some point. There is a tendency with bolted joints for spalling to be induced at the fixing points due to the effects of stress concentrations.

Panel systems avoid the bending moment induced by the load in a frame system, and require only one joint made with direct loading. The largest possible units should be cast with close tolerances to minimise site joints, and omit traditional finishings to mask inaccuracies. The larger the units designed, the greater will be the movements that occur, with consequent demand on sealants used at the joints of façade panels, which will vary according to height of structure.

Joints between structural panel units taking stresses vary with the type (wet or dry) and position of the joint, and should be designed to include for tolerances and creep. Close tolerances are costly to achieve, but joints become more difficult to make as tolerances increase.

Problems relating to the design of joints between structural panel units taking stresses include that of tolerances, which may need to be acceptable for structural, aesthetic, waterproof, thermal and sound resistance purposes. A joint may be required to accommodate tolerances due to manufacture and setting out on site, as well as allowances for working loads. It may also have to exclude weather, allow for thermal and moisture movements, preserve sound and thermal insulation, and withstand factors due to manufacturing techniques and methods of site assembly, such as sandwich façade panel units formed with a cavity to reduce noise and increase insulation between two skins, as well as being designed with structural and weather resistant qualities, and half the weight of dense concrete (Figs. 3.8 and 3.9).

Temperature creep and shrinkage in precast concrete structures necessitate movement joints designed to function without damaging units. Façade sandwich panels and other structural units, which vary the line of action of their loads as the temperatures of the inner and outer skins vary, should be designed to ensure uneven distribution which avoids overstressing.

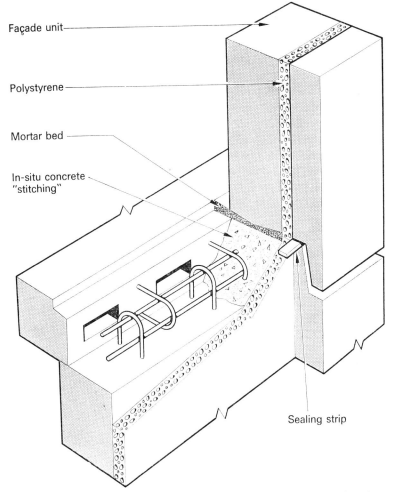

FIG. 3.8   Panel systems: horizontal joint in precast concrete façade unit

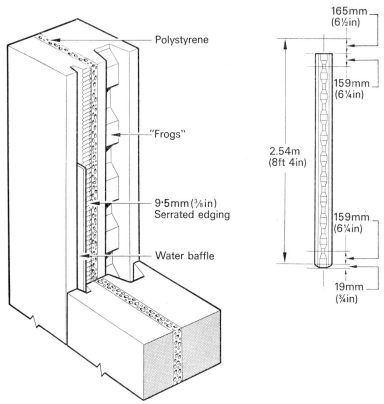

Polystyrene

"Frogs"

9·5mm (⅜in)
Serrated edging

Water baffle

165mm
(6½in)

159mm
(6¼in)

2.54m
(8ft 4in)

159mm
(6¼in)

19mm
(¾in)

FIG. 3.9 Panel systems: vertical joint in precast concrete façade unit

Roof movements due to temperature creep can damage walls. Where possible, insulation with a light reflective surface should be provided above the structural roof slab. Creep deflection of floor slabs can damage partitions and finishes, and must be obviated so far as possible.

Wet joints are costly and delay the erection cycle. Designs should provide for a stable structure to minimise propping units, and enable any grout jointing or 'stitching' to be carried out when required, and not only during erection operations. Units should be designed with bearing areas capable of accommodating reasonable tolerances without spalling at edges, so that they can be placed without fouling any projecting reinforcement.

Joints between plain structural elements such as floor and wall units usually have in-situ concrete 'stitching' poured around additional steel reinforcement to provide continuity and fire protection, and prevent the slabs from sliding apart and forming potential crack lines which may reduce sound and thermal insulation, fire resistance, and structural strength (Figs. 3.10 and 3.11).

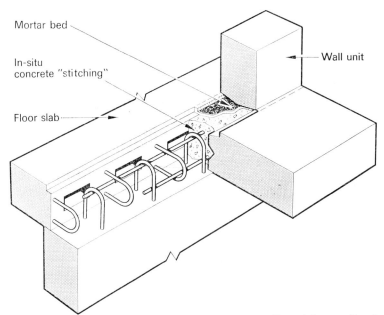

FIG. 3.10   Panel systems: joint of precast concrete floor slab to wall unit

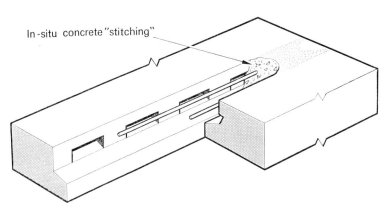

FIG. 3.11   Panel systems: differential joint between adjacent precast floor slabs

7

The function of vertical joints between wall units is to prevent one wall sliding against another, and a 'frog' is provided to prevent this occurring.

Horizontal joints between wall units should be in compression to minimise the cost of steel reinforcement. Where tension occurs, spliced reinforcement joints are more economical to form than joints with plates, bolts and nuts levelled on the lower unit and adjusted when the upper unit has been plumbed, as this form of joint delays the erection cycle (Fig. 3.10).

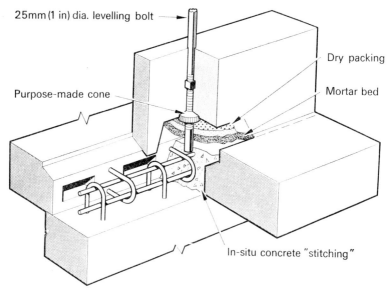

25mm (1 in) dia. levelling bolt

Dry packing

Purpose-made cone

Mortar bed

In-situ concrete "stitching"

FIG. 3.12   Panel systems: levelling device

One economical method of avoiding costly joints at the internal angles of T-plan-shaped buildings consists of forming the angles with poured in-situ concrete to fit the grid module and avoid difficult jointing and weatherproofing of the internal angles.

Landing units and stair flights should be sealed with the minimum of bearings to facilitate levelling operations.

The propping and strutting of units requires minimising for optimum speed of erection. Units should be designed for sufficiently firm assembly which stabilises the structure and supports their dead weights, and construction loads. Attempts to reduce the erection crane's holding time whilst wall units are being fixed include the development of a free-standing storey height unit L-shaped on plan, 8 ft (2·44 m) long × 4 ft (1·22 m) long on return.

Early attempts to provide effective joints between column and beams involved difficulties of tolerances and appearance. Joints must be sufficiently large to permit any concrete placed in them to be compacted by vibration to ensure effective bond between the poured concrete, steel reinforcement and hardened concrete of the units.

The necessity to develop the load-carrying capacity of reinforced concrete frame members through the site joints requires special provision at the ends to transmit forces from the reinforcement, and attention must be paid to the jointing medium.

The construction of precast frames based on storey-height columns enables eccentricities to be imparted by the tendency of the edge beams sandwiched between the column ends to rotate. This may impart additional bending stresses to column ends, and cause them to disrupt at an earlier stage than when subject to pure axial load.

This tendency can be counteracted by improving the resistance to bursting at the ends of heavily reinforced columns to provide a better margin of safety against cracking. In addition, the failure load at this point should be equated to the strength of the column shaft in order to improve the overall carrying capacity, and provide an additional margin to contribute to the bending stresses that might arise from edge beam rotation. The condition of the load application should be improved by the introduction of a soft bedding joint that will permit rotation, or by limiting the area of bedding to accord more nearly to a pin end, thus restricting the eccentricity and moment that can be induced.

It is essential to ensure that reinforcement is not displaced during casting, and that ends of bars are covered to required tolerances which permit easy erection, and maintain an acceptable finished building (e.g. $\pm \frac{1}{4}$ in (6 mm) in 10 ft (3·04 m) for lengths of columns). Closer tolerances (e.g. $\pm 1/16$ in (1·5 mm) require very much more expensive moulds.

Vertical joints should allow for additional lengths of tolerances, and horizontal joints provide sufficient tolerance on the height of the building to maintain correct floor levels.

Horizontal joints between column and wall units can be divided into joints of units in which the concrete can bear the load, and reinforcement is nominal because the units are not required to resist high bending moments; and joints of units in which reinforcement for compression or

tension, and some form of coupling is required. The effect of any movement in the units due to wind or construction operations before a
concrete or mortar joint has reached a satisfactory tensile strength can
reduce the effectiveness of joints. It is essential that a construction
programme allows for the full design strength of any concrete filling to
develop before work begins on the next floor above.

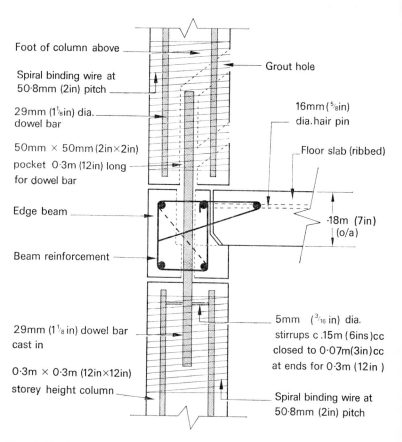

FIG. 3.13   Frame systems: joint in precast concrete frame units

Where the design of a framed structure provides for columns three
storeys in height, plumbing and aligning processes are considerably
reduced. Beams and floor slabs are laid and jointed three floors at the
same time with a stepped technique, the infill panels between columns

being placed and tied into the columns with grouted reinforced joints after the floors have been completed.

The effectiveness of a frame or panel system depends on the strength of all joints being fully developed so that the structure becomes monolithic in behaviour on completion.

The stability of the structures for precast concrete systems needs to be checked on site, as the additional safeguards of continuity and rigid partitioning achieved in traditional building are not normally included.

Industrialised system building based on precast concrete construction is of too recent construction to enable much information to be gained about the most sensitive parts of their structures—grouts in vertical and horizontal joints. But the implications of the failure at the Ronan Point development of multistorey panel system dwellings has proved the vital importance of achieving effective interconnections for large panel construction because of the possibility of accidental loads imposed by explosion or other causes. Specific recommendations to cover these contingencies are incorporated in the *International recommendations for the design and construction of large panel-structures* produced by the Comité Européen du Béton.

BOX CONSTRUCTION

In the U.S.S.R., one form of this type of construction is used for multirise blocks of flats up to twelve storeys in height comprising precast concrete room size boxes weighing 20 tons (20·32 tonnes) each hoisted to position by portal cranes straddling the blocks.

In Canada, a similar form of box construction has been used by precasting three dimensional load-bearing units, each 17 ft 6 in (5·33 m) × 38 ft 6 in (11·73 m) × 10 ft (3·05 m) high of 5000 p.s.i. (351·54 kgf/cm^2 concrete. Units are steam cured in steel moulds for the construction of 158 centrally heated and air-conditioned single family dwellings which vary from one-bedroom dwellings of 600 sq ft (55·74 m^2) to four-bedroom dwellings of 1700 sq ft (157·93 m^2) built up into a multistorey project.

The units weigh 70 to 90 tons (71·12 to 91·44 tonnes) each, and are handled by stiff leg derrick cranes supported by a 70 ft × 70 ft (21·34 m × 21·34 m) base on a moving track 70 ft (21·34 m) wide. Most of the components, including completely prefabricated kitchens and bathrooms are installed in an assembly line method before the roof is connected. A subfloor space in the unit contains all plumbing and electrical services, including a fan coil unit supplied with hot and cold water from a central plant for conversion into warm and cold air and distribution through thin slots in the edge of the floor.

The units are erected one on top of the other, and carry most of the load through walls and piers. They are connected together by post-tensioning and bolting, and incorporated into the structure so that adjacent walls, floors and ceilings of adjoining houses are separated to achieve a high level of insulation from sound and vibration. Additional structural support is provided by 10 ft (3·05 m) high horizontal walkways. These contain the mechanical services, and horizontally transmit part of the load to vertical elevator and stair cores. Overall stability for wind and seismic conditions is provided by the action of the box units and side walks.

The project incorporates shops, offices, covered parking areas, and a network of surrounding playgrounds and parks, at an all-in cost of approximately £27,750 per unit. More than half of the cost is taken up by mechanical handling and factory plant costs, and the learning time required for erection operations. The designers anticipated that in-creased production for outputs of 25,000 dwellings would reduce all-in unit cost to £7,000, but it appears unlikely that this volume of demand will be required.

Precast skeleton structures.

Systems have been developed in Czechoslovakia based on precast reinforced concrete skeleton structures with the main beams running transversely or longitudinally to provide flexible designs suited to various different types and sizes of buildings. Elements are divided into load-bearing and non-load-bearing standardised units to obtain the optimum use of the characteristics of reinforced concrete, reduce weight of struc-tures, and achieve flexible assembly and integration into a series of systems that can be applied to different types of buildings.

Structures are formed of light, medium, and heavy units for dwellings, offices, educational buildings, shops, and other types of buildings. The beams are of uniform length and standardised external finish for all types of systems. Current research is being undertaken to standardise units for structures with large spans taking heavier loads.

Precast concrete box system

Composite precast and poured in-situ concrete construction

Systems for dwellings based on composite precast and poured in-situ reinforced concrete construction have the advantage of obviating complex vertical jointing of precast structural elements. Prefabricated vertical load-bearing units are designed to support poured in-situ concrete floor slabs which compensate for tolerances in the erection of the vertical units, distribute loads evenly over the units they bear on, and provide bracing to the structure.

Vertical units can be cast in several ways. They may form insulated façade panels and all load-bearing walls so that non-structural partitions can be designed with light materials to reduce dead loads; they can be cast with projecting hooks at the top for the steel bar reinforcement of the poured in-situ floor slabs to pass through and help tie the structure together, or designed to form complex structural bathroom and kitchen units of shell type construction incorporating flues, air inlets, waste stacks, services, and all requisite fastenings and attachments in the moulds for the simple site installation of equipment.

Design flexibility can be obtained by adapting the in-situ concrete floors to suit variations in the planning of different dwelling types based on the standardised wall units; and varying surface treatment and fenestration of façade panels incorporating windows which can also function as load-bearing walls.

Some closed systems prefabricate standard plywood shutters on light steel adjustable props which provide fifty to sixty uses for supporting the poured in-situ concrete floors. Vast steel bar reinforcement cages incorporating services are assembled at ground level and hoisted to position in one operation by a spreader frame attachment of the erection crane.

Other systems are based on prefabricated steel shutters with built-in services attached to the steel reinforcing bars, and utilise steam pipes to accelerate the concrete maturing, with controlled temperature to ensure that the concrete hardens overnight.

Composite steel and concrete construction

Until recently, the design of composite beams in structural steel and reinforced concrete was based on elastic concepts assuming a modular ratio $(Z = m/f)$ to determine the transformed section of the concrete area into an equivalent steel area on the hypothesis of complete interaction between the two materials. However, horizontal slip at the interface cannot be completely stopped, and no allowance is included in the theory for concrete creep and shrinkage affecting the stress condition within the beam.

The current approach of ultimate load design based on a specified load factor is more economical, but provides difficulties when selecting a suitable steel beam which balances the concrete slab to give required moment of resistance, as there are normally six basic parameters to be considered for the ultimate load design of a composite section having the plastic neutral axis in the slab. By designing steel columns as composite construction with reinforced concrete, savings of approximately 45 per cent in the weight of the steel columns can be achieved, the volume of concrete remaining constant. A code of practice relating to this method of design is in course of preparation. C.P. 117: Part 1 permits beams to be designed in accordance with this approach, so that full advantage may be taken of the plastic resistance of the steel and the capacity of the concrete casing to take up part of the load and reduce the weight of the steelwork.

The economic design of a steel column to act in conjunction with concrete casing achieves savings in costs by assuming that the yield strength of the steel is reached simultaneously with the crushing value of the concrete, so that both the steel and the concrete casing take their part of the loading in the most economic manner.

Unstiffened plain beams without a concrete casing forming part of steel skeleton frames require fire protection with a dry casing and a mechanical connection between the top flange and a concrete floor slab. When the whole joist is in tension and acts in conjunction with the concrete slab in compression an economic section is obtained when the neutral axis lies within the thickness of the slab.

With composite construction based on elastic theory concrete cased steel beams can be economically designed by deliberately proportioning the composite sections so that the neutral axis coincides with the junction of the underside of the slab and top flange of the steel joist. When based on ultimate load theory, the beams are usually designed without concrete encasement in a similar manner.

Present design rules do not rationally take into account the concrete casing to the columns of a multistorey frame as contributing adequately to the increased strength and stiffness of the encased stanchion. This results in considerable differences of design requirements for a reinforced concrete column and an encased steel stanchion of the same size.

A steel beam designed to act in conjunction with the concrete floor slab must include part of the slab as part of the beam in order to achieve economy by reducing the size of the beam. A more economic concept for a structural steel frame would be to assume that only all the floor loads are supported by the beams and columns, and wind forces are resisted by the floor slabs, and transferred back to suitably positioned stability walls. These strong points would either take the form of flank walls, or of walls forming staircase approaches. Alternatively lift shaft and staircase walls could be integrated to form stiff cantilever core structures in reinforced concrete designed to accommodate all the wind forces, with the perimeter structural steel columns and beams trimming back to the core.

In the U.S.A. the stanchion grids are frequently opened out (e.g. 80 ft (24·38 m) × 35 ft (10·67 m)) to provide uninterrupted floor space which permits open planning. The resulting deep beams increase storey heights, the space between the beam and floor soffit being used for running services installations. This method of design renders structural steelwork much more economical than reinforced concrete, as the volume of concrete required to support such large spans would be excessive compared with the required steelwork, with consequential increase of dead weight and foundation sizes.

The box-shell design of composite construction with steel framework and in-situ reinforced concrete provides for contribution to load support and transverse stability from ancillary elements of the structure. Each medium depends on the other for individual stability, and influences the other in their combined operations.

The problems of design relate to the effective interaction between beams and slab, their extension to the design of the whole structure, and the economic use of all structural elements that can contribute effectively to the stability and support of the applied load. This includes the steel frame, as well as the floor slabs and walls. The framework becomes more complex when the stiffness required to stabilise a tall building is confined solely to the skeleton, as this leads to awkward and costly beam to column connections.

Stability can be achieved effectively by transferring the distributing forces though floors to walls, and thence to the ground. This simplifies beam to column connections, which can be made with only nominal stiffness, and economically joined with friction grip bolts. Floors can be arranged to act as horizontal girders between strong points, generally achieved by continuity of the membrane. Additional reinforcement is not usually required to stiffen the slab for this purpose.

The strong points can be formed from the walls enclosing the stairwells, service areas, or permanent partitions. These act as vertical cantilever girders anchored to the foundations. The elements are conveniently designed with the stanchions and cross-beams acting as tension members enclosing concrete or brick panels to provide complementary compression. Beams may be formed jointly with the floor slab in compression to act compositely with the steel joists.

Composite steel and concrete construction becomes economic when full advantage is taken of the maximum strength available in the combined materials. Where steel beams and concrete floor slabs are designed as a structural unit, the columns must be sufficiently rigid to withstand gravity and wind loads in order to reduce deflection and floor thicknesses. Alternatively, adjacent bays or cantilevers must be provided to ensure semi-rigid construction acting between the limits of design assumptions.

Costs can be reduced by including for the concrete casing protecting steel members to be taken into account when computing their carrying capacity; providing additional steel reinforcement to obtain smaller steel sections and reduced volume of concrete casing, or using composite stanchions.

The ultimate load basis of design enables composite action between the steel floor beams and concrete floors to be achieved with smaller sections by welding upstand shear studs to the top flanges of the joists, and pouring in-situ floor concrete around them so that when the superload is applied, interaction takes place between the beam and floor by transmission of the horizontal stress through the studs. Alternatively, epoxy resins can be used as reliable and safe sheer connectors to withstand either static or dynamic long-term loading. When the steel beams are not completely buried in the floor, exposed sections vulnerable to fire can be cased, asbestos sprayed, or protected by false ceilings.

In general, the intensity and type of superimposed loading determines the most economic span for a chosen floor type, as the spacing of beams is dependent on the maximum economic floor span and the loading of beams and columns. Standardised sections can be minimised if the loads can be transferred axially downwards from the point of application, instead of horizontally.

Floor thicknesses and column and beam sizes are influenced by the methods of wind bracing or stiffening walls. Thus a two-way continuously reinforced floor slab with four edge supports results in a thinner and lighter slab when load and span conditions permit a square structural grid, or the larger side of the bay does not exceed $1\frac{1}{4}$ times the length of the shorter side.

Multi-rise structures up to twenty storeys high with short spans and lighter loadings can be developed economically as flat plate construction.

Reinforced slabs with additional steel reinforcement take increased stresses, and are directly supported by columns without beams to achieve a smaller total volume of concrete than possible with beam and slab floor construction. The absence of beams and aprons simplifies formwork, reduces floor to floor heights, and enables pipework and ducts to be run without obstructions. If design requirements necessitate beams, precast units are generally more economical than those cast in-situ, especially at the perimeter. Freedom of spacing columns and maximum economy are achieved by standardising bay sizes to a module.

The erection of a composite steel frame for a multistorey building requires full integration with the building programme. Independent steel frames erected complete as a self-contained component on prepared foundations before cladding or floor operations commence lose their potential advantages of speed in erection by introducing a time lag before the follow-up trades start, and also the need for fire protection. A fully erected frame does not necessarily speed building operations, particularly in conditions where floors and cladding cannot be handled by tower cranes through the steel frame. Moreover, the skeleton frame requires temporary bracing, which may become extensive when the frame is erected before the floors and stabilising walls.

It is more economical to erect the steel frame for multi-rise composite structures in vertical sections up to a definite height. The frames are erected by steel erectors, plumbed, temporarily braced, and released successively in pairs to the general contractor. A neutral bay can be left between the sections being erected and those being clad. Horizontal section working enables lower floors to be completed before work commences on the upper framework.

Floor casting and construction of stabilising walls on the storey below need closely integrating with releasing temporary braces to the frame. Four lower floors are usually completed before work starts on the upper framework. In bad weather the 'umbrella' floor and the steel skeleton can be used to support polythene cover protection suspended from the frame.

Composite construction, with partial prefabrication of floors and dry casings can reduce site labour and speed operations provided the steel frame erection is effectively integrated with the overall construction programme.

Extraneous factors influencing construction costs

Many unforeseeable extraneous factors can influence construction costs. National and local shortages of labour and materials; credit 'squeezes'; abnormal rainfall during the period of tendering which causes a rise in the water level; sudden increases in the cost of building materials, coal and petrol; change of political party; a greatly increased volume of building commencing or proceeding in the area of the proposed works; all tend to inflate prices.

Costs are also influenced by general factors relating to contract conditions and the many items termed 'preliminary particulars' in Section B of the Current Standard Method of Measuring Building Works. These can represent a substantial proportion of the total construction costs. One recent building contract of approximately £1,350,000 included over £150,000 for such preliminary items, another similar contract of approximately £4,500,000 included over £510,000 for them. Such high costs may be due to uncertainties in the estimator's mind at tendering stage arising from unrealistic current methods of obtaining tenders based on 'accurate' quantities of 'fully described' unit items of 'measured' work fixed in position. These items ignore site transportation and handling problems, the economics of site mechanisation, methods of factory production, and modern construction techniques. The billed unit items do not take into account the effects of repetitive operations on labour outputs, nor provide designers with any conception of the effects of design detailing on costs, because the 'accurate' quantities for different types of work only relate to volume or area, and not to the particular difficulty of individual jobs.

The various obstacles to large-scale planning in cities, such as multi-ownership of land, mixture of land uses, high cost of land, intricate planning requirements, and obsolete building legislation also inflate construction costs; as do price fluctuations in costs of materials and rates of wages which disturb 'fixed' contract prices. Ground with poor load-bearing capacity can abnormally increase the cost of similarly planned projects on different sites.

Maintenance requirements are a major factor of total building costs. Decorations are a significant factor of maintenance costs, and where two different owners pay separately for the initial cost of a building and its subsequent running costs, there may be a tendency at design stage to favour a low initial construction cost with a known high maintenance cost, or vice versa.

The costs of construction very largely determine the aesthetics of modern 'one-off buildings', a factor that could have far less significance for system buildings based on the assembly of well designed standardised component parts mass produced in high serial runs.

In certain earlier periods, the aesthetics of building was determined by entirely different considerations, when men and women were eager to take part themselves in the building of splendid churches, and felt sure that their action in so doing led them towards the Divine Eternal Reality behind visible appearances.

The magnificent results achieved by the Gothic cathedral builders were mainly due to the enlightened and vital spirit of the age, and they still remain to refute the sceptical, materialistic and 'rational' misconceptions of today.

4

Principles of Economic Component Design

General factors influencing the design of standard components for 'closed' and 'open' systems suited to a particular building type, and with limited applications to other similar building types, relate to such factors as:

type of component;
materials, and performance specifications;
size, shape, weight, and number of components suited to the system;
amount of prefinishing and incorporation of different trades and services in one unit;
junction details;
degree of standardisation;
variations on standard designs;
factory production methods;
site erection requirements;
maximum application to different building types;
required serial runs for economic production.

Economic component design should avoid over-specification, restrict variations on standardised units to a minimum, utilise the best properties of selected materials to the utmost, and comprehend suitable methods of factory production and the full capacity and continuous operation of site mechanical handling plant and equipment. This is essential in order to achieve a minimum number of simple standardised repetitive units and their essential variations as suited to each particular building type, or combination of appropriate types, with the least amount of alterations to moulds, shuttering, standardised methods of factory production, jointing techniques and site assembly. Industrial operations can be reduced by sizing units as large as possible to reduce handling, cutting and fitting, and jointing. Component dimensions can be controlled within required tolerances, and ensure safe and rapid site assembly with a minimum number of operations for each part of the building in accordance with the requirements of differing erection techniques.

Non-productive time on site due to one team waiting for another to finish, or more than one team working on one operation at the same time can be reduced by minimising differences of materials and construction techniques, avoiding division of trades, and incorporating components in a prefinished state with the maximum integration of different trades and services in one unit.

Components may be classified as universal components such as bricks, which are valid for all building types, individual buildings, and groups of buildings; components such as load-bearing façade panels which are limited to one or several types of buildings; structural and non-structural components; multipurpose assemblies; sections connecting individual structural units with the finished building; and less complex, standardised and smaller components such as doors and windows suited to the varying requirements of different building types.

Structural elements do not lend themselves to standardisation as interchangeable components to the same extent as do many types of non-structural components. This is due to the great differences of storey heights, finishes, and foundation and structural requirements affecting design. Quite different structural elements are required for one to three storey buildings, four to thirty storey buildings; and buildings over thirty storeys in height.

In general, component types should be related to the size and features of especial importance in a building, such as structural elements; non-structural parts, fittings; services; degree of prefinishing; the optimum integration of different trades into one unit; and maximum application to different building types.

Climatic conditions and available sources of local materials influence component design in several ways. In countries with long cold winter months, precast concrete component production is carried on in factories during the winter period for erection in the comparatively short summer months. In the U.S.A. timber is plentifully available, and most low-rise dwellings are constructed of timber framing, which is simple to fabricate. In Great Britain, most timber has to be imported, and is comparatively costly compared with brickwork and concrete for the structures of low-rise dwellings. In countries with cold climates, materials which are poor heat conductors are better suited to components such as cladding units, whereas in those with hot dry climates buildings which are not air-conditioned should be constructed with materials which provide heat equalisation.

Traditional materials, such as plaster and slates are not suited to mechanised methods of component production. Current advances in the design and manufacture of plastics, laminated skin structures, and pressed metals are insufficient to make them more economical than concrete, steel, and timber for structural units. Technology is enabling raw materials and waste products previously considered unsuited to building technology to be used for construction. Such materials, when used for component production must be of high and uniform quality comparable with concrete, bricks, metals, plastics and timber.

New materials tend to be more expensive than traditional materials because they are based on capital intensive methods of production, usually a monopoly production of one firm, or a group of firms. Unless sufficiently high serial runs are manufactured, and current advances in their methods of manufacture are adequate to render them more attractive, they are unlikely to be selected for component production. However, as the cost of skilled labour has tended over the past years to increase at a faster rate than the cost of manufactured traditional materials, designers are now provided with a more possible economic selection of light new materials, provided that their site erection costs are sufficiently reduced.

The plastics industry has developed from outputs of 106,000 tons in 1963 to 215,000 tons in 1968. Plastics are at present mainly used in building for miscellaneous items such as gutters and pipes, and parts of box units, etc. But the material will probably be more generally used in the future, when system building has advanced to the flexible assembly of complexly moulded light-weight units for various component types.

Functional requirements limit the selection of dimensions for components which can be applied to more than one building type. The size and weight of a unit influences handling and transportation costs, and amount of site jointing. Large heavy units reduce site erection, handling and jointing, but necessitate cranes and other costly mechanical equipment. Smaller and less complete units require more site assembly, fitting, jointing, and increased work of finishing trades. Components should be suited to the full capacity and utilisation of site mechanical handling plant and be designed to achieve simple and repetitive units which ensure continuity of site assembly with the minimum number of operations for each part of the building.

In general, the more that components can be prefinished and assembled into complex elements in the factory, the more site operations and labour can be reduced. A timber-framed cladding panel which incorporates load-bearing functions with cladding, insulation, internal and external finishings, minimises site sorting, handling and erection, and also eliminates time required for drying out wet trades. These advantages are lost unless such components are integrated with the whole sequence of operations and do not involve costly assembly, jointing and making good.

Standardised junctions for a variety of components are difficult to achieve because joint details vary with the material and thickness of a component according to type and structural requirements. Junctions may also necessitate the adjoining component either contributing a joint part of varying thickness, or else none at all.

The British Standards Institution Code of Practice for 'the Control of Inaccuracy in Building', requires that tolerances should be dealt with explicitly, and not implicitly as at present. The aim of the Code is to enable design requirements to be metricised and realised in terms of accuracy in production and assembly. The Institution's publication P.D. 6296 (November 1969), *Metric Standards published and in progress complete to 31st July 1969*, lists the standards already available in metric units, and those being accorded priority treatment.

The type, material and joint dimension of an interchangeable component constitutes a serious limitation to standardised mass production. In general, components and their junction details should be designed with modular coordination and unification of joints, in so far as practicable; with acceptable conditions and realistic understanding of tolerances to meet the performance requirements of each structural and building type; according to the suitability of the particular building type for complete standardised prefabrication; in relation to the number of storeys, as junctions influence structural design and determine the size and other features of structural equipment; with an increase in the installation requirements of sanitary and electrical equipment; and to suit site erection requirements.

Variations on standard designs relate to user requirements; site conditions and environment; building regulations; function and performance requirements, which determine number, size, materials and finish of components; available materials and skills; and type of factory production.

Variations in the assembly of standardised components for 'closed' systems need not slow down the erection cycle provided the number of

8

different component types is minimised, and their basic shape, weight, and method of jointing is similar. For example, four or five heavy structural units can be hoisted to position and fixed in any ordered sequence within a definite planned time so long as they are dimensioned to fit the erection crane's tackle and capacity, and are similarly assembled and jointed.

Variations in construction techniques may seriously delay erection operations. The assembly of precast concrete standardised beams and columns when combined with poured in-situ concrete floor construction may be considerably slowed down due to the obstruction of working areas caused by supports to shutters, and the time required for shuttering and concreting operations.

Any design which breaks the rhythm of the erection cycle increases the non-productive time. Consequently a type of cladding unit which needs scaffolding for erection should not be used with another type that requires cranage.

The standardisation of component production and repetition of site erection operations for increased labour outputs requires architectural and structural plans which assure maximum identity of operations; adequate sized developments which permit sufficient specialisation; and sufficient site space for erection teams to work without getting in each other's way.

A precast concrete system that obviates the use of external scaffolding for component erection needs protection around the perimeter of the buildings at each working level. Concrete elements for perimeters should be designed for erection within the building before inner walls are positioned in order to provide a safe working level as early as possible. When no permanent balustrade or cladding units can be fixed at this stage, provision for some form of temporary guard rail will be required.

Other factors that influence the speed of the site erection relate to the stage of the building programme at which the components are to be introduced; the limitations imposed by permissible tolerances; user requirements affecting component selection and flexibility; the amount of standardisation of non-structural components; and the degree of simplicity of standardised jointing techniques. The later in the building programme components are delivered and erected, the more serious will be the effect of delaying the cycle of site operations.

Design solutions of production and site erection requirements should provide the best relationship between costs of construction and user value of a building, and a wide choice of standardised interchangeable components of varying sizes suited to alternative treatment of the heights, elevations, and appearances of buildings.

The design of more flexible and interchangeable components than those currently produced for closed and open systems should enable an optimum number of selected and variable materials, shapes, colours, and dimensions to achieve an adequate differentiation of heights, masses, surfaces, structures and elevations for each particular building type. By these means industrialised system building can advance to 'component assembly' based on a severely restricted number of essential elements and their variations.

The general principles of component design for the factory production of vast outputs for such standardised interchangeable units are based on the interrelation of the essential common factors of as many different building types as possible to achieve the maximum flexibility of a minimum number of necessary components; the fulfilment of performance and user requirements common to as large a variety of building types as practicable; and the provision of acceptable junction details, joints and tolerances. The value of a building will be reduced if it includes any components which are superfluous for its use and aesthetic appearance.

The standardisation of interchangeable components should be related eventually to an increased application for a wider variety of different building types in relation to building types with identical requirements; building types with similar requirements; buildings with special requirements; and the effects of building heights on structural design, e.g. low-, medium- and high-rise buildings.

Selected interchangeable components could be designed to suit each particular building type and gradually extended to comprehend as many different building types as possible in one component, including housing. A limited number of building type requirements such as for schools, hospitals, factories, offices could be interrelated with a similar number of components; for example, structural frames, partitions, external cladding, doors and frames. Performance requirements and preferred basic dimensions of the selected components could be related to the selected building types. Similar and differing performance requirements could then be divided for all the selected types, and these requirements could finally be related to those for housing.

The final development of the economic mass production of open interchangeable units is based on the unification and eventual standardisation of buildings and components; their methods of assembly and jointing; and the maximum application of these standardised designs to as many different types of buildings as practicable. This necessitates the achievement of more components and varied sizes so that differences in heights, masses, façades and surfaces can be readily obtained by designers through the selection of materials and dimensions which comply with the performance requirements of various types of buildings. The solutions of many problems affecting the harmony of architectural and structural requirements determine the methods of assembly that can be used advantageously on site, and modify individual building requirements. These solutions would also influence effective economic production planned at National level in relation to the quality of buildings; and their environment, climatic conditions, service life, and maintenance.

The full unification of components is not practical. Nevertheless, size, degree of finish, functional requirements, and other universal qualities of components necessitates a certain degree of unified design. The full benefits of system building techniques can only be achieved when systems are based on the assembly of standardised 'open components', and government policy provides for a long-term demand of a large and continuous volume of building.

5

Principles of Economic Component Production

The production of most materials and component parts of buildings is related to capital intensive organisations. System building replaces site labour by the economic production of factory-made structural elements and components that can be handled and erected by mechanical plant. It does not involve contractors necessarily in greatly increased capitalisation, unless limited to one particular type of system based on high serial runs of precast concrete elements mass produced by semi-automated processes in permanent factories to satisfy a vast and continuous demand.

Building contractors' resources are usually widely dispersed, and not limited to one particular kind of construction anywhere. Contractors can hire plant and employ subcontractors as required for their various contracts, and thereby reduce the need for extensive fixed assets and capital. A major part of contractors' costs are direct costs that can be quickly recovered from their employers by monthly interim payments on account.

Even when sponsoring a system based on the site factory production of precast concrete components, required capital investment per operative employed is considerably less than that needed in other industries. For example:

Industry	Approximate capital investment required per operative £
Chemical	7000
Motor car	3000 to 3500
Site factory system	1400

The design of factory produced non-structural components should attempt to correlate the requirements of demand, transportation limits, planning areas, and the required speed of factory production by semi-automated processes. Transport is an essential link between high volume factory production and rapid site erection, and can be simplified provided the type of component manufacture does not require a complex ordering problem in the factory.

Component production should be based theoretically on the estimated overall number of standardised universal components related to a nationally planned building programme in order to achieve the mass production of huge series, with resulting economies due to the variety reduction achieved by optimum standardisation, and increased outputs from site labour due to repetitive operations.

In practice this aim cannot be achieved, due to changes of user during the life of a building; adjustments required by new materials and techniques of construction; transportation problems that would result from an extended national market; special requirements of major individual developments; the difficulty of maintaining vast production runs due to the changing demand for different types of buildings; changes in Government policy; and the whole structure of the building trade and its allied industries. Manufacturers have to provide for the site erection of large buildings constructed from component parts of varying materials, sizes and complexity, which are obtained from many different sources and assembled in close physical association to achieve functional integration. Nevertheless, patterns have been established in other fields that could enable a National effort to be concentrated on these problems, with communication and control methods that integrate many separate parts into a complete operational product.

The output and overhead costs of manufactured products depends on scale and length of series run, and tend to rise when a factory operates at a low level of production due to the high proportion of fixed costs. The development of a building technology based on the flexible assembly of standardised and selected interchangeable components obtainable in the open market requires the development of assembly-line and semi-automatic methods of production, prepackaging, and the acceptance of dimensional coordination and interchangeable jointing.

Present problems of the mass production of standardised units include functional requirements limiting selection of dimensions, and degree of unified finish. These depend on whether components are to be introduced completely finished by mass production methods, or assembled individually in workshops from mass-produced semi-products; and on methods of site assembly and jointing.

Whereas building contractors may be considered as effective organisations conditioned by their ability to obtain, by competitive tender, finance and undertake construction works, most competent and allied manufacturing industries require intensive capitalisation of their assets to operate successfully in a much wider market.

The mass production in vast series of carefully selected materials and 'open' interchangeable standardised components related to long-term National building programmes necessitates component designs which correlate the requirements of demand, planning areas, transportation limits, the effective utilisation and combination of the best properties of the selected materials, and the required speed of factory assembly as necessitated by the high serial runs achieved by automated processes. Such productions also require low cost methods of automation, and the development of semi-automated processes of varying degrees; the creation of new process-dependent industries which will lead to substantial reductions in labour requirements similar to those already achieved in the aircraft industry; and vast capital investments. One polythene factory built in Hungary cost £27 million at 1965 prices.

There are three main categories of production: components produced by the transformation of materials by formation processes of machining to specified dimensions, precasting, and heat or chemical treatment to change physical properties; components produced by the above methods and assembled into complex units such as curtain walling, service cores, box construction; and components mass produced on site.

Types of manufacturing plant include fixed machines with manual control, fixed control programme, or cybernetic programme; complex machines with computerised programme of control; and other degrees in the scale of operations.

Automated methods of increasing productivity at lower costs can be applied to all types of industries, and provide an economic and effective repetition handling in order to benefit workers on the shop floor.

For example, the process involving operatives seated at benches, and picking up and placing pins and studs into holes all day, can be very simply automated at low cost by a vibratory hopper feed. The pins and studs could be correctly orientated from the exit point, fed to a parts placing unit, and married up with the unit part required to accept the pins or studs. The whole arrangement could then be time-cycled for assembly at a predetermined rate to achieve considerable savings on this type of operation, with increased productivity of the complete assembly. This would release operatives employed on the bench for other work.

Automatic assembly and machine loading, and the design and development of special purpose machines need not necessarily involve vast capital expenditure for economic installation provided all elaboration and unnecessary refinements which tend to cause trouble when the machine is in actual operation are eliminated.

The development of manufacturing methods for semi-automated processes and short cycle times involves such processes as ultrasonic techniques for bonding; photoelectric guards for the arrestor mechanisms of machinery; electromagnetic devices such as tape-controlled processes to eliminate hand fitting; and other ingenious devices which substantially reduce labour requirements. But great reliability of increased mechanisation is essential in order to avoid stoppages of production; even one or two insignificant fasteners could shut down an assembly line.

Some manufacturers use pneumatics to simplify the introduction of flow-line production. Cylinders with low pressure compressed air to act as springs are incorporated in roller conveyors in order to obviate complicated mechanically sprung systems and allow complete tension control and rapid machine access. The cylinders are also used for clamping and programmed drilling.

The costs of mass production methods for high serial runs of components relate to type of production, optimum size of plant, and size of serial runs; volume of composition of demand and future developments; degree of automation required for production; investment costs; sources of raw materials, and transport network available; technical possibilities of processing raw materials; power requirements; direct and indirect costs, and number and skill of available manpower; maximum and minimum sizes of components, type of finish, and tolerances and dimensions of finished products; and location and capacities of existing plants.

In general, the higher the capital cost of plant utilised for vast scale productions, the greater the productivity achieved per unit of plant. A single centralised factory with advanced methods of production and transportation related to its high outputs can achieve a quicker amortisation of capital costs than a similar factory operating with a lesser degree of automation.

The main issues involved are to relate mass production methods economically to required outputs; balance production against capital expenditure on plant in order to amortise investments within a sufficiently limited period; and obtain required profits on the total capital employed, and on turnover. For example: a minimum output of 10,000 complete steel dwellings is essential for the economic utilisation of press forming methods of production.

PRECAST CONCRETE STRUCTURAL COMPONENTS

The economic production of precast concrete panel units capable of arrangement into a load-bearing and wind resisting structure is based on general factors which create the environment in which a particular system operates. These include the existence of a special or more general market, scale of output, volume of demand anticipated, economic life of fixed assets, and required return on investment. It is essential to achieve a variety of building types, layouts, and appearances which provide flexible architectural design integrated with structural needs, and satisfy user requirements. Building details and concrete unit profiles should be designed to satisfy performance criteria for at least as long as factory costs have to be amortised.

The minimum number of standardised units is essential for maximum repetition of production, and the achievement of simple jointing techniques. The size and weight of units needs careful consideration. Large panels 20 ft (6·10 m) long, or over, and of standardised storey heights necessitate too many complicated casting processes for site manufacture. Heavy units over 6 tons (6·09 tonnes) each require rail transport.

Type of factory production and mechanisation depends on the extent to which the component design lends itself to advanced mechanisation for high serial runs. Degree of automation for off-site productions should be related to required outputs and amount of flexibility for variations. Any changes in size and detail of standardised units are costly, and can only be made economically for large projects. Requirements of local authorities for variations in standardised systems to suit their individual artistic demands can increase the costs of their dwellings by as much as $33\frac{1}{3}$ per cent.

The location of a factory affects transportation costs and risk of damage to units in transit. Handling and transportation in the factory and on site should be minimised, and daily outputs programmed and phased daily to integrate with erection requirements.

Off-site factory production

When possible, an off-site factory should be located in public areas near good roads, within 25 to 40 mile (40·23 to 64·37 km) radius from sites to be served, and have ready access to public utility services to avoid additional costs for providing requisite 500 K.V.A. electricity supply. Access to the factory should be provided for incoming deliveries of materials and outgoing transportation of units to sites, with different spaces allotted in factory areas for loading and manoeuvring trailers to avoid traffic jams.

A high proportion of transportation costs relate to loading and unloading trailers; approximately one hour is required for each operation. Thus the difference in cost of transporting units to sites 1 mile (1·60 km) and 25 miles (40·23 km) distant from the factory relate to the time passed on route; four loads being made to the sites 1 mile (1·60 km) distant as compared with two and a half loads to sites 25 miles (40·23 km) away.

When comparing comparative merits of off-site and on-site factory production methods, transportation costs from a proposed off-site factory should be compared with the costs of handling units by a site factory crane to erection cranes located near adjoining structures, and of site transport from the temporary factory to distant blocks.

Off-site factory production is based on semi-automated assembly floor-line processes with highly specialised operations carried out at successive working stations. A quick turn around in the cycle is achieved by lifting units from the moulds into the stacking yard as rapidly as possible without rehandling.

Over-capitalisation in factory mechanisation due to over-estimated volumes of demand in relation to economic production can be avoided by laying out new factory buildings on the approximate basis of double the amount of existing outputs, with only sufficient machinery installed to satisfy current volumes of demand. This ensures there will be at least a sufficient requirement for economic single shift production if the estimated demand falls below anticipated peak periods after the factory is in operation.

If too much costly machinery has been installed so that high-volume production with two shift work is essential to obtain an economic return on capital investment, reduced demand will result in decreased outputs with the machinery working at under capacity, and loss of profit.

Costs of installing a permanent factory for the manufacture of precast concrete panel units can vary from approximately £60,000 to £600,000

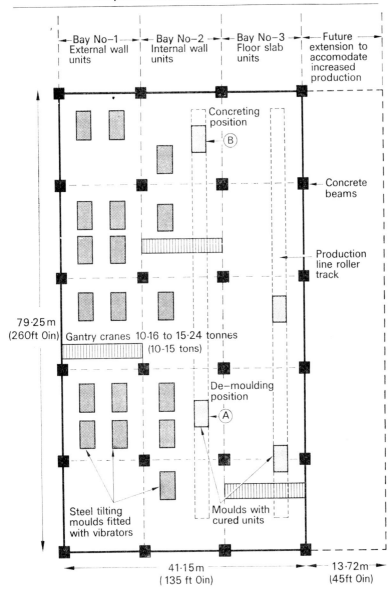

FIG. 5.1   Plan for off-site factory production for daily concrete outputs of 2300 cu ft (65·13 m³) of units

and upwards, according to scale of production and degree of mechanisation and automation utilised. A factory to be set up on production line basis for manufacturing precast concrete panel units requires a minimum of machinery and plant sufficient for the sustained production of approximately 600 dwellings, with daily outputs of 2300 cu ft (65·13 m³) of units based on thirty to thirty-six component types. Successful production on this basis can enable total site labour of all erection teams to be reduced to approximately 800 man hours per dwelling.

Production based on daily castings to achieve demoulding after twenty-four hours requires factory layouts based on some form of transverse and multiple through bays, with special cranes to ensure the smooth and continuous handling of units. More rapid results can be obtained in factories which maintain continuous operations with accelerated concrete curing and two shift work. By using semi-automated self-stripping and erecting multipanel precision-made steel battery moulds fitted with electrical heating elements, and working three shifts, continuous production can be maintained of single units such as plain wall and floor panels with a tolerance of 1/16 in (1·5 mm).

In cold winter months continuous operations are ensured by preheating the mixing water at night to provide a concrete placing temperature 15·5°C (60°F). The moulds are heated to maintain the rapid production of units for demoulding after twenty-four hours (or less). Subsequent maturing is effected on storage racks.

Manufacturing bays, moulds, and air, water and electrical services should be suited to the techniques required for producing each different type of unit. Transverse bays with offices, stores and workshops can be located where required in the production bays, and added to suit expansion of the factory. The main batching and cement site equipment should be planned normally along one end of the factory, with a rail mounted conveyor belt and a receiving hopper for direct off-loading from lorries to feed aggregate to ranges of storage compartments. These should be of different size for several weeks continuous production.

Although inspection and close concrete quality control is essential, a deviation of 500 lb per sq in (35·15 kgf/cm²) to the next highest standard mix may be provided when a lower strength mix is specified, as the extra cost of the cement is negligible compared with the costs of more effective quality control.

For production of daily outputs not exceeding 3000 cu ft (84·95 m³) the factory stacking yard would be normally of sufficient area to take several weeks stock of units, plus an additional two weeks 'buffer' stock, and of approximately similar area to the factory production bays. Six or seven trailers would be sufficient for daily deliveries to sites.

Deliveries need phasing to ensure units can be off-loaded direct from the trailers and hoisted into position without need for a stacking yard on site, and consequent double handling. Delivery times should include allowances for hold-ups due to breakdowns and traffic jams. If efficiently timed, deliveries should be normally up to within twenty minutes of scheduled times.

Example of economic production for daily outputs of 2300 *cu ft* (65·13 m³) *of panel units.* The production cycle for internal wall panels would usually be based on a team of twelve to fifteen men working one shift, with a concrete conveyor delivering mixed concrete from the batching plant to required positions on the roller line. This line produces the units as it moves along the production bays, each operation taking approximately fifteen to twenty minutes.

The cycle of operations would generally take from 2 to 2½ hours, and comprise: placing the mould filled with cured concrete on the roller line; demoulding the concrete; cleaning and oiling the mould; placing reinforcement, electrics and other inserts in the mould; pouring concrete; placing topping mix; and finishing surface of topping. Concrete would be cured by ambient temperature maintained in the factory at 18° to 21°C (65° to 70°F) by oil-fired warm air heaters to provide good working conditions, or by similar means to permit natural concrete curing on a 24-hour cycle.

The cycle of operations for the production of floor panels would be similar to that for the wall panel units, but without the finishing operation, if screeded on site. The operations for the production of façade panels would vary according to external finish, type of insulation, and type of unit. A plain flank wall unit takes less time to cast than a unit with a window opening, and may require approximately four to five hours.

When standard units have to be varied to suit architectural or structural requirements, the team of twelve to fifteen men would need to be doubled.

Higher outputs for panel systems with units 20 ft (6·10 m) long necessitate larger factories with more costly machinery, and site erection cranes with greater lifting capacity. But total factory production costs would be similar to within approximately 10 to 15 per cent.

SITE FACTORY PRODUCTION

The most efficient location for the installation of a site factory and stacking areas is related to the shape of the site, available space, building layouts, access for materials deliveries, required volume of production, type of construction, mechanical plant utilisation, and required finishes.

The main problems include minimising double handling, and integrating production with erection requirements. These are solved normally be siting the factory within reach of the buildings, and setting up the batching plant near the site entrance. Where space is restricted, ready-mixed concrete can be used to supplement limited batching plant, or even for all castings.

The ideal position for a factory is at a central or other convenient position, so that the factory portal handling crane is within reach of the erection tower crane to ensure as direct a lift as possible from the factory into stacks adjoining the buildings. No difficulty is involved on sites developed with only single or multiple tower blocks. But on sites with low-rise or mixed developments, units will require transport. Stacking areas should be located immediately adjoining the factory so that furthermost blocks can be completed first to avoid transport problems through finished areas.

A site factory in a centralised area for manufacturing precast concrete panel units, some of which are to be transported and erected on other sites, comes within the terms of the Factory Act Regulations. These involve certain additional requirements to the Building Regulations, and include reporting the existence of the factory to H.M. Inspector, displaying Factory Forms 1, 43 and 31 on site, installing fire alarms in the factory, obtaining certified means of escape in case of fire, providing hot water for washing, and incorporating practical safety precautions, good drainage facilities, and clear gangways between moulds. A site factory should contain adequate shelters, manufacturing bays, and services suited to the production techniques for each type of unit. Layouts of moulds and stacking areas should be carefully checked against the radius and lifting capacity of the factory cranes to ensure maximum utilisation.

Major plant requirements comprise mixers, moulds, subsidiary plant for curing concrete, steel fabrication areas when reinforcement is not delivered to site ready cut and bent, and shelters which vary according to type of factory. The main types of lifting plant required are tower cranes, overhead travelling cranes, and portal cranes (Plate 1).

In order to provide efficient equipment and conditions for curing cubes and undertaking sieve analysis and other tests, a small size laboratory should be set up, and liaison established between the factory and erection teams regarding quality, improvements, and availability of units.

Factory manufacturing bay areas for preliminary programming

can be estimated on an assessment of three to four times the total floor areas of the buildings to be erected each week, and a basis of mould utilisation averaging four castings per week. For example:

Floor areas of buildings to be erected   5400 sq ft (501·68 m²)
Maximum weekly rate of erection   5400 × 1·2
6500 sq ft (approx.)
(609·87 m²)
∴ Approximate area of factory bays   6500 × 3·50
23,000 sq ft
(2136·77 m²)

The size of the factory can be determined more accurately by scheduling the number of units required each week and calculating the number of moulds required on the general basis of five castings per mould per week. Some moulds would be based on six castings per week in order to attain six repeats when needed, and avoid unnecessary mould duplication. Where only a few units of a particular structural type are required, they can be made in a single mould to make up the number to four repeats, thus permitting one free day for mould modifications.

These calculations can be improved as casting and erection teams become fully trained. On contracts planned with experienced teams it is practicable to produce ten castings a week of structural units with shift working.

The percentage of covered space to the factory production lines normally should be approximately 60 per cent, varying according to the time of year when precasting is at its peak. If casting is to be undertaken during the winter period, this needs increasing to 75 per cent.

Limited volumes of production on single sites require standard manufacturing bays set up with a series of 30 ft (9·14 m) wide × 20 ft (6·10 m) long mobile shelters formed of light steelwork covered with any suitable material, to run on rails. Electricity, water and steam services should be constructed with appropriate outlets adjoining the moulds. The rails for the shelters can be secured to timber inserts cast in the oversite concrete so that two men can move the shelters away from the moulds when steel reinforcement placing, concreting, and lifting operations are proceeding.

The electrical installation for the factory requires socket outlets to mould beds positioned to minimise cables trailing to vibrators. Intake and switch gear housings should be placed clear of portal and tower crane tracks to prevent a trap being formed between the housings and moving cranes.

Steam installation pipes need lagging to prevent operatives contacting hot pipes, with control cocks designed to prevent accidental operation.

A good psychological effect on site operatives can be obtained by their working in a factory which is not too stuffy, with facilities provided for washing and change of clothes. As some men may be allergic to mould oil, oil spraying should not be permitted, but barrier cream and neoprene (or similar) aprons and gloves provided.

Factory crane requirements for a single tower block are comparatively simple, as both the casting and erection cranes usually provide adequate coverage to all moulds. Multiple tower blocks developed on one site, involve the problem of siting the factory within reach of each block. Part of the factory lifting equipment should include a tower crane with an extended track to reach the stacking areas for adjoining blocks. These methods are unlikely to enable all blocks to be reached directly when more than three tower blocks are to be constructed on one site, and transport should be provided to deliver the cast units to required locations for erection operations.

The choice of a factory portal or tower crane depends on comparative cost economies, and the space available on site for stacking and casting units.

Portal cranes have several advantages where site space is not too restricted. Cranes up to 6 tons lifting capacity can perform along the production bays all concreting operations, including casting, striking, placing and lifting units. In the initial stages of a contract, the crane can be used for the erection of the production bays, and also for the erection of the building up to the first five or six storeys. The crane can be turned through 90° to increase its portability and flexibility, and be easily transported across a site for repositioning. Setting up and erection time is much faster than that required for a tower crane of comparable performance, and is consequently less expensive in terms of manhours. The portal crane does not require such a heavy track as a tower crane, and avoids the lifting problems normally associated with cantilevered jibs, such as wind interference, diminishing permissible load with outward travel of the hoist, and inherent structural dangers.

Overhead travelling cranes can provide a useful secondary support over battery pits on sites where a tower crane is used as a major factory lifting appliance.

The speed of the erection cycle determines maximum crane utilisation and rate of factory production. This erection rate, and the design of the type, size, number and finish of the units to be manufactured, influences the number and type of moulds required, methods of casting, type and amount of factory plant and equipment, duration of the casting cycle for each unit; the nature of shift work; and the size of production bays, stacking, and storage areas.

Mould layouts and stacking areas should be carefully checked against the radius and lifting capacity of the proposed tower crane to ensure its maximum utilisation. The displacement of the factory cranes should provide coverage to all moulds and mixing plant so that in the event of a power failure, work to the moulds can continue.

On sites with a single tower block of box-shell construction, mould utilisation is the key factor to output. Economic casting speed would be about 4000 to 5000 cu ft (113·27 to 141·58 m³) per week, with one factory crane for casting purposes used to the maximum, supported by the erection crane, which would tend to be under-utilised.

On normal sites with two or more tower blocks, and an erection rate of eight dwellings per week, at least two factory cranes are necessary. One should be a tower crane used for delivering the finished units within reach of the erection cranes, or for loading on to trailers. The other crane should be a portal or overhead travelling crane set up over the 30 ft 0 in (9·14 m) factory production bays, and used solely for concreting and initial stacking. To avoid problems of clashing, a tower crane can be used with a shortened jib.

The work loads between the two cranes needs to be carefully balanced between the operations of concreting horizontally-cast moulds, concreting vertical moulds, striking and stacking horizontals, striking and stacking verticals, striking and stacking tiltings, and lifting and loading to trailers horizontal and vertical units.

When an increased rate of production is required for two different types of tower blocks, the factory should be divided into two parallel production lines, one for each block type, with an additional crane common to both sections for loading and stacking units.

Vaster production series require the installation of a more permanent type of factory with heavier cranes for casting large and more complex units with a greater degree of pre-finishing.

Production costs

In general, production costs are influenced by installation, running and dismantling costs of the temporary factory, plant and equipment; mould costs, affected by increased utilisation due to accelerated maturing of concrete and shift work to increase outputs;

9

materials costs, affected by surface treatment and final colour of the units;

labour costs, affected by the integration of the casting and erection cycles;

type, size, finish, and number of units, as indicated in the table on page 113.

Plain and simple units can be economically cast on site. Units of intricate design are better suited to off-site production under more controlled conditions. Unless the same shaped units are used on every floor, additional costs will be incurred for altering moulds for any different units used at various floor levels.

Large panel units reduce the number of joints required for smaller units, but involve increased time and costs for more extensive cutting, shaping, and accurate location of steel reinforcement in the moulds; more accurate casting and working of larger area façade panels with a facing mix, sandwich layer, and adjoining backing mix; costly precision made steel moulds capable of supporting the dead weight of a panel weighing several tons; and cranes with comparatively high lifting capacities to handle and stack units. In general, optimum economy is obtained by standardising moulds for a minimum number of units, accommodating variations of span and loading in standard basic profiles by adjusting the amount of reinforcement within the sections to achieve design requirements, and varying lengths with stop ends.

Materials costs are influenced by availability and type of aggregates, (the use of local aggregates and sand provides maximum economy); type of cement; design of concrete mix, and quality control; amount and type of steel reinforcement; method of fabrication (cage or mat) and placing in the mould; technique (ordinary reinforcement or prestressed), and number and type of inserts; and type of materials for insulated panels.

The following types of batching plant are generally suitable for normal on-site concrete productions:

1. For outputs up to 6000 cu ft (169·90 m³) per week, a type of mixer with scraper and electrically driven three compartment aggregate storage, or similar equipment. An 18/12 mixer is suited to plain structural concrete units, and a 10/7 mixer to exposed aggregate mixes.

2. For outputs over 6000 cu ft (169·90 m³) per week, a 21/14 gyramixer with automatic drag line, leading boom, and five-compartment aggregate storage bins, or similar equipment. This type of plant can produce a batch of mixed concrete in 20/30 seconds, with a mix output of 30 cu yd (22·93 m³) per hour. As the feed rate of the boom is only 15 to 26 cu yd

(11·47 to 19·88 m³) of aggregate per hour, two automatic loading booms are needed to feed the aggregate in to obtain maximum utilisation of the mixer, which requires a 30 to 40 ton (30·48 to 40·64 tonnes) cement silo to serve it.

FACTORS INFLUENCING COSTS

PRODUCTION COSTS
are influenced by

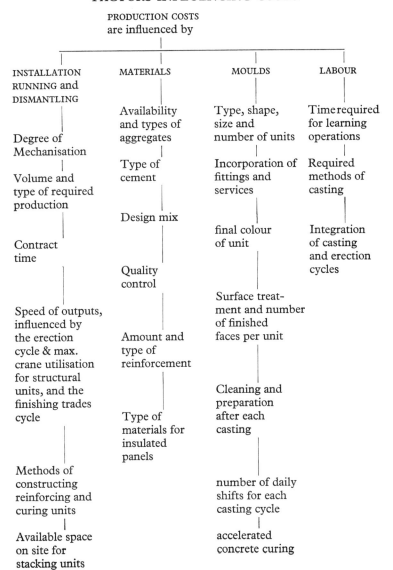

INSTALLATION RUNNING and DISMANTLING	MATERIALS	MOULDS	LABOUR
Degree of Mechanisation	Availability and types of aggregates	Type, shape, size and number of units	Time required for learning operations
Volume and type of required production	Type of cement	Incorporation of fittings and services	Required methods of casting
Contract time	Design mix	final colour of unit	Integration of casting and erection cycles
Speed of outputs, influenced by the erection cycle & max. crane utilisation for structural units, and the finishing trades cycle	Quality control	Surface treatment and number of finished faces per unit	
	Amount and type of reinforcement		
Methods of constructing reinforcing and curing units	Type of materials for insulated panels	Cleaning and preparation after each casting	
Available space on site for stacking units		number of daily shifts for each casting cycle	
		accelerated concrete curing	

Storage bin capacities should be 50/60 cu yd (38·23 to 45·87 m³), of which 20 cu yd (15·29 m³) is dead storage; and a minimum area of approximately 60 ft × 55 ft (18·28 m × 16·76 m) should be allowed for the plant, excluding lorry access.

The mixer may be completely operated by one man, who can control all the aggregate handling and mixing operations, but skilled maintenance is essential.

Where more than five aggregates are required to cover exposed aggregate mixes, staircase and other special units, an additional mixer should be provided. On sites where space is extremely limited, ready-mixed concrete can be economically used, either for all castings, or to supplement outputs of limited batching plant.

The final colour of a concrete unit depends more on the colour of cement and fine aggregates used than on the coarse aggregates, and on surface treatment. The colour of the cement is of less importance with some exposed aggregate finishes, as the proportion of cement to aggregate visible may be relatively small, and only affect the general tone value of the slab. With an ex-mould casting, where the surface is untouched after release from the mould, the cement is the dominating factor.

Natural aggregates vary greatly in colour and cost. Crushed brick, tile, and other manufactured materials are even more expensive than coloured natural aggregates, as they require crushing and grading.

The type of surface texture to be produced depends on scale of texture; size of aggregate related to viewing distance; aspect of façade related to weathering; particle shape and surface characteristics of the coarse aggregates, which affect weathering and the reflection of light from the surface, and whether the finished surface is untouched from the mould, or further treated. Processes such as grit blasting remove laitence from the finished surface and minimise risk of crazing from too rich a mix, or too high a water/cement ratio.

The surface pattern of a slab is related to size and shape of unit; texture and colour of surface; arrangement of slabs and joint treatment; the use of profiled effects produced either by casting against relief moulds, or in sand or moulding clay; and the use of exposed aggregates.

The number of finished faces to each unit affects methods of casting and costs. One exterior finished face can be readily achieved by casting a thinner facing of the required facing material, with a backing of ordinary mix concrete. One or two return faces to be finished in addition can be readily obtained from the returns of the facing mix, provided the width dimensions are not greater than the thickness of the facing. If all faces of a unit are to be finished, the mix for the casting can be made of special white coarse and fine aggregates, and white cement where a textured or exposed aggregate finish is required. Alternatively, ordinary coarse aggregates and white fine aggregates with white cement can be used where the surface is untouched after finish from the mould. In the latter case, any subsequent removal of laitence from the ex-mould surface will expose the ordinary aggregate and spoil the finished appearance of the unit. A mottled surface can be obtained by using coloured coarse aggregates, white fine aggregates, and white cement.

External wall panels, beams and columns can be finished more economically in the moulds rather than by applying mosaic, tile or other finishes applied later. A self-finish costs less, and concrete shrinkage tends to cause applied finishings to fall off, or crack.

Steel reinforcement depends on the type of unit to be produced, and may be either delivered cut and bent to required shapes ready for placing in the moulds, or be cut and fabricated on the site by factory flow-line methods. Reinforcement cages should be detailed so that the cranes can pick up and place them in the mould without distortion, and correctly fitted to maintain specified concrete cover.

Internal wall panels are cast normally without any reinforcement other than that required for handling. Floor panels are reinforced, usually with mesh fabric, which although more costly than steel bars require less site labour for fabrication and placing.

The removal of cast units from the moulds, transportation, and handling operations may require special reinforcement and different lifting points or devices from those used for placing. Irregular shaped units involve problems in handling stresses during demoulding; as the unit is lifted off the crane, a great deal of weight is put on one corner.

Mould costs are based on the number of castings to be obtained, plus the direct costs of cleaning and preparing each mould after casting; placing the concrete in the mould, curing, and lifting and handling units to the stacking yard.

All units should be cast as large as possible with minimum tolerances for handling by suitable cranes; prefinished in the moulds to minimise wet trades; and cast on the basis of assembling preformed standard parts for placing in the mould. Preformed inserts should be ready before casting to avoid mould changes. Inserts for precast units, whether bolts, service fittings, or cores for holes must be carefully fixed and rigidly held in the moulds to avoid any displacements or twists during casting the concrete, as any slight irregularities can seriously interfere with the erection programme.

The optimum number of moulds required for site factory casting is related to the total number of castings obtainable from each mould, the contract period, and the number of daily castings planned to suit erection requirements or stock piling.

When the volume of demand is such that a larger number of moulds would be uneconomic for production, the units should be produced in fewer moulds well in advance of erection operations commencing on site, and during site preparation and foundation works.

Vibrators used for vibrating concrete in metal moulds should be designed to vibrate vertically in order to prevent segregation, and vibration should be carried out to each pour of concrete from the skip to the moulds.

Concrete which has a low slump to provide high early strength should be discharged direct, so that the rate of flow can be regulated or stopped at any point of discharge where units are being built up in the moulds.

A typical economic mould layout for the site casting of panel units for box-shell construction should be based on production lines 30 ft (9·14 m) wide, with a maximum length of 200 ft (60·96 m); minimum working space around all moulds of 2 ft (0·61 m); and moulds of standardised sizes grouped under battery-cast walls, standard floor slabs (horizontal), standard wall slabs (horizontal and tilting moulds), exposed aggregate units, and units with special finishes. Battery moulds requiring large pours of concrete should be placed nearest to the batching plant.

Moulds for casting panel units are necessarily constructed of heavy steel to withstand constant vibration, maintain accurate tolerances, and provide required surface finishes for large volume production, and can cost approximately £12,000 each (and upwards) according to type. Variations in modular sizes of wall panels can be obtained with extendible moulds and stop ends to vary lengths of panels standardised in height.

The accuracy of finish in site casting varies according to the accuracy of the moulds, but normally enables $\frac{1}{8}$ in (3 mm) textured plaster to be sprayed on direct to concrete ceilings, and $\frac{1}{4}$ in (6 mm) to $\frac{3}{8}$ in (9 mm) thick wood floated rendering to be applied direct on concrete units. Units with wider tolerances require less expensive moulds, but involve additional jointing media, and take longer to erect.

Mould designs for non-automated site factory production are based on number and types of moulds required for the design of panels required by the system. The number of moulds of each type is related to the correlation of panel types provided by the possibilities of the system. This determines the weight and radii at which the panels have to be handled, and the total number of panels required for a project; detailed designs of mould bodies and mechanisms; and of incorporation provisions needed in moulds for entrances and canopies; access balconies, staircases, fire protection requirements, lifts, internal and external finishes, plumbing, heating and electrical installations, and fittings; assembly details of the above units relating to mould versatility; details of foundations and jack pits required by moulds; details of hydraulic, mechanical, electrical, heating, water and compressed air installations and equipment required for each mould and injector; and layout of service mains in the factory, including welding plugs and crane power.

Current developments of mould design for panel production include the extension of battery casting techniques to curved and patterned cladding, and other types of shaped panels; the evaluation of the 'Chevron' technique to produce self-supporting L-shaped elements of varying sizes and thicknesses to eliminate awkward corner jointing; and methods of spraying and pressing concrete units.

Both curved and grooved cladding panels which are insulated and lined internally can be produced on site in battery moulds. Special lifting gear, and a belt conveyor facilitate handling concrete from the mixer to the moulds.

The shape of the units to be produced determines their methods of casting.

Tilting moulds for horizontally cast floor panels subject to wash and spray techniques achieve a more rapid turnover from the mould before the slabs have gained sufficient strength for horizontal handling. Floor panels can be economically cast with electrical conduits run in, and screeded off ready to receive a vinyl or similar floor finish.

Battery moulds for vertically casting plain panels enable a series of units to be cast with two finished faces. This can be achieved economically by casting the panels in series with two parallel smooth faces free from blow holes for lifting directly into the building from the mould, thus avoiding multiple handling, transportation costs, and expensive finishing operations. With horizontal casting, the slab has to be picked up before placing in its vertical position. Panels up to 18 ft (5·49 m) long and weighing 6 tons (6·10 tonnes) each can be battery cast and handled by travelling tower cranes on specially constructed rails.

Problems arise when designing moulds for external load-bearing façade panels which incorporate door and window frames, intermediate insulating layers, a variety of internal finishes, and raised, sunk, or exposed aggregate finishes to provide flexibility of appearance. Economical methods of vertical battery casting for this type of panel need to be developed to provide sufficient space for pouring and vibrating the concrete on either side of the sandwich layer.

Insulated wall façade panels are usually cast horizontally face down to obtain a relatively thinner and more expensive concrete finish, and a profiling from a template for external patterned finish; to utilise sand bed techniques for exposed aggregate finish; and to accord with the particular shape of the unit, and its erection requirements; for example, positioning of starter bars, incorporation of fixings and other inserts.

Panels are cast alternatively horizontally face up when it is required to obtain an internal face which is very accurate in plane and free from irregularities and marking; to accord with required unit shape, e.g. a ribbed panel incorporating structural steel, with a dished centre to lighten weight; to enable the aggregate to be exposed by spray and soft brush techniques; or to profile by sculptured techniques.

One economic method of vertical battery casting for such façade units involves profiling the divider plates, or grit blasting the external face of the panel to expose the aggregate after demoulding, and applying an insulating skin to the internal face of the unit either in the factory, or on site.

Systems which incorporate complex structural core units use more costly moulds which enable ducts, flues and service stacks to be cast with requisite pipework and attachments for fittings. Load-bearing components forming kitchen and bathroom units can be cast to combine in one mould many operations that would be separated in traditional building, with an accuracy of production that achieves rapid site installation of requisite equipment and fittings.

Moulds of lighter steel are used for casting beam and column units for frame construction. More open planning can be obtained by standardising moulds for repetitively casting sections to the maximum of their load-bearing capacity, any required increase of column spacing being obtained by prestressing techniques.

Lighting systems for dwellings constructed of panel units can be provided economically by integrating a complete wall lighting scheme in the wall panels. The method of fixing prefabricated electrical conduits within the moulds necessitates dimensions of repetitive conduits varying by not more than $\frac{1}{8}$ in (3 mm). All holes in accessory outlet boxes, except those required for fixings, should be taped over, and all open ends of conduits corked or taped during casting.

Boxes for switches, socket outlets, wall brackets and similar fittings should have rotary adjustable lugs to overcome any casting errors, and obviate any distortion caused during concreting operations from affecting the fixing centres. Points should be located on the socket outlet ring circuit to avoid extensive deviation from a perimeter ring current, and standardised types of conduit cast in the moulds. Socket outlets should be of a type where the twin unit has two horizontal fixing holes for use in conjunction with the rotary adjustment lug.

Wall bracket lighting outlet boxes should be fitted after casting with a three-way through-connection block of 10 amp rating, with terminals suitable for $2 \times 7/0.029$ cables. Bracket fittings can be wired with $23/0.0076$ flexible cord, and connected to connector blocks inside the outlet box, the third terminal in the connector block being used for earth wire.

Some composite systems based on precast concrete wall panels and poured in-situ concrete floors integrate a radiant heating system which is fabricated in a template at ground level, and integrated with the steel reinforcement for the poured in-situ floors. The electrical wiring system for lighting is fully integrated in the structure by casting in the wall panels flexible plastic type cables and outlet boxes, and assembling in the site factory all wiring required for the in-situ floor slabs.

Factors influencing speed of site factory production

The main factors influencing speed of factory production relate to: methods of constructing and reinforcing units, speed of concrete curing, the different daily outputs required for each type of unit, the number of daily shifts required to be worked for each separate casting cycle, and available space on site for stacking units.

The optimum curing cycle will vary according to design mix and type of materials for each unit. In order to maintain long-term strength and durability, panels generally should be kept moist throughout the curing cycle, and for some time afterwards. But with some types of structural units, it may be more advantageous to ensure that a large proportion of shrinkage has taken place before their incorporation in the structure. Thus some loss of moisture would be desirable during curing, choice depending upon the position of the unit in the building.

The cycle of operations and the approximate times for a team of four men employed on the production of sandwich façade panels 8 ft × 12 ft (2·44 m × 3·66 m) and 12 in (0·30 m) thick, formed with a 2 in (51 mm) insulation sandwich layer between 6 in (153 mm) structural and 4 in (102 mm) backing concrete, and cast horizontally in steel tilting moulds would be:

	Hours
Striking mould from previous unit	1
Cleaning mould	1
Applying mould oil	$\frac{1}{2}$
Placing inserts	$\frac{1}{2}$
Fixing steel reinforcement	$\frac{1}{4}$
Placing 6 in (153 mm) structural concrete	$\frac{1}{2}$
Cutting and placing insulating panel, and spacing and fixing ties	1
Packing 4 in (102 mm) concrete backing	$\frac{1}{2}$
Exposing aggregate surface ⎫	$\frac{1}{2}$
Stacking panel in yard (after curing) ⎭	$\frac{1}{2}$
Cleaning exposed surface with acid (after stacking)	$\frac{1}{4}$

The concrete would be left to cure in the mould overnight, and stacking and cleaning operations carried out the next morning.

The casting cycle and approximate times required for manufacturing internal wall panels 15 ft × 8 ft × 7 in (4·57 m × 2·44 m × 178 mm) thick in vertical batteries of five or six would be:

	Hours
Striking mould from previous unit	1 to $1\frac{1}{2}$
Cleaning mould	2
Applying mould oil	1
Placing inserts, e.g. fixing blocks, electric conduits, inserts for holes	$3\frac{1}{2}$
Fixing steel reinforcement	1
Placing concrete in mould	$1\frac{1}{2}$
Curing concrete	5
Stacking panels in yard	1
Treating surface finishes in yard (next morning)	1

Under normal conditions, factory operations would be staggered for two single shifts of eight and a half hours each per day in order to obtain two casts from the moulds. One team would commence at 6.0 a.m. and the other at 8.30 a.m. Both teams would be engaged in preparing reinforcement and inserts when waiting for the concrete to cure.

With production requirements based on a three-minute cycle mix of concrete from a 1 cu yd (0·76 m³) capacity mixer to place the concrete into its mould within twenty minutes, the casting cycle and approximate times required for manufacturing floor panels 10 ft (3·05 m) × 12 ft (3·66 m) × 6½ in (165 mm) thick with one team of three men working one daily eight hour shift to complete horizontal casting operations of one panel would be:

Striking mould from previous unit	10 to 15 minutes
Cleaning mould	10 minutes
Applying mould oil	2 minutes
Placing inserts	6 to 7 minutes
Fixing steel reinforcement	15 minutes
Placing concrete in mould	20 minutes
Surface treatment	20 minutes
Curing concrete	6 hours
Striking concrete from mould	10 to 15 minutes
Stacking panel in yard	10 minutes

The turn round of moulds for constant use is economically based on a 24-hour cycle, so the design of a concrete mix should provide sufficient strength for demoulding at twenty-four hours, with a strength of 1450 lb per sq in (101·94 kgf/cm^2) at eighteen hours.

The casting and curing of concrete at temperatures over about 50°C provides a quicker handling of units, and enables two daily casts to be obtained from steel moulds, but involves strength loss of up to 50 per cent, which can be compensated by using a richer mix with more cement.

Rapid turnover without loss of strength can be obtained at temperatures up to approximately 50°C. The minimum casting per mould requires temperatures above 16°C for both casting and curing. Below this temperature gain of handling strength would be insufficient for daily turnover.

It is desirable that no violent changes should occur during the casting and curing cycles. Concrete should not be cast at 20°C and then rapidly cured at 40°C. If conditions necessitate casting at a considerably lower temperature than that required for curing, temperature increase should be gradual.

Steam curing accelerates concrete maturing by causing it to expand, and increases productivity by enabling moulds to be used more frequently for casting, so that two or more mould casts can be obtained in one shift. As the costs of materials and labour are constant for each casting, economies achieved relate to the more rapid casting and striking from the moulds. Thus a 13 ft × 8 ft (3·96 m × 2·44 m) wall panel can be steam cured in half an hour, and then demoulded, a process which normally takes from two to five hours.

Some continental systems are based on methods of battery casting and high temperature concrete curing with double shift work to obtain five prefinished units from moulds ready for stock piling in sixteen hours. By these means, utilisation is achieved of only one-fifth of the number of moulds that would be required for horizontal casting with an output of only one or two units per sixteen hours.

Economical types of steam plant for the site factory curing of concrete include a mobile steam generator unit which provides a steam output of 550–572 lb/hour at a pressure of 142 lb per sq in (9·98 kgf/cm^2) with a fuel consumption of 5·5 Imperial gallons (25 litres)/hour of diesel or gas oil Type B.S. 2869: 1957 Class A. This type of generator requires an electricity supply of 440 volt three-phase, and a water supply of 59·4 Imperial gallons/hour, and is suited to production requirements up to 3000 cu ft (84·95 m^3)/week during winter months. For larger productions of about 6000 cu ft (169·890 m^3) a week and over, a unit with a vapour boiler and fuel capacity of 1000 gallons (4546 litres), giving a 1000 lb/hr steam output at 150 lb p.s.i. is suitable. Fuel consumption is at the rate of about 9·2 Imperial gallons (41·82 litres)/hour of diesel or gas oil. The unit requires a 440 volt three-phase electricity supply, with water softeners and electrical time switches, and an enclosed shelter. An insulated tank at high level with a capacity suited to concrete production should be provided, through which steam may be used to heat the mixing water. Approximately 28 gallons of water is required for each cubic yard of concrete mixed.

New operatives require approximately two to three weeks to learn the various manufacturing techniques required in a temporary site factory. A team of thirteen experienced men employed on a daily 8½ hour shift for the production of large panel units for the box-shell construction of dwellings on one site would have a normal weekly output of approximately 4000 to 8000 cu ft (113·27 to 226·54 m^3) of units. It would not be more economical for the teams to work two shifts per day in order to increase their productivity on sites to be developed with only one to three tower blocks unless sufficient stacking area was available on the site for the simultaneous production of the units required for all the blocks; the additional erection cranes required could be economically utilised; and adequate team strengths were available for the finishing trades to follow up erection of the structures.

Site factory outputs are limited by the finishing trades' operation cycles, and optimum utilisation of mechanical plant and equipment for handling and erecting the structural elements.

When increased weekly outputs of about 10,000 to 12,000 cu ft (283·17 to 339·80 m³) per week are required for larger projects, economic single shift work could still be maintained, although an additional factory crane would be required to deliver the factory finished units within reach of the erection cranes and trailers. Economic shift work depends on carefully balancing manufacturing techniques with daily production requirements for each type of unit. A daily output based on the production of x interior wall panels, y façade panels, and z floor panels would be geared to the required ratios by determining whether to utilise more moulds with less shift work, or fewer moulds with increased shift work, according to type, size and construction of each unit; required output of each type; any limitations imposed by erection equipment; layout of buildings; space available for stacking finished units; and the overall contract period.

In general, shift work may be economical on a private development project in order to obtain a quicker return on the employer's capital investment in the form of rents. On local authority developments, where subsidies are required to be paid out when the dwellings are occupied, there is not the same drive for rapid erection, and construction is usually based on more economic but slower construction with completion of one single block followed by a second block, trade by trade.

In order to ensure safe handling, concrete units should reach a satisfactory stage of their curing before removal from the moulds (e.g. 1500 lb per sq in (105·46 kgf/cm²) or 40 per cent of their 28-day strength), and be identified with their date of manufacture in order to prevent green units which have not reached their design strength being built into the structure.

Efficient stacking of units is essential for site operatives' safety. Stacks should not be positioned close to moving plant so that a trap would be formed between the fixed stack and the machine; a minimum clearance of 2 ft (0·61 m) is essential for safety. Odd units should not be placed outside the normal stacking areas, as they may foul crane tracks and access ways, or be caught up by another unit whilst being slung into position by cranes. Units should be supported at suitable points in the stacking yard to avoid permanent deformation due to their low strength of concrete at this stage of their maturity. Direct and bending stresses in the lifting loops, bars or bolts should be checked, as units damaged in stacking can be dangerous when lifted from the stack by cranes.

Adequate packing is essential in order to prevent damage and fracture to the units. Floor panels stacked horizontally should be separated by such means as timber packing placed one above the other up the stack, with sleepers positioned over the bolt holes when the slab is even. Good access should be provided to the top of the stack. Long runs of vertically stacked wall units require an elevated walkway the entire length of the stack to ensure quick and safe access to any position.

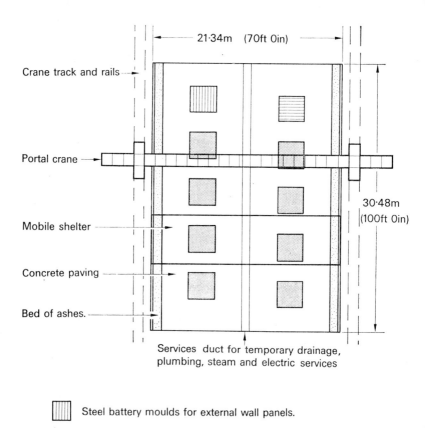

FIG. 5.2 Site factory plan for production of precast concrete units for 400 dwellings

Considerable care is required for the transportation of units around the site. Hard standings for trailers should be provided at loading or unloading points, as vehicle wheels may sink into soft ground and unbalance their loads. All units should be chained to their transport vehicles, and units travelling vertically on 'A' frames should be well secured with clamps.

Factory production of panel units for 400 dwellings

The following example indicates the procedure required for setting up a site factory for the production of precast reinforced concrete wall, partition and floor slab units suited to the box-shell construction of multistorey dwellings on an assumed basis of 400 dwellings, planned in four twenty-storey blocks for completion within a period of 100 weeks.

The factory floor indicated comprises precast paving slabs bedded in sand around the moulds, with a service duct in the centre, and a bed of ashes laid between movable polythene framed shelters and the portal crane track. About 40 cu yd (30·58 m³) of concrete would be required for supporting the steel moulds and battery pits, and bedding the portal crane tracks.

The plant required would include a 70 ft (21·34 m) portal crane, a 21/14 mixer, a steam generator, and stacking racks. The work load of the portal crane would be based on lifting approximately 280 units per week to provide a 15½ day erection cycle per floor geared to daily factory outputs of 850 cu ft (24·07 m³) of precast concrete units.

The floor slabs would be produced in horizontal moulds, and the wall slabs in vertical battery moulds. The precast units required for each floor would comprise:

> 100 floor slabs
> 80 cladding units
> 50 internal wall panels
>   5 staircase panels
> 45 internal partition wall units
> ‾‾
> Total 280 units per floor, comprising a total of 13,000 cu ft (368·12 m³)
> ‾‾
>   of precast concrete.

Factory production of panel units for 1000 dwellings

The type of site factory required for larger outputs (e.g. for 1000 dwellings) would necessitate differently planned manufacturing bays and a more permanent type of temporary structure, additional cranes, and increased areas of production bays and stacking yards as indicated in Fig. 5·3.

Plant requirements would include one portal crane for each production bay; one mobile tower crane spaced to control all movement of units; one 18/12 concrete mixer with track for two skips serving each portal crane and the tower crane, one steam generator unit, and approximately 2000 sq ft (185·81 m²) of stacking area made available adjoining the track of each portal crane.

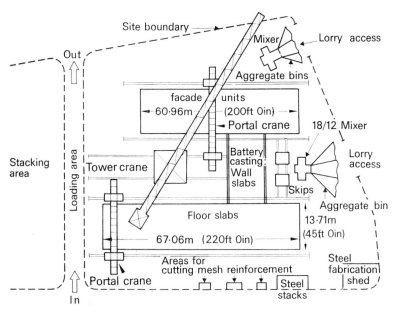

FIG. 5.3   Site factory plan for production of precast panel units for 1000 dwellings

Approximately 5000 sq ft (464·52 m²) of additional stacking space should be allocated in a convenient area of the site.

Factory production of units for larger outputs

Increased volumes of site factory production for more dwellings necessitate more highly intensive capitalisation for larger and more permanently constructed factory buildings, with maintenance sheds for vehicles delivering units from the factory to required locations on site; a greater degree of mechanisation for production, requiring more costly machinery, plant and equipment; large areas of handstandings and stockyards; fencing, gates; and additional staff, which would include a foreman, quality control inspectors, production planning and materials ordering staff, concrete engineers, plant and cost clerks.

A housing project comprising 4000 low- and high-rise dwellings of composite precast and poured in-situ concrete construction would be based on site factory production of wall units for yearly outputs of 1000 dwellings working one shift per day. Additional capacity would be provided for increasing outputs to units for 1500 dwellings working two shifts per day. The type of factory installed on site would have a closed roof, with two bays of sliding roof provided at one end, and an internal gantry crane for handling units and placing them in the stacking yard. The layout of the manufacturing areas would include two casting halls, one for floor panels and horizontal facings, and the other for vertical complex units, staircases and miscellaneous units. Stores, welding shops, a boiler house, carpenter's shop, fully equipped fitters' shop and approximately twenty trailers would be required.

All moulds for precasting would be of precision-made steel to provide flexibility for varying lengths of standardised wall units by the insertion of stop ends. The curing of units would be normally by steam. External wall panels would be cast with a polystyrene insulation sandwich layer, and fittings, doors and windows inserted in the moulds. After casting, the panels would remain in a vertical position to simplify handling operations. Horizontal moulds would be jacked up vertically to avoid stressing, and lifted into the trailers by crane for transporting and hoisting to final positions in the various buildings.

Average daily outputs of precast units based on two castings a day would vary from between 3000 to 4000 cu ft (84·95 to 113·27 m³) of concrete, according to site erection requirements. The average time required for producing one unit would average approximately two and a half to three hours, excluding twelve minutes for inspection and making good pinholes in finished surfaces. Average approximate times for the cranes to handle one unit to position would be fifteen minutes, and for a team to erect, joint and point the unit, about ½ hour.

The effects of increased scale of outputs on factory production costs of precast concrete panel units is relatively insignificant within fairly confined limits. The following assessments of site factory costs at 1967 rates are averaged over all types of large panel units for the box-shell construction of dwellings based on weekly outputs of 8000 to 10,000 cu ft

(226·54 to 283·17 m³) of concrete units for 300 dwellings, the minimum volume of demand for economy:

	p
Factory installation, maintenance, and dismantling	4
Steel moulds	5
Casting	35
Plant	5
Concrete sandwich materials	22½
Steel reinforcements	12
Factory staff	4
Insurances	2½
	90
Add Handling and transporting unit to position and erecting	10
	£1 (=100)
Add Contingencies, overhead charges and profit, say 25 per cent	25
Approximate total cost per cu ft of concrete unit produced and erected in position	£1·25

By doubling such outputs, a saving of approximately £100 per dwelling could be achieved on the total cost of system built housing, of which approximately 33⅓ per cent relates to traditional site and foundation works. Increased outputs for 1000 dwellings would probably achieve a saving of approximately £125 per dwelling. This would be a limiting reduction, because vaster outputs necessitate either a much larger or more expensive type of site factory, or else a second factory to maintain speed of assembly and erection.

Other effects of increased outputs relate to additional requirements for heavier and more costly types of cranes and transport vehicles to handle larger and more prefinished units to keep pace with erection requirements.

The main advantages to be gained from the increased scale of production relates to a certain limited economy of construction costs, and to the advantages obtainable from the construction of large numbers of dwellings of a higher standard than those built by traditional methods due to the greater precision and better finish achieved by factory methods of controlled production; more rapid construction with less site man-hours; improved labour management relations arising from better working conditions and more opportunities of obtaining increased bonus payments; and the beneficial psychological effects achieved from operatives readily seeing the quick effects on output of their increased efforts.

6

Programming and Control of Site Mechanisation and Erection Operations

PROGRAMMING

Traditional building construction is a labour intensive activity, with the speed of craft operations mainly determined by the ability and drive of the operatives related to effective bonus schemes, availability of work and materials, and the design of the buildings to be erected. The productivity of industrialised system building is also influenced by these factors, but more especially by the detailed design of mechanical plant and equipment used for semi skilled operations, the general sequence of erection operations, the composition and strength of erection teams for specialised trades geared to the mechanical plant serving them, and the integration of factory outputs with more rapid erection requirements.

The speed of system building is determined by the critical operations of the floor to floor erection cycle, which is mainly influenced by type of structural design. Thus when several teams are employed on in-situ concrete operations based on crane handled shuttering and concrete skips, maximum crane utilisation may result in one or more of the teams being idle at times. When central core construction is planned to proceed well in advance of general floor construction, attempts to increase the speed of other operations may only result in more idle time.

Effective preplanning and site control of all phases of industrialised system building is essential to ensure that all erection teams are fully occupied and can move freely from one operation to another without delays, maintain continuity of construction and plant operations, and minimise non-productive time and site on costs.

For fast cycle repetitive work seconds count, and careful consideration should be given to the sequence, timing and most economic method of all erection operations. Simple erection devices can be used to plumb, level and line precast concrete units for jointing. The comparative advantages of manpower or suitable mechanical plant and its positioning must be determined before work starts on site in order to achieve uninterrupted construction. The momentum of system building depends on optimum utilisation of plant and labour, efficient safety and welfare measures, provision of artificial lighting during winter months, adequate protection for operatives during adverse weather conditions, facilities for servicing and repairing mechanical plant, and effective bonus schemes. In general, the fewer separate erection operations required, and the more standardised and repetitive they are made, the easier will be the organisation and progression of erection processes.

In order to achieve a high labour output, equitable bonus targets should be established for the phased operations of all trades and sub-contractors' men integrated with the planned erection cycle. This programme may require frequent revision during the progress of the works to suit changed conditions, such as shortage of materials and labour, alternate methods of construction, bad weather, and other unforseen circumstances.

Slower building with less mechanical plant and equipment tends to reduce idle time, but increases overhead costs, and delays the return on employers' capital investments. The use of more mechanical plant to replace site labour combined with efficient control over materials, component deliveries, labour and mechanical plant can minimise non-productive time and achieve faster construction, savings in overheads, and a more economic return on capital investment and turnover.

Non-productive time can be reduced at design stage by standardising components, erection requirements, and simple jointing techniques. The specialisation of erection tasks enables labour output to be increased by the operatives' improved facilities for carrying out the same operation repeatedly.

Maximum economy of labour and speed of site erection is achieved by architectural and structural designs which provide a maximum repetition of standardised site erection operations with sufficient working space and access to operatives inside the building; and site layouts that permit adequate manoeuvrability of mechanical plant, continuous operation of cranes, and efficient utilisation of all other plant and equipment selected for total construction operations.

System building has brought the construction industry more into line with manufacturing industries by the introduction of factory methods of production and industrial problems of the shop floor. These profoundly affect the control of a contractor's profits. The main control ratios are profit/total capital employed, which indicates the efficiency of assets utilisation; and total capital employed/turnover, which indicates the efficiency of circulatory capital expenditure. This is largely obscured by the allocation of fixed capital in the ratio that is not turned over during the financial year.

An organisation based on a building system requires the control of both finance and production due to the rapid speed of construction, which is strongly responsive to the introduction of capital. Increased receipts, which are influenced by rapidity of earnings, should be related to return on capital as well as market demands. Required profits on capital investments should be established in relation to planned productions.

The table following indicates how the introduction of capital and speed of construction should be controlled by financial planning.

Method of planning to control capital investment in relation to speed of construction

	Period of contract Weeks	Value of contract £	Gross profit 10% £	Assets employed £	% return on assets	% earned per week	Cash earned per week £
A1	30	500,000	50,000	200,000	25	0·83	7667
A2	20	500,000	50,000	220,000	22·7	1·135	2500
B1	18	500,000	50,000	230,000	21·74	1·20	2778
B2	18	500,000	34,360 (6·8%)	230,000	14·94	0·83	1909

In example A2, capital of £20,000 (a second erection crane) was introduced to reduce the contract period to twenty weeks. By obtaining this speed of construction it would be possible to reduce the gross profit on turnover to 7·3 per cent and yet still obtain the same weekly return on capital employed of 0·83 per cent per week, i.e. the estimated profit can be reduced to £13,580 (i.e. the difference between 10 and 7·3 per cent) and still be improved by reducing the contract time.

In example B2, increased assets yields a proportionally much smaller decrease in contract time, but as the amount introduced is relatively smaller, the percentage return earned per week is increased. This represents greater earnings in terms of cash flow per week. Thus a contract price which yields 6·8 per cent on turnover yields the same return on capital (i.e. 0·25 per cent) as obtained in Example A1. The speed of a project should be related to its profitability in terms of total capital invested. Alternatively, turnover, capital, and speed of construction should be used to achieve the optimum return on capital investment.

Phasing materials and component deliveries to suit erection requirements

The ordering of phased deliveries of materials and components for housing developments comprising about 500 dwellings on one site should be based on the delivery of structural units and cladding direct to the erection cranes. Materials and non-structural components should be delivered to storage compounds for packaging into dwelling types and storing until required for lifting into the buildings at shell erection stage, or carrying in at a later stage.

The speed of industrialised building requires corresponding business efficiency aids to management. Computer techniques are used for accelerating management decisions and speedily evaluating a complex series of unrelated data in detail. Computers can cut down the work in preparing lists of units for developments with a considerable variety of dwelling types and units. For example, fifty different cladding units painted five different colours represent 250 types of this unit alone.

An effective computer system can aid rapid and flexible control over preplanning and costing by taped programmes for ordering materials to phased deliveries. Estimated costs can be compared with the current costs of all jobs in progress by a detailed breakdown which forms a pre-expenditure control budget enabling all price variations between estimated and actual costs to be readily determined. Payments and outstanding balances due to subcontractors can be calculated rapidly on the basis of coded budget programmes. Monthly efficiency reports which provide detailed information about differences in costs and quantities of resources and sub-contract works are quickly obtained.

Computerised forward weekly delivery lists can be prepared for materials to be sent to storage compounds, and allocated into a list of materials to be carried into buildings from storage compounds, a list of building types (in weeks), and a list of materials to be delivered direct to the cranes.

Materials lifted to position at erection stage should be included in the weekly erection lists and ordered in a fixed number of weeks ahead equivalent to the period of stock held in the storage compounds.

Materials to be handled into the buildings after erection stage can be timed by adding on the period from erection to fixing time, and deducting the stock period.

Materials delivered direct to the crane involve a more laborious process, as a sequential list should be prepared for every unit in order of erection, analysed into loads.

All these methods of scheduling materials deliveries can be computerised by feeding the computer with a list of dwelling types, and the amount and numerical code numbers of each type of unit; a list of the units' numerical code numbers against the equivalent design code numbers; a list of week or day numbers; and the amount and type of dwellings in each day or week.

Five basic types of schedules for dwellings are required for computerised production control:

a delivery schedule on a time basis, giving the amount and types of units required each week;

an erection schedule of units delivered direct to the crane, giving a sequential list of units in order of erection broken down into trailer loads, with delivery dates against each load;

a quantity schedule for each block, or part of a block, giving a list of the units required for that particular portion of the project;

labour content schedules with the total manhour content of each dwelling type and component, as a basis for assessing bonus payments;

price schedules, or cost plans, with the prices of various components for each dwelling type.

Whilst computers can provide extremely useful tools for such pedestrian applications it cannot be too strongly emphasised that a computer is only as good as its programme, and this has to be thought out by fallible man, and related to logic and mathematics, which are extremely limited tools for research into hidden realities. For mathematical reasoning is not completely free from inherent contradictions, and contains deeply hidden assumptions for which there are no valid logical proofs. Any deduction established only repeats in other words what already lies concealed in the premises 'nothing new or original is discovered'.

It is too frequently forgotten that the fundamental propositions of arithmetic are neither true nor false, and consequently all attempts to fill the gap in our 'number system', such as 'irrational', 'imaginary', 'complex', 'hyper-complex' and 'ultra-real' numbers, as well as 'classes' and 'theories of sets', in order to extend the 'system' so that a 'number' can represent graphically a point on the axis of a 'rectangular Cartesian co-ordinate system' to indicate 'time' or a 'dimension of space' are doomed to failure because they are based on misconceptions.

It is not generally understood how dangerous and misleading values obtained by statistical methods can be. They can never be completely accurate or comprehensive and at best are subject to errors of at least $\pm$ 3%. The fallacies inevitably concealed in such a method can be highlighted by comparing, for example, statistical values of 100 in year 1 (which subject to $\pm$ 3% = 97 or 103) and 105 in year 2 (which subject to $\pm$ 3% = 102 or 108). Thus by comparing 97 and 108, an increase of plus $11\frac{1}{2}$% is indicated for feeding into a computer, and a comparison of 103 and 102 shows a decrease of minus 1%.

Preplanning the erection cycle

In the complex network of concurrent, overlapping and interrelated site operations, speeding the time of a single operation may actually increase costs without decreasing the contract time, because other critical operations have not been speeded up as well. Quickening the time of all the operations may well result in excessively increased costs being incurred in relation to the reduced time achieved.

The critical path method of sequence analysis aids preplanning by making it possible to establish which particular operation, or sequence of operations can be speeded in order to obtain the most economic reduction of time by isolating those operations whose starting and finishing times are critical, and must be strictly kept in order to complete the contract to date. The amount of flexible time ('float') included in each non-critical operation can be evaluated within which it can be started later, or be completed more slowly than originally programmed without affecting the completion date. Non-productive time can be minimised by adapting the speed or sequence of non-critical operations to maintain the steady full employment of the planned labour force over prolonged periods. Mechanical plant and equipment can be programmed for optimum utilisation, instead of being used to complete operations in spurts followed by idle times, and the uneconomic use of additional equipment brought on to site to meet short peak loads can be avoided.

Site layouts

Site layouts should be planned flexibly to coordinate and control access, movement, plant, service runs, traffic routes, and factory administrative and work areas in relation to the different phases of construction and the contract time, in order to ensure a smooth flow in the cycle of operations.

Administrative areas should provide adequate temporary offices, stores and welfare units which avoid obstructing work areas, and maintain free access to storage compounds and points requiring maximum labour control.

Site factory and stacking areas should be determined by available space, access for deliveries, required outputs, type of construction, and layout of buildings and plant in order to minimise double handling, and integrate production with erection requirements. Where space is restricted, ready-mixed concrete can be utilised to supplement limited batching plant, or even for all castings.

Construction areas should be sited to minimise movement and handling, and permit storage of the least amount of materials and components required for the erection operations.

On large development schemes in city areas, economy can be sometimes achieved by allocating a separate storage area for subcontractors' deliveries, the general contractor being responsible for their transportation to required locations on site in order to avoid lorries waiting before being able to enter the site.

Transportation routes and temporary roads should be effectively located to avoid restrictions on earthworks, and service runs. Movements of mechanical plant can be routed either by planning two-way traffic systems, or by one-way circular routes with turn rounds and passing bays according to the site layout and phased operations. Vehicles for transport should be related to power, surface condition of planned works, capacity, and shape, size, and weight of units.

Wet sites necessitate tracked machines, whereas sloping sites may obviate the use of rail mounted cranes. A site surrounded by adjoining tall buildings may require a derricking jib crane, rather than a horizontal crane, in order to clear the buildings as it slews round.

On sites to be developed with several multistorey blocks based on the site factory production of precast panel units, the most economic but slowest method of site erection relates to single block construction, where the foundation team constructs the foundations, and moves to the next block when its work has been completed; the 'non-repetitive' teams then construct the work from ground to first floor, or such floors as are 'non-repetitive'. During this period, the site factory should have produced the units required for the three floors above. These are erected next, and the finishing teams then follow on in the floors erected. This cycle of operations continues, so that by the time the roof is placed on the first block, all the units for the three first floors of the second block have been manufactured and erected.

Where a development provides for six or more blocks, more economical construction would be based on doubling factory production outputs and cranage, and similarly erecting two blocks at a time, because the time for completion of all the blocks, and their numbers and layout influences the choice of structural type and team strengths related to cranage.

In general, in-situ concrete construction is more economical than precast concrete construction for smaller developments such as 250 dwellings on one site; non-repetitive designs, and widely separated blocks. Such site layouts and small volumes of demand do not justify the costs of setting up a site factory.

Economic precast concrete construction requires larger projects, efficient design of structural elements and jointing techniques, and block layouts spaced sufficiently close for rapid erection operations. Thus blocks should be laid out so that two cranes and two erection teams can operate three blocks, or three cranes and three teams can operate six blocks.

When all the buildings are to be completed at the same time, the most efficient site layout normally would take the following form:

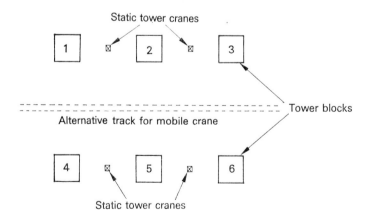

so that when block 1 has been completed, the erection teams can proceed to blocks 2 and 3.

If the blocks were to be widely spaced apart as indicated in the following diagram:

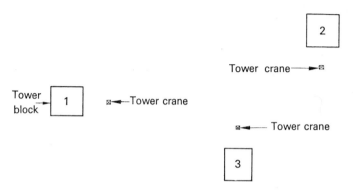

it would be more economical to construct them with in-situ poured concrete, and three cranes and associated erection teams.

On sites where only one block of dwellings is to be constructed with in-situ concrete, one crane and erection team of ten men could complete one floor of five dwellings each week. This would involve a certain amount of non-productive time (approximately 20 to 30 per cent) according to circumstances, and would not provide the operatives with sufficient incentive to increase their efforts in order to gain a bonus for improved outputs. But when two similar blocks are to be developed on one site, and suitably positioned so that they can be served by one crane, outputs of the associated erection team can be increased to achieve weekly completion of one floor in each block, a total of two floors per week. This procedure minimises non-productive time, because the operatives can fall back very readily from the first block to the second without disorganising the team, and provides an incentive to work harder with the opportunity of increasing their productivity from approximately 50 to 70 per cent in order to obtain a good bonus.

When three similar blocks are to be developed on one site and suitably positioned for erection with two tower cranes, three associated teams would be needed, one for each block. If only two teams were operating, the men in each team would be split up in order to fall back on the third block, and by so doing, would lose their integrated output. By operating three teams the situation becomes similar to that when only one block is to be developed on a site, and there is insufficient incentive for the men to increase their efforts to gain a bonus.

When four blocks are to be developed on a site, it is more economical to operate with two cranes and two associated erection teams of fifteen men each to achieve a situation similar to that required for the economic construction of two blocks.

It is usually more effective to construct long blocks for a mixed development scheme comprising low- and medium-rise dwellings up to four storeys high with a small portal crane on tracks, rather than tower cranes. If the buildings to be constructed were taller, greater economy could be achieved by using two climbing tower cranes suitably positioned, as the cost of laying the track and sleepers for the portal crane is avoided, and two tower cranes provide more versatility in handling different kinds of materials and components, and can keep the operatives more readily employed in order to speed the erection cycle.

The preliminary erection programme

After determination of the building, plant, services, and site factory layouts, a preliminary overall erection programme can be planned on the basis of a bar chart indicating separately all the principal repetitive erection operations of the system which are to be undertaken within the contract time, and all non-repetitive work in the substructure and above up to the level at which repetitive system building starts.

This procedure enables cost comparisons to be made of the most economic alternative methods of construction. For example, the use of climbing tower cranes rather than static cranes, or of sliding shutters instead of prefabricating shutters in large sizes for handling by crane. Once the broad overall programme has been decided, critical path planning can be introduced to indicate the amount of spare time each operation includes before the starting and finishing times of 'critical' operations which cannot be delayed or prolonged without extending the contract time.

The most economic cost to time relationship of erection operations is that best suited to the total labour, plant and materials requirements for the whole of the programmed works in order to optimise the contractor's return on his investment in the contract works, and lead to a reduction in competitive tender prices. Construction costs tend to decrease as output per team of operatives and related mechanical plant increases. Ill-planned speeding of erection operations can result in higher costs being incurred for overtime, shift work, over-sized erection teams, unnecessarily large or additional mechanical plant, and different and more costly methods and techniques of construction.

One advantage of industrialised system building is that site work can be split into well-defined operations capable of being carried out by various types of teams without their interfering with one another. This method of procedure replaces the traditional 'criss-crossing' of teams from house to house on low-rise development schemes by a train of teams following one another around the site, their work having been preplanned so that no one team can proceed slower or faster than its neighbours. The leading erection team determines the speed of the whole cycle of operations, and is separated by a 'buffer' period of about one week from the succeeding teams, which are each similarly separated in time one from the other. These 'buffer' periods act as a safety valve to achieve day by day variations without involving non-productive time, as where the labour content of different dwelling types vary, one team will tend to catch up with, or fall too far behind the team in front.

Comparison of traditional building methods with system building techniques for low-rise developments indicates how the latter can minimise non-productive time being incurred on site (see Fig. 6.1).

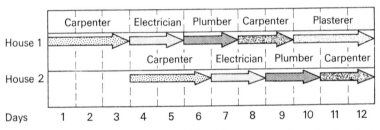

FIG. 6.1   Trade teams for two traditional houses on a low-rise housing development

This table of trade teams is not based on any particular form of traditional construction, and indicates the planning of trades where each trade is intimately connected with all the others. The carpenter team is represented as completing its first task in house no. 1 by day 3, and moving into house no. 2, where its task is completed by day 6. By this time, the following team of electricians has completed its task in house no. 2 on day 5, but cannot start work in house no. 2 until day 6 because the carpenters are still there. The electrician team either has to wait a day, or else be occupied elsewhere. Similarly, when the carpenters have finished in house no. 2 on day 6, they are unable to return to house no. 1, as it is still occupied by the team of plumbers.

These situations result in a confusion of trades either waiting on their predecessors or else holding up their successors. When multiplied on a large development project by several hundred houses, site management is presented with a typically confused problem which can only be solved with traditional methods by building much more slowly.

With low-rise developments of dwellings, mobile erection cranes become the leaders of a series of teams which follow the cranes around the site and enable operatives to carry out their preplanned tasks at a fixed speed. Each crane and its associated team composed of a crane driver, banksman, and two erectors, is completely isolated from the other cranes, and must erect and finish their dwellings to programme in order that the teams can receive a bonus payment at the end of the week. With high-rise developments, the cranes are selected and laid out with sufficient mobility to bring the required materials and components to the waiting erectors stationed at planned positions. The type of crane required depends upon the plan shape, size and height of the structures to be erected, block layouts, site contours, ground surface conditions, access space, contract time, and site conditions.

In programming erection operations for system building, the optimum effects of repetitive tasks on labour outputs can be achieved best by dividing the whole of the contract works into a large number of simple, well coordinated processes based on effective and satisfactory bonus incentives. By these means a high degree of specialised tasks can be undertaken for the assembly of standardised components geared to a common rate for the erection cycle by independent teams of operatives moving freely between different working areas of the building in accordance with the general work rhythm.

All the separate tasks should be listed, and the most important key operations selected on the basis of their regular occurrence, for which time cycles are estimated. The planning of the remaining operations should be based on these cycles to provide a rhythm for the various teams to follow in an integrated sequence, with only one team occupying each defined work area in order to avoid interference of one team with another. Sufficient space should be made available so that all the different teams can work simultaneously without any loss of time, and start work on the next floor above as soon as their work on the floor below is completed.

Properly planned and coordinated factory production and site operations reduce the space required for teams working inside the building, which can be reduced when components are delivered prefinished. Wet processes involve more space, which if not made available slows down the whole erection cycle, reduces productivity, and adversely affects the operatives' bonus payments, thereby damaging good labour–management relations.

The general rhythm of work may have to be adapted as occasion arises in order not be break up the erection teams, or re-employ additional men. When key operations depend upon a technological process such as the time required for concrete to mature, or the hoisting capacity of mechanical handling plant and equipment, the number of men can be reduced.

With work carried out in a closely organised and sequential manner, the interruption of some operations will affect the whole construction process, and may cause secondary delays as subsequent trades overtake those originally stopped. Thus heavy rainfall over the weekend can delay earthworks and concreting operations programmed for the following week.

Non-productive time due to bad weather can be reduced by transforming as much site work as possible to factories in order to obtain the optimum dry assembly of prefabricated components, adopting methods of construction which enable the shell to be rapidly roofed in, and taking into account monthly data supplied by the meteorological office covering the duration of weather capable of stopping or delaying operations.

Bad weather can delay the erection cycle and increase the construction costs due to operatives being prevented from working. High winds exceeding 33 m.p.h. can delay the working of tower cranes, and heavy rain can hold up concreting operations and the in-situ jointing of floor to floor connections. But the operatives mainly affected by bad weather are bricklayers and general labourers. Additional manhours will be required to make up reduced productivity in bad weather and for making good damaged work.

The approximate times normally allocated to erection operations when pre-planning a preliminary overall programme for housing projects would include:

	Per cent
site installations	10
excavations, foundations, drains	8
traditional works	3

site erection of pre-fabricated structural units	44
internal finishings and services	20
external finishings	2
general site works such as maintenance of plant, safety measures, clearing and tidying site, storing and checking materials etc.	13

Good site management can reduce non-productive time to within approximately 10 to 15 per cent of the total manhours employed. And effective bonus incentive schemes can reduce non-productive site service time to within 20 per cent of the total effective operational time.

EFFECTS OF REPETITIVE OPERATIONS ON LABOUR OUTPUT

The repetition of identical site operations reduces construction time by increasing labour output, achieves savings in indirect costs by the greater utilisation of mechanical plant and ancillary works, and reduces on-costs by the increased use of such items as stores, site offices, and temporary roads.

The processes of repetition relate to the organisation and specialisation of methods of site assembly and jointing. These involve a learning phase and a routine acquiring phase, which gradually induce increased speed of operations dependent on degree of accuracy required for an operation; type, size and number of components to be erected; techniques of construction and jointing; type of mechanical plant and equipment utilised; and the number of men forming the erection team. Larger teams require more time to learn an operation—greater effort is needed to coordinate their work—and bonus incentive targets. Increase of labour productivity is disturbed by operational discontinuity, due to non-identity of operation, executional discontinuity caused by a break in team sequence or changes in teams, process restrictions, and bad weather.

Decrease of operational costs is not directly related to increased labour outputs because wages are based on bonus schemes and incentive payments, which may not be linked to actual increases of labour productivity. This dissociation may become a source of difficulty when bonus payments for all the different teams on a site are pooled and distributed equally amongst each man, instead of the payments being made to individual teams on the basis of their increased outputs.

When calculating the gradual improvement of labour due to repetitive operations, the number of men required for undertaking the different operations may be taken as constant, and the time taken by each process gradually decreased in order to reduce the number of operatives whilst maintaining a constant speed for the whole cycle of operations.

The effects of repetitive operations on labour outputs comprise only a part of the results due to introducing large series of standardised components into building operations. Other factors which affect the time of individual erection operations depend on the design and methods of prefabricating and transporting units, the locations of factories manufacturing materials and components, scale of production, contract time, restrictions imposed by site conditions, and site organisation.

FACTORS IMPEDING THE ERECTION CYCLE

Some of the adverse factors that delay erection operations are outside the contractor's control, such as traffic jams in city areas holding up deliveries to site, components damaged in transit, winter darkness. Other factors relate to weight of components (the heavier the unit, the more time required for handling to position), over-complicated jointing details, failure of the factory or outside component manufacturer to maintain planned production targets, inefficient selection of mechanical plant and related erection teams, breakdown of plant, power failures, and dissatisfaction of the men with their bonus targets.

Some adverse conditions that delay the speed of erection operations come into effect only as the number of storeys in the building increases. Men take longer to reach and leave their work positions; handling and hoisting of materials and components to increased heights takes longer; movement becomes more difficult as wind strength increases and affects the handling of lighter materials and components; propping requirements for structural elements become more stringent; and weather conditions at heights of 50 ft (15·24 m) and above become more unfavourable.

BONUS INCENTIVES

Bonus incentive schemes for site bargaining were introduced in the immediate postwar conditions of a vast reconstruction programme and acute shortage of skilled labour in order to permit payments over the standard union wage rates to be made to operatives, provided that they were strictly related to increased labour productivity. The intention was to afford operatives an opportunity of increasing their earnings by increasing their outputs of work.

There are no nationally agreed target times or standard methods of measuring work for bonus payments that can be applied to industrialised building projects for several reasons. In some areas, national bye-laws can be superseded in favour of local bye-laws, which may institute different conditions with easier task requirements; and craft methods of working differ in different parts of the country. Contract periods vary, so that men employed on a six-month contract require quicker results from their work than men employed on two-year contracts, who can be educated to understand that their bonus targets are truly profitable. This enables tighter targets to be operated on long-term contracts than on short-term contracts. As a result of this lack of uniformity, national rates of wages are of but little importance in most areas throughout the country, because bonuses may not be factually related to productivity, and whilst increasing operatives' earnings, undermine the standard rates on which their bonus earnings depend.

The trade unions' retention of a rigid traditional craft structure in the face of continuing changes in work content due to mechanisation and new techniques of construction can lead to inefficiency and delay. Thus the erection of a system building designed with a structural precast concrete frame and poured in-situ concrete floors may be slowed down by a union rule which prohibits labourers during breaks in the cycle of assembling and erecting precast concrete units from assisting other labourers working with carpenters on shuttering operations.

Before the 1939 war strict intercraft and craft labour demarcation lines reflected real divisions in building operations, and served to provide a measure of work security and wages for labour. Thus a plasterer will pick up mortar with a trowel, but not with a shovel, as it is a labourer's job to mix the plaster and place it on the plasterer's spot board.

New techniques and mechanised processes require new levels of skills, in many cases capable of being carried out by labourers upgraded to semiskilled status with adult retraining. Yet the union structure usually prohibits any process requiring a specialised technique, however limited, from being performed by anyone other than a craftsman trained through traditional apprenticeship, often with attendant labourers. As a result, skilled men are frequently underemployed, the shortage of craftsmen is aggravated, and the savings in labour that can result from new mechanised processes may not be fully obtained because craftsmen may have to be retrained for each new operation. The production of concrete is in the hands of unskilled and semiskilled labour instead of apprentice-trained artisans. This necessitates improvement in both the production and finishing of site concreting operations, and can involve additional materials costs for extra cement to ensure specified strengths, as well as technicians to attempt the effective quality control of site mixed concrete.

Industrialised building employs a new type of operative termed an 'erector', whose knowledge and skill is considerably less than that of a craft tradesman, but requires a knowledge and awareness of mechanical plant, the sequential operations in the erection cycle, and an understanding of the way components must fit together. A recent agreement on balanced teams of craftsmen and labourers for industrialised system building operations enables experienced erection teams to be built up on a site to a certain extent, but necessitates some erection operations which are basically continuous to be divided in order to accommodate two or more unions. Moreover, such teams when established on a site do not usually remain for other jobs.

Efficient system building can achieve high labour productivity with human satisfaction through the reduction of adverse effects on labour operations due to heavy physical labour, dust, bad weather, isolation, and lack of zest.

Of the several different types of financial incentive schemes operated in the Building Industry—profit sharing, piecework, hourly plus rates, and earned bonus—that normally best suited to system buildings with accurately scheduled and established times of repetitive operations relates to team bonusing based on standard and measurable performances. Payments made on the basis of 'in lieu bonus' or 'inspired' guesswork due to lack of bonus surveyors may well bear no relation to production, and become a mere increase of rates.

Although bonus schedules are usually drawn up at the start of most large industrialised system building projects as a basis for negotiation, less than half of the skilled labour force may be covered, and serious problems can occur which eventually lead to strikes. Where several specialist subcontractors are employed on a site, each firm may have its own different incentive scheme. This can result in the union representatives' demands for equal or pooled site bonuses, to which skilled operatives and craft tradesmen often object. When forced into operation, such incentive schemes can slow down the work of skilled men, and lead to output targets becoming so costly that a job may close down, even when operatives are earning double the average national earnings with their bonus payments.

A well operated bonus incentive scheme is essential to obtain the full benefits of costly factory production and mechanical plant, and should be related to the outputs of the whole cycle of erection operations, and measurable targets which the men can check each week. Bonus payments should provide an equitable return to all operatives employed, irrespective of whether they are craftsmen, labourers, or employed on non-productive work such as unloading, cleaning out latrines, or assisting storekeepers, as all these operatives indirectly increase the general productivity of the works.

The targets for each individual task should be negotiated separately for each erection team and contract, but certain basic principles apply. The method of calculating bonus payments should be fair, easily understood by all the teams, and enable operatives to obtain at least 50 per cent of the benefit derived from any time that is really saved. Tasks and their targets should be clearly specified, issued in advance of work commencing, and remain unaltered except by mutual consent. It is essential that goodwill is maintained by scrupulous integrity. If a technique involving additional plant is introduced to speed erection, targets should be adjusted so that the related operatives can gain 50 per cent of the increased saving, otherwise the men will tend to slow down their rate of working.

No maximum should be placed on earnings, and allowances should be made for delays which are outside the teams' control. A target may be fairly assessed, but prove unprofitable to the operatives due to inefficient management. For example, carpenters working on second fixings may find their work continually held up by delays in obtaining materials, or the uncompleted work of other trades. An economic balance needs to be made between productive operatives and non-productive operatives indirectly serving them. This balance can be maintained only if both groups of operatives put forth equal efforts to increase their work outputs.

All bonus payments due should be paid regularly on the next pay day after the work has been assessed.

In general, the size of a contract should control the targets set for a particular duration so that the operatives can look forward to a measure of continued bonus earnings, and do not tend to slow down their efforts through fear of being unemployed when the contract is completed.

A good bonus incentive scheme should entail the observance of all safety, health and welfare requirements; maintain required standards of workmanship and efficient plant utilisation; minimise wastage of materials and temporary services; permit the continued training of apprentices; and enable site service operators to earn higher wages based on increased outputs that are only indirectly related to increased productivity of the contract works.

If a bonus scheme does not satisfy men employed on tasks which are not directly productive, their cost of serving tradesmen may be increased from about 19 per cent to as much as $33\frac{1}{3}$ per cent due to a lack of incentive to increase their outputs. For example, four men who 'couldn't care less' might be unloading materials where only two men were required to undertake the job in the same time, because their weekly bonus payments amounted to 50p whereas their craftsmen brothers were earning weekly bonuses of £10.

Mechanical aids, stock-piling, extra transport deliveries, and a high level of organisation can enable productive operatives to maintain a constant high level of output, and high bonus earnings. But the balancing of their increased outputs with the outputs of the service operatives requires all the non-productive site labour to make comparable efforts, otherwise the number of men required for site servicing can become out of all proportion to the number of productive operatives, and prevent teams from earning a reasonable bonus.

Target schedules should therefore be agreed so that the increased efforts of site service operatives achieves a reduction of the men so employed. Productive operatives should not profit at the expense of site service operatives by the introduction of methods which increase their output and require additional site service. All operatives should be encouraged to cooperate and understand the costs involved and bonus earnings obtainable by their combined efforts.

One method of achieving these results is for an agreed percentage of the average productive operative's bonus to be assessed as between operatives of direct service to teams, including unloaders nominated by the site works committee at, say 60 per cent; fitters, and drivers etc., at say 50 per cent; and other site service operatives nominated by the committee at, say, 30 per cent. Such a method provides the site service operatives with a keen inducement to maintain strong efforts, as they stand to lose approximately four times as much as the productive operatives. By making the site works committee and bonus surveyors responsible for agreeing the actual names of men to be included in any particular group, they are kept informed of new operatives entering the site service teams.

In order to improve the general level of welfare in the building industry, instead of casual employment and incentive schemes, more permanent labour forces should be built up who can receive payments based on length of service bonuses, pensions, and profit sharing. These inducements would help to create contentment, staff loyalty, and encourage operatives to do their best, instead of tending to slacken off their efforts towards the end of a contract through fear of working themselves out of a job.

CONSTRUCTION PLANT ECONOMICS

The building industry's method of operation, with almost complete separation of the functions of project initiation, design and construction, and dependence for continuity of work on competitive tendering and the availability of short-term capital to finance long-term investment, influences the rate at which mechanisation of the industry can be economically justified. Contractors' investments in plant should yield a financial return that compares favourably with alternative investments; and involve considerations of capital costs, operational and maintenance costs, anticipated revenue from construction operations, investment grants, depreciation allowances, and corporation tax.

Profitable building with mechanical plant is based on economic financial investment, accurate forecasting of operating conditions, efficient programming and budget cost forecasting in relation to actual outputs and wear on machines under prevailing site conditions, maximum utilisation of a plant fleet operating on a variety of different types of contracts, and financial control of operations by trained staff to achieve lowest overall cost in the shortest time per unit of machine output.

Rapid construction with mechanised building is strongly responsive to the introduction of capital investments in plant. Increased revenue, which is influenced by speed of earnings, should be related to return on capital as well as market demands, and required profits established in relation to planned productions.

Plant investment

High interest rates and other restrictions on capital make the outright purchase of plant increasingly difficult. It is essential to tender and obtain work that will keep the majority of the plant fleet reasonably utilised, to investigate design modifications of new models that reduce operating and maintenance costs, and to service and maintain plant efficiency.

Investment grants and tax allowances mitigate income tax payable on plant investments, which need balancing in relation to the plant fleet as a whole, and the labour force employed.

Investment in extra plant planned to shorten a contract might achieve higher gross profits and additional contracts, but net profits may not be increased because of the need for increased investment and interest charges in relation to cash flow, and the tax element on increased profits.

Capital for investment in new plant should:

Not be in too small a ratio to fixed assets, and the range of required equipment available in the market; and should be provided on the basis of the balance of costs and income from current contracts, and finance obtainable in the cheapest market.

Profitability of investment is influenced by forecasting marginal effects of purchasing plant as against not so doing in order to estimate the yearly outflow of funds on purchases, and the inflow of additional income resulting from the investments.

Cash flows can adversely affect the benefits of sound investment due to under-certification of work completed each month; late payments of certificates; fluctuations in the use of plant; accidents; operational losses due to bad programming, ineffective supervision, down time, etc.

The amortisation of capital investments from income is achieved by depreciating plant purchases plus interest to determine annual depreciation costs, and adding the cumulative maintenance costs as a basis for budgeted internal hire rates charged to sites.

Plant depreciation

Plant depreciation represents the true spending of invested capital, and indicates the gradually decreasing value of a machine caused by: *deterioration* by wear, which takes place gradually and increases with age. Various grades of steel are used to increase the robustness of the wearing parts of machines, and increase the costs of different models: drop-forgings of high-tensile (hardened and tempered) steel for parts such as track shoes, rollers, excavator bucket teeth, etc.; case-hardening steels with a carbon content of 0·20 per cent for such parts as track bushings; and quench—annealed high manganese steel, primarily used in cast wear parts such as excavator buckets and excavator teeth, used where heavy impact stresses arise (e.g. excavating shattered rock).

Obsolescence (due to improved models becoming available any time before an original machine is worn out which can achieve the reduction of maintenance and operating costs).

Economic decline, which commences with deterioration, is quickened by obsolescence, and increases more rapidly with age.

Methods of depreciating plant investments depend on type of plant, as some machines have longer working lives than others due to their construction and work loads. Methods adopted should aim to increase depreciation values during a machine's earlier life when maintenance costs are comparatively low and larger profits can be earned, so the later economic decline will be aided by decreased depreciation values, and tend to even out overall economic decline.

The 'straight line' method of writing down plant is a purely linear function, and can prove misleading. For example:

	£
Cost of machine	10 000
Working life, five years	
Salvage value	750
	£10 000–£750

$$\therefore \text{ Depreciation value per year} = \frac{£10\,000 - £750}{5}$$

$$= £1,850$$

The method tends to undervalue capital investment costs and over value maintenance costs at the beginning of a machine's working life, e.g.: as in the example shown in Fig. 6.2.

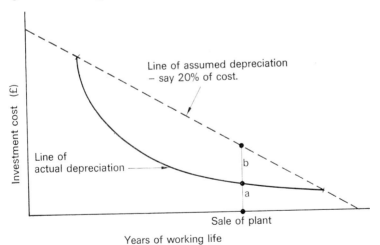

FIG. 6.2   Investment costs and value maintenance

a = actual residual value of machine after this period of working.

a + b = assumed value of machine by 'straight line' method.

If the machine were sold at that time, a loss would be incurred.

The reducing balance method of depreciation is recognised by H.M. Inspector of Taxes, and provides increased depreciation values and greater tax relief during the earlier life of a machine. For example:

Year	£ Per cent	Depreciation
1	$10\,000 \times 25$	2500
2	7500×25	1875
3	5265×25	1405
4	4220×25	1055
5	3165×25	790—balancing allowance

Economic life of plant

The period during which a machine can be operated at a profit is influenced by typical characteristics. For example, derrick cranes include a high proportion of their total costs in structural members and have a longer economic life than tractors, which have a high proportion of their costs in moving and wearing parts. Other influences include: amount of care and maintenance provided, site conditions, number of hours operated at maximum productivity, operator skill, and obsolescence (e.g. a mobile crane with a telescopic jib reduces the operating costs of cranes with strut jibs due to speed of erection, and elimination of rigging time).

The actual operating hours of a machine are based normally on the hours of work for operatives laid down in the Working Rule Agreement, less deductions for down time, adverse weather, meal breaks, etc., e.g.:

	Weeks	*Weeks*
Weeks in a year		52
Less		
Bank holidays	1	
Overhauls and repairs	2	
Transportation on and off site	2	
Idle time (e.g. wet periods meal breaks, etc.)	8	13
Total		39

On this basis yearly operating time averages about thirty-nine out of fifty-two weeks, normally about 1600 to 2000 hours for most types of plant. Static cranes which are subject to stoppages due to high wind velocities normally operate less hours, usually between 900 and 1000 hours a year. But all types of machines may be operated for longer hours when worked overtime at peak periods, or to make up delays to programmed work.

Most machines are unlikely to complete their revenue earning on only one major contract, or be operated for the whole of their potential life. Some organisations aim to maximise profits from investment grants and optimum disposal values by purchasing machines for intensive utilisation before major repairs are incurred. Other firms keep their plant fleets operating for as long as machines remain serviceable, and only purchase replacements when machines wear out, or additional plant is required for new contracts.

Both policies have certain disadvantages. When a machine is kept for only a short period, average depreciation costs are high due to frequent investments in new machines. When kept for a long time, average total operating costs over a prolonged working life tend to be high due to obsolescence and increased maintenance costs in later life; and salvage values (if any) will be low.

Plant replacement

Plant replacement is a matter of probability, and cannot be determined with scientific accuracy due to unknown site conditions and operator skills.

As average annual depreciation costs are more rapid during the early period of a machine's life, and average annual maintenance costs rise steadily with age, these total costs pass through a minimum beyond which it will be uneconomic to keep a machine, i.e.:

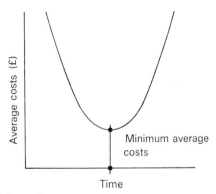

FIG. 6.3   Machine maintenance costs

The best time to dispose of a machine can be determined approximately from its cumulative costs of: depreciation, replacement—which involves both increased purchase price and decreased value of the pound—maintenance, down time.

When these costs begin to balance the amortisation of fixed and operating costs, it will be more economic usually to dispose of a machine rather than keep it, unless previously rendered completely obsolete by new models.

The following diagram indicates one method of determining when it may become economic to dispose of a machine:

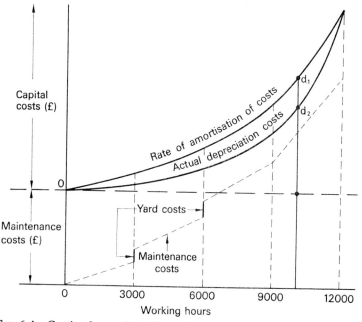

FIG. 6.4   Costing for machine disposal

When the curve to point d_1 is not so steep as that to d_2, it will be more economical to dispose of plant at d_2.

Plant provision

Plant provision may include: allocation to sites of machines available in the plant depot, or from other sites; hire from outside firms; hire purchase; additional outright purchase, or lease on a guaranteed 'buy back' agreement. This has the advantage of securing a defined fixed depreciation cost but the disadvantages of uncertain maintenance costs and restriction to one particular manufacturer.

Plant purchases in relation to the total plant fleet and overall economy may be influenced by the unexpected release of a machine from site, or a new contract which increases the need for a particular machine.

In general: firms with a substantial plant fleet own machines which are used most frequently, and hire plant at peak periods for special jobs of limited duration, or in periods of credit squeeze.

It will not be economical to operate a machine which is idle in the depot if it is not suited to the particular task to be undertaken, or hire a machine from outside sources at a lower rate than that for a suitable machine available in the yard.

When work in the future can be ascertained, investments in plant are more certain, but when future requirements are uncertain, or there is a period of 'credit squeeze', the tendency is to hire rather than purchase plant.

Plant budgets

A plant department should be able to obtain sufficient profits to hire out plant to sites at internal charges which enable site management also to make a profit. The department's financial performance can be controlled in relation to a yearly budget programmed to link a long-range plan with a strategic plan for current contracts, replace plant in accordance with optimum operating periods and re-sale values, and optimise plant utilisation within the firm's ability to obtain new contracts.

A new plant budget is prepared usually by the depot after consultation with management and the contracts department in relation to capital available, plant records based on an efficient costing system, current and anticipated contracts.

The total value of the budget should bear some relation to the total depreciation of the plant fleet throughout the year, increased costs of purchases, and the demand for various machines.

Plant purchases

Purchases to replace machines and meet contract requirements involve considerations of: type and amount of work to be undertaken, age and obsolescence of plant to be replaced, the need to match with existing plant, availability of suitable models, initial capital costs, interest and service charges, amount of initial investment grant and annual tax allowances available, records of hired plant to guide purchases, and advantages of productivity and decreased labour and maintenance costs of comparable machines in relation to anticipated working life and estimated profits. Machine modifications which reduce costs should also be taken into consideration, e.g.

tractors—tracks and rollers which are sealed against dust and dirt, do not require greasing, and provide a working life of about 5000 hours.

gear boxes—powered shift transmission which enables gear changes to be made while a machine is moving over rough ground.

braking systems—hydraulically controlled and immersed in oil can reduce operator fatigue and simplify operations. Some models are manufactured with disc brakes.

Before finally deciding on the purchase of a large and costly machine, a scheduled assessment should be made of its definite and possible future work (see Fig. 6.5).

Machine	Ref. No.	1968												1969	
		Jan	Feb	Mar	April	May	June	July	Aug	Sept	Oct	Nov	Dec	Jan	Feb
Static tower crane		◄— PARK ROAD —►									◄– – New Lane Tender – –►				
38 RB		◄— SMITH STREET —►				◄— NORTH AVENUE —►					◄– – Southgate Tender – ►				

FIG. 6.5   Plant assessment schedule

Hired plant

Some types of specialised plant can be hired more economically from outside sources (e.g. heavy rollers), other types cannot be hired easily, and may have to be bought, despite probable limited utilisation. Machines which normally have too infrequent applications for purchase, such as rubber-tyred mobile jib cranes, are usually hired for occasional lifts. Both the complete purchase or complete hire of all plant utilised would not be economical—there is an optimum balance needed to minimise costs and maximise production.

Decisions to hire plant for a particular contract are mainly influenced by: hire rate, transportation charges (which may be high for large machines, or include travelling time to site), period of contract and amount of work to be undertaken, facilities for maintenance and repairs, available storage space off-site when the plant is not in use.

The advantages of hiring plant include: use of up-to-date machines, wide choice of available plant, and the opportunity to test new equipment before deciding to buy. Adequate servicing of machines is only required intermittently, and there is reduced need for capital, work shop space, fitters, and trailers. Plant depreciation is paid for only whilst a machine is operating on site. The cost of hiring plant is a charge against revenue, and there may be advantages in not investing capital in machines which may be left idle due to unsuccessful tendering.

The main disadvantage of hiring plant is that no capital asset remains for disposal after considerable outlay.

Cost comparison of owned and hired plant

The hire rates of an outside firm are normally $33\frac{1}{3}$ per cent (and more) greater than the internal hire charges of a well-organised plant depot, as external hire rates include for heavy maintenance costs, transportation to sites, high depreciation costs due to the need for providing latest and most up-to-date machines, uncertainty of continuous hire, overheads, and profit.

The economic problems of the plant hire industry differ from those of the construction industry. A plant hire firm's decisions to purchase new plant depend on demand based on shortages likely to occur during the machine's economic life, and acceptability of a machine when disposed of in the secondhand market. The rate of return anticipated in current hire rates to provide satisfactory profits, the need to optimise salvage values, and the provision of a highly efficient maintenance service are all factors in such a firm's administration.

If the supply of any large machine exceeds demand for any length of time, financial losses will be incurred. Inadequate depreciation can result in salvaging plant at a loss. Over-cautious depreciation requires substantial profit on resale to avoid serious financial loss. The most advantageous method of depreciation for plant hire firms enables written down values to be just below real secondhand value at any time.

A method of comparing the economic advantages of buying or hiring a machine is based on the equation:

$$R_n = \frac{C + {}_1\Sigma^n R - D}{H}$$

where
R^n = estimated operating rate based over n years,
C = net capital cost,

$_1\Sigma^n R$ = sum of repair costs (excluding overheads, etc.) to year n,
D = disposal value,
H = total hours operated over n years.

For example:

	£
Net cost of machine	8250
Sum of repairs over five-year working life	1500
Disposal value	750
Estimated working life	5 years
Operating hours each year	1800

$$\text{Estimated operating rate} = \frac{£8250 + 1500 - 750}{1800 \times 5}$$
$$= £1 \cdot 25 \text{ per hour}$$

which provides a reasonable basis for comparison with quoted hire rates.

Plant costs

Total costs of owning and operating plant include:

fixed costs, which are incurred whether or not a machine is working, decrease as utilisation increases, and include: net capital cost after deduction of grants, tax allowances, any disposal value, interest charges, administration expenses, licences and insurances.

operating costs, which vary according to amount of utilisation as influenced by site conditions and operator skill, increase with increased utilisation, and comprise: fuel, oil, consumable stores, labour and supervision, transportation costs, erection and dismantling costs, and all other expenses of operating plant on site (e.g. mats for excavators in muddy ground, maintaining haul roads; tying back the mast of a static tower crane to the structure to gain increased working height).

Maintenance and repair costs, which increase with age, are strongly influenced by operator skill (e.g. wear on tyres and tracks), and include: costs of upkeep, spare parts, labour, consumable stores, down time, etc. Optimum standardisation of equipment reduces costs by minimising delays due to a spare part being unobtainable when required.

The true measure of plant performance is represented by *the unit cost of outputs per working hour*. This varies greatly according to ground strata, contours, site working conditions, programmed operations, operating techniques, maintenance requirements, and supervision.

Control of maintenance costs

Estimated maintenance costs for budget purposes are based on cost records of similar machines previously purchased. Actual costs vary considerably according to type of machine, servicing requirements, operating conditions, operator skill, and amount of care and protection provided on site.

A plant depot's cost system to control the upkeep of plant by inspections, overhauls and replacements, would include normally analysis sheets to establish budgeted internal hire rates, upkeep books for different types of plant to record each machine's phased budgeted costs and actual costs at 1000 hour intervals. These would be supplemented by plant cost charts, labour and materials record cards, stores requisitions, and summary sheets with details of maintenance costs, overheads, utilisation, and revenue—to provide management quickly with up-to-date information regarding the economic position of any machine.

The Plant Cost Chart (Fig. 6.6) indicates one method of comparing phased budgeted costs, and actual maintenance costs.

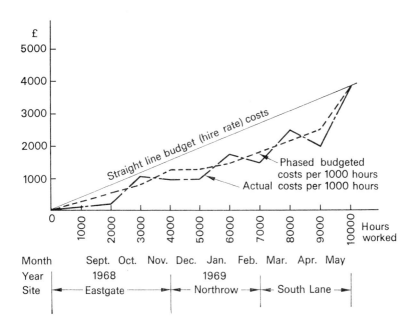

FIG. 6.6 Budgeted hire rate for tracked excavator

The back of the chart would record cost details of depot materials and labour, and site materials and labour.

Plant utilisation and productivity

Utilisation as a time-based function relates to the period a machine is on site divided by the total time it is actually operated, and requires maximising for economy. Two other factors are required to connect utilisation directly with productivity: the ratio of a machine's optimum potential output to actual output under site conditions, and the labour hour content of the operator and labour team. For example: A concrete mixer with potential outputs of 30 cu yd/day (23 m³/day) and actual outputs of 25 cu yd/day (18 m³/day) operating four out of eight hours a day for a 40-hour week, would have:

$$\text{Utilisation (in time)} = \frac{20}{40} \times 100 = 50 \text{ per cent}$$

$$\text{Productivity factor} = \frac{20}{40} \times \frac{25}{30} \times 100 = 25 \text{ per cent}$$

which would be influenced further by the number of men employed in the concreting gang.

Improved productivity under site conditions might be possible by using the mixer more constantly, decreasing machine cycle time, and reducing labour requirements.

The inadequate utilisation of plant can result in the non-recovery of fixed costs. Economic utilisation depends on minimising costs and maximising outputs by correct selection and matching of equipment, maximum utilisation of all machines operating on site, trained operators, sound operating techniques, effective supervision, efficient maintenance to obviate breakdowns, and optimum balancing of men, machines and time to fit in with the construction programme.

On large earth-moving contracts wasted seconds in five-minute operating cycles, and poorly maintained haul roads can incur substantial losses of revenue. For example, a fleet of scrapers push loaded for ten seconds longer than necessary can reduce outputs from twelve to ten cycles per hour resulting in a hidden loss of thousands of pounds a year.

All labourers and operators driving plant on sites need adequate instruction. Operators should be allowed extra time outside normal working hours for daily and weekly routine maintenance. On large contracts with many machines, routine jobs and servicing to avoid breakdowns are undertaken normally by servicing teams.

The highest costs of plant breakdowns relate to loss of production, standing labour, and disruption of the construction programme, which can prove extremely expensive. Actual outputs rarely match rated or calculated outputs on account of the difficulty of obtaining maximum efficiency on site due to downtime, idle time such as meal breaks, setting out work, refuelling, waiting on other plant, restrictions on manoeuvrability, etc., and adverse weather conditions.

Improved plant outputs depend on: method studies to determine the most economic sequence of operations within a representative cycle of work, using a specific type and number of machines; efficient programming to minimise idle time (e.g. lack of planned overhauls, badly routed haul roads); operator skill, effective operating techniques, efficient supervision, and satisfactory bonus targets. In general, utilisation and productivity factors are improved whenever a machine is worked for a substantially longer period beyond the estimated normal time upon which budgeted hourly costs were based, as the original purchase price is being recovered in a shorter period.

Machines used repeatedly, or for long spells on operations incurring heavier wear and tear (e.g. piling, grabbing, etc.) than more balanced work may also require adjustments of their budgeted hourly costs. These costs may either need decreasing or increasing according to the particular conditions involved.

Mechanised site operations are highly sensitive to any delays and interference with productivity. Speed of construction depends on the sequence, timing and most economic method of erection operations, and the comparative advantages of manpower or suitable mechanical plant and its positioning in order to achieve uninterrupted construction.

In order to ensure a smooth flow in the cycle of operations, site layouts should be planned to coordinate and control access, traffic routes, movement of materials, etc., site factory productions, and work areas in relation to the different phases of construction, and the time available to complete the contract.

According to the particular conditions of a site, operational efficiency may be increased by, for example: selecting a machine to fulfil a number of functions; utilising a range of machine sizes, or accepting a lower range of efficiency for separate operations by selecting a compromise size of machine to reduce plant costs by increasing utilisation; sloping fill, or bottom of basement excavations, to obtain good drainage at the end of a shift; and meeting peak load requirements in a different way, e.g. by using ready-mixed concrete deliveries.

In addition to sound plant provision, good management in all its aspects is essential for economic mechanised construction.

The effective use of mechanical plant and equipment on a recently built high-rise office building with low-rise podiums for shopping areas constructed on piled foundations and involving extensive demolitions in a crowded city area included the use of tower cranes, compressors, pile frames, concrete batching plant, and sliding shutters. By these means, savings of approximately 50 per cent in time and 20 per cent of total construction costs were achieved in comparison with traditional and less mechanised methods of construction utilising more site labour.

In general, the more working hours that can be obtained from a machine during each year of its life, the lower will be its operational costs. In the U.S.S.R. and most European countries with a controlled economy, longer working periods, and considerably less safety and welfare provisions for site operatives than required in Great Britain, plant is operated for a very much longer time each year over periods extending from eight to ten years, or until the machine is no longer serviceable.

Such increased use of plant does not achieve economy in total construction costs without efficient overall planning and site control, or result in increased human welfare and happiness.

SITE CONTROL

Economic system building necessitates 'flow-line' methods of production and erection to simplify site management and enable daily assembly operations to be controlled through a 'management by exception' technique. This consists of checking to ensure that each erection team is up to required strength, and fully equipped with materials and information to carry out its planned tasks for the day. Teams which are under strength in labour or ability can be especially dealt with, and the remaining teams left alone to carry out their planned tasks at definite speeds geared to factory production in order to ensure that the men will not run out of units to assemble.

The 'line-of-balance' technique developed by the National Building Agency for programming and controlling repetitive housing is based on the natural construction 'rhythm' of dwellings, and can provide a valuable technique for avoiding uneconomic design.

Efficient site organisation and control can reduce costs and ensure continuity of erection operations by eliminating unnecessary idle time.

Before a site can be controlled effectively, weather and ground conditions, sources of local labour and materials, positions of public utility services, the subsequent disposition of plant and activities, and the effects of any tying back to the structure of a static crane etc. must be thoroughly investigated; and the site layout planned to induce 'flow line' site production.

Site planning features mainly relate to the movement of men, materials and plant; locations of services, storage and administrative areas; disposition of work activity areas; access to and exit from the site, maintenance facilities, and control. The main problems involved relate to available time, type and layout of structures, completion requirements, and any shortages of labour or materials.

Materials handling requires planning and controlling to maintain continuous operation at optimum capacity, and all activities should be timed and planned to assist one another.

Vehicles for site transport need relating to power requirements, surface conditions of planned work areas; and the capacity, shape, size and weight of units.

Adequate safety precautions should be provided at floor edges wherever practicable by components designed as cladding units, or balustrades cast in with any balcony units.

When the design of a system does not include such units, falls are possible, and temporary guard rails must be provided with the first operations of the erection cycle. Holes in floors, and lift shafts should be protected with suitable covers, and rails positioned across lift door units. Immediately staircase units have been placed and provide working access, they should be fitted with temporary handrails.

Tower cranes are potentially the most dangerous machines used in building, and involve hazards relating to: the erection and dismantling of the crane where site contours are uneven, wind effects, access to driving positions and for maintenance, human failures under working conditions such as careless or incompetent driving, incorrect signalling or slinging, risk of overloading, and several different firms of subcontractors working together.

Passenger hoists around the structures of tall buildings can speed the time of men leaving and returning to their positions at meal breaks and the beginning and end of work periods.

Some systems suited to high-rise dwellings utilise a small mobile canteen which is hoisted by crane to each erection floor level, one man being detailed to fetch all meals required for the team. Larger labour forces which require increased canteen facilities may necessitate one canteen at ground level and a second canteen installed on the tenth floor level of structures over twenty storeys in height to minimise non-productive time.

Artificial lighting for outside work during months of winter darkness can reduce loss of time during shorter working weeks. The approximate costs of installing a temporary floodlighting system are about £100 per tower, plus 53p per 100 sq ft (9·29 m²) of site space illuminated. These costs can be reduced when some of the initial equipment is reused on other sites. The well planned use of flood lighting can guarantee a full working week plus overtime to a planned labour force, aid site security, and provide greater safety during hours of dusk during early morning and evening.

Tools and materials should be stock-piled and readily available for use as and where required. This requires careful control to avoid impeding access to working areas, and minimise double handling, which can be reduced by unloading deliveries as near as possible to required positions for erection.

Timber and similar materials should be protected from the weather, and fragile materials placed where least likely to be damaged. A stack of soft facing bricks placed on unsuitable ground can result in 25 per cent breakages caused by settlement after very heavy rain at weekends.

Aggregates should be stored where they can be fed by road transport, and placed adjoining batching plant without need of further handling. This prevents careless operatives allowing the materials to spread and become trampled into the ground during mixing operations. Wherever practicable, long bank runs to and from mixers should be avoided by the use of skips handled by cranes.

Steelwork should be stacked near erection areas and delivered to site in the correct order of units to suit erection requirements.

Components should be suitably grouped near cranes and hoists so that they may be handled and hoisted where required in one operation with a minimum change of the crane's position. The lengthy site storage of components increases risk of damage, and units should be erected as soon as possible after delivery to site.

Plant programming

The efficient utilisation of site mechanical plant and equipment increases production and labour outputs; and speeds erection operations at reduced overall construction costs by performing work that cannot be readily undertaken manually, eliminating heavy physical work, and maintaining production when labour is scarce. The type and extent of site mechanisation for a particular project will be influenced by the nature and amount of the work to be undertaken; contract time; site conditions and restrictions; the layout, type, size and heights of the buildings to be constructed; the sequence of erection operations as determined by structural design, techniques of construction; and number, size and weight of components to be handled; the technical skills required for operating the machines; the type of craftsmen and quality of unskilled labour available for site erection operations, and the capital costs or hire charges for the plant.

Efficient site mechanisation is achieved when all plant is being utilised in conditions which enable it to provide continuous optimum performance; the apportionment of operatives to plant ensures that both the machines and related teams of operatives are kept actively employed to maintain steady outputs, with a minimum of idle time; and the tasks of handling and fabricating components are separated so that teams undertaking a limited number of specialised repetitive tasks can work freely and continuously on site to rapidly assemble and erect standardised prefabricated components.

Manual labour can be employed on more isolated operations, but conditions may arise on site when it will become more economical to utilise machines in order to produce a superior result, or avoid expensive delays, even if the plant selected cannot be used to reduce costs.

The planned work load of any separate item of mechanical plant should be balanced and integrated with the working of all other plant on site in order to fit in with the overall construction programme, as the actual output of a machine does not solely depend upon its own potential, but also on the limitations which follow. For example, the effective output of a concrete mixer is limited by the rate at which the concrete can be poured and transported to placing points, and will be lower for placing in columns than in mass foundations.

Plant work loads can be planned by programming the outputs of each machine and related labour team to achieve maximum productivity under site conditions. It is essential to gauge the correct pace for each task, balance plant outputs in a sequence of operations, and match related plant and labour teams in a complete cycle of operations. These should be planned so that all machines arrive on site for continuous working at optimum capacity and go off site on completion of their tasks.

Programmed outputs should include realistic job efficiency factors related to site conditions which provide adequate flexibility to adapt the general rhythm of operations to suit changing circumstances, and avoid breaking up erection teams or employing extra men.

The work loads of tower cranes for maintaining fast erection floor cycles need systematic planning to meet daily changing requirements due to accidental happenings. Detailed operational work load schedules can be prepared from activity charts which show the estimated time of all operations and their sequences.

According to the particular conditions of a site, operational efficiency may be obtained by selecting a machine to fulfil a number of functions, meeting peak load requirements in a different way; utilising a range of machine sizes; or accepting a lower rate of efficiency for separate operations by selecting a compromise size of machine to reduce plant costs by raising the level of its use.

Plant utilisation records can aid site management to spot ineffective working without delays. Work study techniques can establish correct methods of matching and operating equipment at maximum efficiency. The accurate information obtained can be used for comparing alternative methods of construction, and forecasting work schedules to improve site organisation and avoid wasteful tasks.

Mechanical aids to labour

The development of profiles, jigs, hand-powered tools and mechanical aids to both skilled and unskilled labour can achieve considerable savings in time and costs. For example, compressor tools and hand-powered tools for cutting, drilling, sawing, hammering and plugging; cartridge operated fixing tools for plugging and rapidly fixing battens and steel sections to brickwork and concrete; spraying machines for painting, and pumping mortars and plasters; oxygen (thermic) lances for drilling concrete and rock. Bricklaying machines have been developed capable of laying 800 bricks per hour, which is equivalent to a brick-layer's output in one working day. One type of machine travels along a track of scaffold tubes to lay bricks at rates varying from ten to twenty per minute, the mortar for jointing being gravity fed from two hoppers in a continuous operation. Thus the machine requires an operator, and a skilled bricklayer for supervising and pointing the brickwork. The degree of plumb and evenness of the work depends upon accuracy in positioning and levelling the track; true economy is un-certain.

Completely automatic brick panel building machines can prefabricate brick panels 6 ft (1·83 m) or more wide and of storey heights for handling and transporting to site in steel jigs. The machine incorporates a pneumatic handler that picks up bricks direct from the production line, and transports them for loading into the machine's tray. Horizontal and vertical jointing of the panels is relatively simple, and avoids structural complications. Automatic machines are available for high speed application (150 ft (45·72 m) per minute) of industrialised joinery primers and undercoats to all types and shapes of straight timber with sections up to 12 in (304 mm) wide × 6 in (152 mm) high.

Earth moving plant and equipment

One of the main factors influencing excavation costs in the U.K. relates to the serious effects of soil and weather conditions on the outputs of mechanical and earth moving plant and equipment. The natural moisture contents of earth fill materials are relatively high usually, and rainfall and low evaporation during winter months normally limits large excavation works to periods from March to October, or less.

Economic earth moving by machines is affected by the composition and properties of the soil to be moved; the form and dimensions of the soil-cutting tool; the engine power of the machine related to its operating cycle and capacity; ground contours and surface conditions; and the weather.

The weight of materials to be excavated is affected by the moisture content of the soil in its natural state. This strongly influences the capacity of load and working performance of the excavation plant, as the heavier the material, the greater the motive power required to move it. Some materials can be bulldozed or loaded into a scraper in their natural state, other materials require loosening, or even blasting before removal, and their increase in volume for removal after excavation varies considerably.

In general, the soil-cutting tool of an excavator is acted on by the force of the resistance offered by the soil to the digging, and may be considered as the sum of the reactions exerted by the soil on the cutting tool, the magnitude and direction of which depend upon the type and design of the tool; the shape and size of the cross-section of soil excavated; and the kind and state of the soil.

In order to minimise the effects of wet weather, soil should be excavated from a vertical face and transported to the fill or disposal areas by plant whose operation is not critically affected by the wetting of the ground surface, and all filling should be placed in the thickest possible layers and compacted immediately.

The output of mechanical plant such as tractors, scrapers, bulldozers and shovels is particularly influenced by site conditions. These conditions also affect the internal site transportation of spoil, as lorries and dumpers tend to become bogged down on wet sites, and have to travel with reduced loads, but the outputs of heavy machines are not affected to the same extent.

Excavations should normally be carried out so that dig and disposal operations are maintained continuously with the minimum of waiting time and the most economical form of earth support or method of raking back earth sides, in relation to site conditions.

Choice of plant and equipment is influenced by loadability, weight, moisture content, swell, and degree of hardness of the materials to be moved; total quantities of earthworks; method of soil disposal; correct balance of the number and size of haulage units in relation to the number of excavators as required by the building programme; haulage distances to tips and spoil heaps; weather conditions; time available to undertake the work; the experience, skill, and bonus targets of operators; and efficient maintenance and repair facilities. These factors determine the average outputs and costs of plant per unit of time.

Earth moving machines may be classified according to purpose, nature of working operations, mounting, and type of control.

Types of plant available include earth moving machines that handle the soil as the machine moves forwards such as bulldozers; grading machines that shape excavations to required formations, such as powered scrapers; compacting equipment such as rollers, tampers, and vibrators; excavators that dig the soil and load it on to trucks or other transporting facilities for disposal to a place of deposit, such as crawler-mounted shovels, digger-loaders, draglines; and 'universal purpose' machines which cover a variety of digging and loading operations, and can also be used as cranes.

Bulldozers provide a great variety of uses such as stripping off turf or top soil, removing bushes or stumps of trees, spreading and levelling earth filling; pushing spoil from excavated areas to spoil heaps; back filling trenches and pits. They can also be used for auxiliary jobs such as clearing a path for scrapers and dumpers, or helping scrapers forward when their bowls are filled.

Scrapers are most usefully operated on moderately wet sandy soils and loams which fill the bucket to full capacity, but are not economical in use on loose sand, which does not adequately fill the bucket, soils containing large stones, very heavy soils which require ripping up before utilising a scraper, or moist clay or earth, which sticks to and clogs the walls of the bucket. They are the only type of equipment that can load, haul at high speed, and spread loads.

The low speed of crawler tractors limits the operating ranges of towed scrapers according to site conditions. Self-powered scrapers with a travelling speed two or three times higher than crawler vehicles are more efficient for longer distances. With good ground conditions, a rubber-tyred tractor scraper unit which requires push loading can move more excavated material at less cost that a track type unit, whereas a loaded scraper moving over a sandy surface requires a crawler tractor.

The earth-moving capacity of modern scrapers has increased to the extent that a fleet of three scrapers can provide a capcity of 1000 cu yd (764·5 m³) an hour over a 6000 ft (1828·80 m) haul. Dump trucks with diesel electric drives are manufactured in ranges up to 240 tons (243·85 tonnes) and scrapers with diesel engines producing a total of 1900 horse power in ranges up to 78 cu yd (59·64 m³) capacity for use on large development schemes.

Powered revolving excavators with intermittent operation and several different readily fitted working attachments are manufactured as 'universal' machines to provide a variety of digging and lifting operations. The main parts of the machine comprise:

(*a*) Front attachment, e.g. face shovel, back acter, dragline, grab bucket, trencher, crane mast. Dragline attachments are used for excavating deep cuts from spoil heaps or 'dumplings', and generally in conditions where a large outreach is required, as the boom of the dragline is twice and even more times longer than that of a digger-loader. Digger-loader attachments with a pivoted loader-beam and bucket are used for excavations below the level on which the machine stands. They can provide an increased reach over a normal bucket attachment, with a fast lift and dump which speeds the loading cycle. Detachable trenchers with buckets and pivoted loader-beam extension for hydraulic operation are capable of excavating trenches up to 3 ft (0·91 m) × 11 ft 6 in (3·50 m) deep, and grubbing up any tree roots encountered. The operating member in the form of a bucket, shovel, drag line etc. excavates the soil, carries it a short distance, and dumps it into a pile or on to transporting facilities, and returns the operating member back to the digging face to complete the machine's cycle of operations. Under average working conditions, a shovel type excavator will fill and empty its bucket about forty-four times an hour, and the back-acter about thirty times an hour, outputs varying according to the nature of materials to be excavated, and depth and type of dig.

(b) *A turntable* carries the power plant, engine, or winches, and operates at a faster speed when used with digging attachments than when operated as a crane. The machine is usually powered with either diesel engines, electric drive powered from an electricity supply, or diesel electric drive. Increases of engine speed and power of lifts can be obtained with hydraulic action, and operational control of a machine quickened with compressed air.

(c) *A tower frame*, takes the weight of the turntable mechanism and operating equipment; and

(d) *the running gear* comprises crawler mounting for operation on ordinary soils; widened caterpillar tracks for soft, very moist or boggy soils; or truck mounting with air-tyred wheels designed to carry the excavator on a normal or reinforced chassis.

When the machine is used as a crane, a hydraulically operated jib mast is fitted instead of the excavating arm, the positive movement of the hydraulic cylinders in both directions resolving the problem of jib hoisting with a suspended load. The jib is raised by the hydraulic ram used for raising the excavating arm, and provides the excavator with manoeuvrability and load lowering operations controlled by engine speed.

A multipurpose crawler mounted excavator with crane attachments, instead of two machines, can achieve economies on smaller sites after excavations have been completed provided that the crane capabilities of the excavator are adequate for the handling work to be done. Such a machine can be used for levelling out small slopes, and its hydraulically controlled movements make it possible to use the machine for stripping or finishing operations, which until quite recently had to be undertaken with a high input of manual labour.

In general, low capacity multipurpose machines are suited to small contracts, and high capacity single purpose equipment to large earth moving contracts.

When undertaking earth moving operations, an excavator generally works with a dumper truck or tipping lorry for the disposal of the spoil, so that the cycle times which the machines take to complete their operations must be related to layouts, contours, strata, and surface of the site.

The motive power of vehicles transporting spoil to places of fill or deposit is influenced by weight of load, ground resistance, the retarding force of gravity when pulling up hill, and the surface of the ground over which it travels. Where higher power is required over short hauls and ground conditions make scraper utilisation difficult, bulldozer equipment can be used economically up to approximately 100 lin yd (91·44 m) push. But for hauls up to a maximum of 450 lin yd (411·48 m), tractor-drawn scraper units are more economical.

Where the nature of the excavated materials or haulage distances preclude the use of scrapers, it is usually more economical to use wheeled transport. Dumpers are uneconomical on long hauls, and are not generally utilised at distances over half a mile from excavation to tip. However, it may be sometimes advantageous for a vehicle to travel a longer distance over the site following ground contours, rather than travel a shorter distance over rough ground.

The application of power to earth moving plant has been developed over the past decade to such an extent that, for example: walking draglines are manufactured for open cast mining that can dig and dump 3000 tons (3048 tonnes) of material in 35 minutes, lifting 100 tons (101·6 tonnes) at a time; multi-bucket trenchers are manufactured for quarrying chalk at cement works with potential outputs exceeding 1000 tons (1016 tonnes) an hour; hydraulic trenchers with a winch and clamshell attachment can excavate trenches up to 100 ft (30·48 m) deep; mobile 'chain trench diggers, for continuously excavating trenches up to 4 ft 6 in (1·37 m) deep can achieve outputs of 600 cu yd ($459m^3$) in sand; self-propelled mass excavators with direction and depth of cut controlled automatically by sensors tracing a single guide line that can excavate 2500 cu yd ($1911\ m^3$) per hour by cutting a trench 26 ft (7·92m) wide, and up to 5 ft (1·52 m) deep at speeds of 25 ft/min (7·62 m/min) according to depth of cut and soil.

A transverse conveyor with a series of high capacity belts monitored by electronic sensing devices removes the spoil from the machine's auger a distance of up to 150 ft (45·72 m) to either side of the machine for dumping.

When operated without the conveyor, the machine can dig 3500 cu yd ($2676\ m^3$) per hour.

The effect of this vastly increased power is to 'compress' time to such an extent that wasted seconds due to ineffective planning, supervision and control can result in very substantial financial losses.

Concreting plant and equipment

The selection of plant for site concreting operations presents problems of materials storage, quality control, speed of production, and handling and transportation of mixed concrete to placing points dependent upon the nature of the contract, site conditions, and the building programme.

All plant selected, and its related labour teams should ensure the continuous production of good quality concrete to specified mixes in relation to the inflow of material and subsequent movement of the mixed concrete to points of placing, and be capable of conveying and placing the mixed concrete in relation to the speed of production and locations required by site conditions.

Detailed planning to determine the capacity of site mixing plant and rates of concrete outputs and handling requirements throughout the concrete period, should be related to the total volume of concrete required, and fluctuations in demand during the construction period. These can be supported by deliveries of truck mixed concrete for occasional peak periods. The size of any one mixer should be related to the capacity of the plant needed for transporting and placing the mixed concrete so that the mixers can be discharged as quickly as possible. Placing times should be estimated first, then transportation times. Hourly outputs depend on type of concrete being placed (e.g. beams, slabs, walls), which affects speed of pouring; the volume of concrete that can be transported and placed within the hour; and the job efficiency factor—i.e.: the number of minutes actually worked per hour according to site, construction, and weather conditions. Calculated mixer outputs usually need increasing to cover break-downs and finishing operations quickly before winter darkness.

Automatic weighers, mechanical loading of mixers, and cement silos for large volume productions can increase outputs by 20 to 40 per cent, although they necessitate mechanical placings by conveyors to ensure continuity of outputs, and deliveries to required work points.

The mixing time of concrete varies according to type of mixer, but it is the number of revolutions of the machine (generally about twenty) that determines adequate mixing.

Batch mixers have an optimum cycle time of two and a half to three minutes based on the minimum time for loading the dry materials into the mixing drum, adding water, and properly discharging the drum, and on a method of handling concrete which enables the batch to be discharged at maximum speed as soon as properly mixed.

A wide range of powered dumpers, monorail transporters, feed hoppers, belt conveyors, and mechanically operated pumps are available for transporting concrete at high speed to positions of placing. Their selection depends upon the nature of the contract, volume of concrete to be transported, and its placing positions under site conditions. The final selection of concreting plant and equipment should be related to the handling of all other materials and components required by the overall construction programme. Thus maximum economy for a large volume of concrete productions might be obtained by using automatic weighers and a 14 cu ft (0·40 m³) capacity mixer with a related team of operatives composed of a driver and one labourer in order to minimise non-productive time when the demand for concrete became inter-mittent, but other site conditions could determine greater overall economy would be achieved by using a skip hoist and a smaller capacity mixer, because various components had to be handled by crane.

Where conditions permit, maximum economy and ease of supervision can be achieved by selecting one mixing plant strategically located to produce average concrete production requirements throughout the period of the contract, supplemented by deliveries of ready-mixed concrete to serve occasional peak periods of increased demand. But if the contract works are widely dispersed, greater economy might be obtained by setting up several smaller plants at strategic locations.

Truck mixers for supplying ready-mixed concrete can be used to speed productions when programmed so that each delivery truck can be discharged rapidly direct into position, normally in foundations, or at ground level. Where concrete is required to be placed beyond the limited reach of the delivery truck's discharge chute, a belt conveyor with chute attachment can be fitted to the truck-mixer in order to place concrete at a 25 ft (7·62 m) radius from the truck, or at heights of approxi-mately 10 ft (3·05 m) without the chute.

Ready-mixed concrete requires specifying in relation to workability, type of cement, cement content, quality and maximum size of aggregates, and any admixtures.

A high discharge rate of truck-mixed concrete can be achieved for large volume productions in foundations over short construction periods by setting up concrete pumps and several chains of belt conveyors to achieve high outputs for daily placing. But it is uneconomical for deliveries to be taken at a higher rate than they can be placed. Methods adopted for reducing the site operating time of the trucks include decanting loads into a wet hopper so that the concrete can be drawn at rates suited to site handling equipment, providing sufficient skips for handling by crane, or detachable type bodies for handling by dumpers, and providing trailer skips for transporting complete truck loads by monorail.

When concrete deliveries can be off-loaded direct into chutes for placing in mass concrete foundations, 6 cu yd (4·59 m³) trucks at eight minute intervals can achieve the placing of 450 cu yd (344·05 m³) of concrete per day. By increasing deliveries to 4-minute intervals, outputs can be doubled to 900 cu yd (688·10 m³) per day.

In freezing weather, the concrete can be delivered at (10°C) (50°F).

The siting of mixing plant in relation to the layout of multistorey buildings determines the erection tower crane's times of slewing, trolleying, and hoisting. It is essential to match skip capacity to the mixer and crane, because when working at high speeds the rate of hoisting becomes a critical factor in the concreting cycle. In some circumstances, time may be saved by hoisting two mixes in one skip, rather than in two skips. The most economical type of skip should be easy to control manually whilst discharging its contents—with side discharge for vertical members and bottom discharge for horizontal slabs—easy to clean, and of strong construction.

The speed of erection for a composite concrete system based on precast concrete structural vertical elements and poured in-situ concrete floor and roof slabs needs careful adjusting to the rate of concrete productions. Where structural requirements demand a high continuous output of concrete over long periods and site conditions permit, economic production can be achieved by the use of a large central mixing plant located in the most suitable position for minimising deliveries to pouring points.

The hoisting and use of shuttering for the in-situ concrete are key operations. The optimum number of shuttering units which are used in regular rotation provide a definite and readily controllable operational floor. During bad weather, electricity heated panels fixed to the shuttering can keep the supported concrete at regulated temperatures to eliminate delays in curing.

Handling plant and equipment

The economic handling and complete movement cycle of materials and components on site requires the cooperation of manufacturers with the contractor to achieve an economic system of delivery so that units can be delivered prepackaged or prepalleted for quick unloading, or delivered on vehicle platforms left on site for collection after the units have been hoisted to their required positions. The use of selected mechanical aids and equipment to off-load lorries can reduce labour required for unloading. Efficiently planned operations of integrated and well maintained handling plant and equipment, dependent upon the optimum use of their limited capacities, is essential for economic construction.

Hoisting problems are complicated by wide variations in the nature, shape, size and weight of materials and components incorporated into a system. These may include steel bar reinforcement, heavy concrete panels, prefabricated shutters, sheet metal trunking of all shapes and sizes, sanitary fittings, bricks, heavy plant, and machinery

The off-loading of lorries can be speeded by the delivery to site of manufactured units packaged, crated or strapped together in standard-ised weights and sizes in non-returnable packings, such as palletised bricks; packaged concrete blocks; packaged flooring in 'house sets' containing the exact square feet of flooring per dwelling, and ready to lay without further covering. Each set of flooring can be packaged in heavy duty polythene, and fastened with tough nylon bands, with the edge of the pack protected by wooden slats so that the boards can be unloaded by crane and handled direct to required positions. Portable elevating belt conveyors can be useful for handling bricks, tiles and similar materials to higher scaffold levels. High lift fork trucks that can travel over rough ground and have a lifting capacity of 35 cwt (1·78 tonnes) to heights of 30 ft (9·14 m) can provide economies on low-rise contracts. Machines such as 'humpers' can be used to off-load packaged and palletised materials and distribute them speedily over the site. Steel 'stillages' and racks designed to take large built-up components such as cladding units delivered in three-storey heights can be con-veniently located for off-loading and handling direct to position by crane. A number of tower crane attachments have been developed to meet special handling requirements. These include hoppers for bulk materials such as aggregates so that a crane can unload a full 5- to 8-ton (5·08 to 8·13 tonnes) load in a few lifts and transport the loaded hoppers to required positions with comparative ease. Patent devices such as 'porta-forms' facilitate handling table forms to position. Lifting cages can be used to handle packaged precast concrete blocks and bricks; multitine crane forks which can enter the cavities of 12 in × 12 in (305 mm × 305 mm) hollow flooring blocks enable a stack weighing 1 ton (1·02 tonne) to be off-loaded direct from lorries delivering to site. Mechanical aids are available which enable precast concrete units to be lowered slowly and gently into their final positions with accurate positioning and alignment.

Where two tower cranes are used for erection operations the arcs of their jibs must intercept in order to obtain complete coverage of the

13

building and stacking areas for materials handling. Adequate precautions must also be taken to avoid their jibs and hoist ropes colliding as the cranes slew round by the horizontal booms of any tower cranes set at different levels.

The critical point in movement handling occurs when the direction changes from horizontal to vertical, and vice-versa. Materials for the substructure and ground floor of a building require horizontal rather than vertical handling, and where practicable should be performed by lorries delivering loads to the site for placing in the final positions direct from the vehicles, and with versatile machines such as 'humpers'.

Vertical handling is of greater importance with tall buildings, where units should be stacked fairly close to the base of the buildings in order to reduce distances of horizontal handling

In general, it is essential to distribute units to localised stockpiles in order to maintain continuous erection operations. Larger units can be off-loaded from trailers and handled direct to position, or else remain in a storage area until required for erection.

All unnecessary movements of materials and components should be eliminated, so that loads are moved to positions by the most direct practical routes by suitable handling equipment with as high speed as possible in relation to capital cost and operating efficiency.

Plant for horizontal handling includes motorised barrows, mobile cranes, dumpers, trucks, railed transporters, conveyor belts, ready-mixed concrete trucks, and pumps for moving large quantities of concrete.

The horizontal handling and movement of materials and operatives on site is strongly influenced by the provision of adequate and well routed temporary roads, the layout of buildings, and any site restrictions. Wet sites necessitate tracked machines. Sloping sites may obviate the use of rail-mounted cranes. Confined sites may not provide sufficient space for mixing or transporting plant, and necessitate the use of truck-mixed concrete and small line mobile pumps. Limitations of access may reduce the size of plant that could have been used economically for large volume productions of concrete, or for site factories.

Outputs of handling plant are determined by type of construction works, rate at which units can be moved, speed of operation to which the plant contributes, locations of pick-up and delivery points, and type and weight of load to be handled. In general, the ratio of weight of equipment to load carried should be the minimum for maximum economy.

Where ground conditions are bad, or access to work positions limited, horizontal handling can be speeded by monorail transporters with power-driven vehicles, which can tow wagons of $\frac{1}{2}$ cu yd (0·38 m³) capacity filled with concrete at speeds of 100 lin yd (91·44 m) per minute on a single rail supported by adjustable stands. The machine does not require a driver, and can be started by the mixer driver and stopped automatically. Where there is a regular and continuous flow of materials between fixed points, a simple type of wire rope for conveying palletised bricks off-loaded from fork-lift trucks can be used for their direct transportation to required work points. A type of electrically operated fully con-veyorised plant with outputs of over 80 cu yd (61·16 m³) per day can be used for precasting various types of prefinished concrete units. The machine requires only two men to operate the batching and conveying plant from two main points, and can be laid out with parallel steel joists between which the moulds are cramped. Concrete is fed from the batching plant into a 120 ft (36·58 m) long mechanised conveyor system.

Types of narrow-belt conveyors run at a fast speed have a high output in relation to their weight, and can be joined together in series to carry concrete to placing points. A train can be readily set up and dismantled when each length of conveyor is articulated, and on wheels. To ensure concrete being fed from the mixer at a steady rate, a short length of conveyor with a wide belt running at low speed, and a large receiving hopper can be used. These enable a complete batch of concrete to be discharged from the mixer and feed a series of narrow-belt conveyors at a required and steady rate.

Mechanically operated static pumps can be used for conveying large quantities of concrete. Piston-type pumps can deliver a steady flow of concrete through a pipeline which remains full when the pump is stopped by insertion of a stopper in the end of the pipe. Compressed air from a container can be used to push the stopper and concrete out of the pipe line. Pneumatically-operated type pumps can blow a batch of concrete from a vessel at high velocity down a pipe to a baffle which reduces the velocity at placing points. The pipes should be cleaned out after each batch has been shot. Both types of pumps can deliver concrete a distance of several hundred feet horizontally and about 100 ft (30·48 m) vertically. Overhead runways can be used economically for paint spraying or pointing façades when no fixed scaffolding has been erected to elevations, or where the frequency of materials flow does not necessitate a con-veyor.

Plant required for lifting and hoisting materials and components includes small mobile platforms, barrow hoists, platform hoists, elevators, and cranes.

A variety of platform hoists with speeds ranging from 175 ft (53·34 m) per min to 250 ft (76·20 m) per min, according to height of building, have been developed for carrying goods only; goods and/or passengers; and concrete in self-tipping skips for continuous pouring operations.

Self-contained hoist assemblies are manufactured to accommodate electrical floor limit switches, and gates with self-supporting prefabricated tubular towers carrying a centre-slung type combined platform and automatic concrete elevating plant, or a passenger hoist, with complete interchangeability of respective hoists within one basic tower.

Twin hoists operate on a counterweight principle, with geared electric winches up to 5 ton (5·08 tonne) capacity, and controlled speeds of ascent and descent arranged for remote control. They are particularly suited to handle precast concrete units and façade panels with precision and accuracy of landing.

Passenger hoists can travel vertically almost as rapidly as tower cranes, and have the advantage of not being held up by the high winds which prevent cranes working. Operatives can normally reach their work positions in a multirise building up to approximately ten storeys in height by means of the staircases as constructed. Structures above that height normally require hoists for operatives and cranes for hoisting components, irrespective of structural type.

The comparative advantages and disadvantages of selecting tower cranes or hoists with similar economic range for handling materials and components on medium-rise structures relate to: the comparative costs of hiring or purchasing each type of plant, providing skilled drivers, power, hauling the equipment to site, and erecting and dismantling it; possible effects on techniques of construction such as simplification of shutter design, possibility of more economic assembly of steel reinforcement on ground and rapid hoisting to positions; comparative savings in labour. For example: versatility of crane to hoist shutters, fabric reinforcement, steel bars, and feed bricklayers: the increased labour productivity per floor constructed that can be achieved by efficient cranage to eliminate manhandling materials and components from the top of the hoist to fixing positions.

Other relevant factors include programming labour requirements to compare the number of men required to carry out operations without idle time utilising hoists or cranes. The comparative efficiency of each operation is determined according to which type of plant entails the simplest method of carrying out the works. For example, whether two hoists instead of one crane necessitate more supervision for the efficient distribution of materials and components; or the comparative costs of temporary works such as scaffolding in relation to each type of plant.

In general, platform hoists with lifting speeds up to 300 ft (91·44 m) per min. are suited to placing materials within the shell of a structure when required in positions out of reach of the erection crane. Some systems based on in-situ concrete construction with simple prefabricated standardised shutters for structures up to ten storeys in height can be economically constructed by using hoists without a tower crane.

Cranes

The main problems of cranage relate to base stability, tendency to tip over, decrease of lifting capacity with working radius, and continuity of utilisation. The economic handling of materials and components by cranes is based on minimising crane movements in both horizontal and vertical planes, and relating work loads to the crane's lifting capacity in order to minimise the number of lifts, and speed erection. Efficient crane utilisation depends on the correct selection of cranes for each particular programmed work load by planning to maximise load/working radius covering the optimum area of construction, unloading and stacking areas; continuously maintained crane working at each particular assembly operation; the provision of effective safety devices; regular and efficient maintenance; the correct matching of the erection teams and other related mechanical plant with the crane's operations; and the skill of drivers and banksmen.

Tower cranes

A tower crane has a truly vertical mast and is capable of withstanding wind loads of 5 lb per sq ft plus twice the safe working load. Cranes that do not fully meet these requirements involve heavier insurance only obtainable for limited periods.

Electrically operated tower cranes are required for the erection of tall structures. They are usually of telescopic pattern constructed with a support in the form of a tapered gantry of flat frame which carries the travelling mechanism; a mast of either lattice steel framework or large diameter steel tubes, fabricated in several sections to facilitate erection and dismantling; a revolving structure and boom with travelling trolley; a counterweight, which compensates for the weight of the boom and part of the load weight being lifted; and controls.

The operating members of the crane comprise the boom, hoisting pulley and load handling attachment, with hoisting, slewing, travelling, luffing and jib mechanisms. The crane can lift upwards to required heights before reaching out to distribute loads over the whole plan area of a tall building, thus eliminating horizontal handling at ground and floor levels above.

There are four basic types:

1.   *Telescopic static cranes* with built-in drive, remote control, climbing gear, and provision for adding sections to the mast. The crane is positioned outside the structure, and is suited to point blocks and buildings that can be covered by the jib, supplemented by platform hoists for subcontractor's materials. Erection and dismantling costs are high, and extra expense is incurred for foundations and tying back the mast to the structure in order to obtain increased heights above the crane's free-standing height.

2.   *Mobile cranes on rail tracks* able to travel with full rated loads. This type is suited to long, narrow, tall buildings, or a series of buildings on level sites where the length and preparation of the track is economical.

3.   *Short masted climbing cranes* which use the building structure as a foundation. They are suited to extremely high blocks on restricted sites. The base of the crane and its load are usually spread over three floors. The crane can cover the building with a comparatively short jib and few mast extensions, but has the disadvantage of lack of coverage over ground storage areas.

4.   *Small mobile tower cranes* which can provide greater economy than mobile jib cranes on medium-rise developments over four storeys high when a jib crane cannot cover the far side of a structure without moving to alternate sides for erection of upper floors, or where two cranes would otherwise be necessary.

The main factors that influence the versatility, selection and costs of tower cranes relate to type of crane, length of boom, height of free-standing mast, lifting capacity in relation to working radius, speed of lift, type of control (remote or cabin), type of chassis, power and safety requirements, building layouts, type and height of structure to be built, site restrictions, and the building programme.

Tower cranes must be designed to obviate the risk of being tipped over by an excessive load or load moment in accordance with the requirements of B.S.S. 2573 and 2799. Operations should cease when wind velocities exceed 38 m.p.h., or 5 lb per sq in (0·07 kgf/cm^2) according to load.

One type of safety device utilised automatically changes the safe load lifting capacity of the crane while keeping the load moment constant. This makes it possible to increase the weight of the load at shorter jib lengths. Other types of weigh load indicators show the load weight on the hook and maximum permissible load at any radius by black and red pointers on a dial; when the two pointers coincide, danger point has been reached and the alarm is given.

Statutory safety requirements include the testing of crane slings and lifting gear by the manufacturer before use, and by the user every subsequent six months.

One of the most critical factors of effective crane safety and maintenance relates to regular lubrication of the crane's wire ropes throughout their working life. It is essential to ensure that the size of the wire ropes is exactly suited to the dimensions of the pulleys and rope grooves in the sheaves of the drum, as the rope will become trapped and damaged if there is not a fit; and that an efficient banksman with good communication with a well trained operator are employed.

On sites where the Area Electricity Board may be unable to provide sufficient power for site requirements (which can exceed 300 K.W.A. for a single factory), one or more temporary transformer stations may have to be provided on site, with cable ducts carefully located to minimise abortive runs.

The required motive power for electrically driven tower cranes varies:

Tower crane plant	Horse power range
Hoist motor	3·0 to 80
Slew motor	1·5 to 15
Travel motor	1·0 to 10
Grab or derricking motor	1·0 to 10

In order to select the correctly sized tower crane required for handling large heavy units to any great height, it is essential to establish the maximum load to be lifted to its maximum height; the maximum free-standing height of the static mast under the lifting hook, both when in operation and not working; and the safe lifting capacity of the crane in relation to its working radius.

The smaller the tower crane, the lower the free-standing height of its mast. Beyond this critical point, special steel tie-off frames must be fitted to connect the tower mast of a static crane to the structure for greater stability, and increase the effective height of the crane around a fixed point.

The lifting capacity of the crane is greatly reduced when it trolleys beyond the stay bars or ropes, due to the bending moment induced on its jib.

Types of tower cranes at present manufactured are designed to accommodate the varying requirements of approximately 150 different systems, with maximum unit loads varying from 5 cwt to 13 tons (0·25 to 13·21 tonnes), and available ranges varyng from cranes that can lift a few cwt at 30 ft (9·14 m) radius to those capable of lifting several tons at 100 ft (30·48) radius or more.

The following examples indicate the range of variation in lifting capacity of a static type tower crane with a maximum free-standing height of 174 ft (53·03 m) under the hook:

Radius in ft at centre line of mast		Lifting capacity of crane	
(ft)	(m)	(cwt)	(tonne)
45	13·72	200	10·16
59	17·96	144	7·31
80	24·38	101	5·13
99	30·17	76	3·85
118	35·97	60	3·05

At heights above 174 ft (53·04 m) the crane would have to be tied back to the structure for support, and above 300 ft (91·44), the crane's capacity would have to be slightly derated to the weight of the rope on the hoist drum.

Required speeds of lifting are influenced by the total tonnage to be hoisted, the nature of the site, the height of the structure to be erected, and the building programme. This determines the size and number of cranes needed to maintain the speed of the planned erection cycle. Work loads should be accurately calculated, not based on average lifts and average theoretical time cycles, because in practice delays inevitably occur in lifting and placing loads, and a load of insignificant weight may have to be lifted to maintain continuity of the erection cycle.

The rig of the block system determines the crane's hoisting capacity and speed of lifting. Greater capacity within a crane's specification can be obtained by changing the rig from twofold to fourfold, an operation which only takes a few minutes. A twofold rig can achieve a faster speed, but with only 50 per cent of the maximum load taken by a fourfold rig at reduced speeds.

Lifting speeds with a twofold system involve a winch with two 40 h.p. motors to obtain lifts in high gear up to 30 cwt (1·52 tonnes) at 328 ft

(99·97 m) per min, and lifts in low gear up to 100 cwt (5·08 tonnes) at 132 ft (40·23 m) per min. Beyond these capacities, the requirements of B.S. 2799:1956 provide for a safety factor of 6:1 on the hoist rope's breaking strength, which necessitates a fourfold system to obtain lifts up to 60 cwt (3·04 tonnes) at 132 ft (40·23 m) per min, and up to 200 cwt (10·16 tonnes) at 66 ft (20·12 m) per min.

Lowering speeds are influenced by the type of gear box incorporated. Fast lowering of the hook at 400 to 500 ft (121·92 to 152·4 m) per min in order to maintain fast erection cycles incurs extra costs up to about £1500. Creep speeds are required for commencing a lift, and for lowering a load into position.

The weight, shape and position of a unit affect the time of crane working. Precast concrete wall units have to be propped, floor units positioned and levelled, and staircase units similarly but more delicately handled.

Simple erection devices to plumb, line and level precast concrete units are essential for economy. The final lowering of a unit into its position is a critical point. It must be dropped without further movement other than propping in order to avoid too many lateral movements of the crane, which has to hold and steady the unit, as well as handle it into position.

The difference in crane time hoisting units above tenth floor and up to twentieth floor levels does not vary by more than approximately 10 to 15 per cent increase of the time required for hoisting to lower levels, because the speed of the crane's lift can be quickened by changing to a faster gear. However, wind velocities are greater at high levels, and can hold up the crane's operations to delay the erection cycle.

Mobile jib cranes

A mobile jib crane is defined as 'a crane capable of travelling under its own power other than a crane that travels on a line of rails'. They are particularly suited to low-rise developments and can provide versatility of operation by fitting requisite attachments for excavations, convenient self-erection, and a realistic load/radius with a comparatively small base machine, without wasting working area. The number of changes in a crane's position depends on the sequence of construction operations. When programmed so that one block is to be completed before moving on to the next block, less movement is needed than when programmed for floor by floor erection cycles of adjoining blocks.

The working load and radius of these cranes are governed by the gradient on which the crane stands and the proportion of base machine stability (crawler size and counter weight) to mast height/fly jib length.

The use of high tensile steel for the masts can double normal lifting capacity.

Rubber-tyred and truck-mounted jib cranes are provided with outriggers which increase the bearing surface of the crane, completely relieve the springs and wheels of the load, and increase the load-handling capacity of the crane. Crawler and rubber-tyred mast cranes are driven by an engine mounted on the turntable. Truck-mounted cranes are similarly powered but with a separate motor for driving the running gear. When travelling, the crane is operated from the driver's cab, and for load handling by the motor mounted on the turntable.

An economical machine on low-rise developments would normally be crawler mounted, able to handle 5 to 6 tons (5·08 to 6·10 tonnes) at 80 to 90 ft (24·38 to 27·43 m) radius, and up to 8 tons (8·13 tonnes) at reduced radius, with ability to self-level and minimise the need for preparing working platforms on sites sloping at 1 :10.

Slinging

It is essential for both safety and economy that the correct type and method of slinging is used for all loads.

Slinging should be undertaken so that wherever possible equal tension is maintained in each sling leg during handling and lifting operations, pick-up points are equidistant from the load's centre of gravity, and the crane hook is positioned vertically over the centre of gravity when beginning and during lifting operations.

Unbalanced loads when essential can be lifted horizontally by using sling legs of equal length, with the attachment points equidistant from the centre of gravity, and a rigging screw incorporated in the sling legs for fine adjustment.

Lifts of heavy precast panels may require special lifting tackle such as adjustable lifting beams with a variety of centres for lifting points for wall and cladding units, or 'scissor' beams with floor lifting points for floor slabs.

Problems of tandem lifts with two cranes require careful planning, and involve a competent supervisor, balancing of loads, and communication between drivers by radio or a central banksman in order to coordinate operations.

Portal cranes

Designed on the principle of a beam supported by two columns, electrically operated portal cranes can travel at creep speed on two widely spaced rails with a fixed span and height. They have the advantages of constant load/reach characteristics and operation unaffected by high winds. No counter balance is employed, and as the load is spread over four points, maximum wheel loading is lower than with other forms of lifting equipment. The crane can be adjusted to variable spans and heights before erection through standardisation of the legs and beam. On sloping sites the crane's tracks should run parallel to the line of contours with its legs extended on the downhill side.

Portal cranes compare favourably in cost with tower cranes when used for work involving similar lifting capacities up to about 20 tons (20·32 tonnes), and are particularly suited to long buildings of precast concrete construction up to about twelve storeys in height.

Attempts to obtain both the full use of a standard tower crane and the performance features of a heavier type of overhead crane at an economic cost have resulted in the manufacture of a tower/gantry crane which consists of a standard 15 ton (15·24 tonne) tower crane model converted into gantry operation by introducing an auxiliary mast. The boom of the basic crane is slewed and positioned on top of the auxiliary mast to form a portal crane with a capacity of 15 tons (15·24 tonnes) throughout an effective straddle span of 125 ft (38·10 m), with lifting heights up to 195 ft (59·44 m). The auxiliary tower can be removed in order to free the machine for normal tower duties.

Derrick cranes

The capital cost of derrick cranes are comparatively low compared with other types of cranes for heavy lifts, but versatility of operation is more limited. Their main advantage consists of the ability to maintain heavy lifting capacity at greater radius than possible with tower or mobile jib cranes.

A guy derrick, which has a vertical king post larger than the jib, can be economical for erecting steel framed structures where site restrictions necessitate erection within the building.

A scotch derrick with long jib and short vertical centre post is more suitable when the crane can be sited outside the structure.

Crane utilisation in relation to building layouts and site restrictions

Cranes should be sited on a work load and movement basis to cover as much of the construction area as possible. Their positions are influenced by the accessibility of loading and unloading points, and the effective radius at which the loads can be safely lifted.

The arrangement of an unloading area within the crane's working radius should be determined to minimise double handling, and enable the crane to unload and hoist programmed deliveries of maximum weight as planned with suppliers. Materials and components should be hoisted into position, and not placed within the minimum radius of the crane's hoisting capacity.

On sites with limited storage space for stacking materials and components, economy can be achieved by feeding the main erection tower crane for the structure with a small mobile crane which ferries components from a main stacking area located elsewhere, the crane area being restricted to stacking for daily lifts.

To achieve optimum economy, all cranes should be sited to achieve optimum coverage from access roads and materials stacks to placing positions in the building, and permit vehicles to be unloaded on or adjacent to roads, instead of entering a site and becoming bogged down in wet weather.

The road access to low-rise developments influences the selection of the type of crane to be used economically. Where the buildings are sited close to a road so that a crane can function from it, rubber-tyred mobile mast cranes may be suitable. But if a crawler-mounted mast crane is selected, the distance of the buildings from roads is not of such importance. This type of crane normally operates on firm level ground; slight deviations may tend to make the machine unstable, but do not radically affect its boom stresses. These conditions have the reverse effect on mobile tower cranes, as off-level working is more critical.

The following examples indicate how economies in time and manpower can be achieved by the use of strategically positioned cranes for unloading and handling materials to required locations in a building:

(a) Palletised bricks in packs of 400 can be off-loaded from delivery lorries and handled to position in approximately fifty minutes with one crane and two slingers, a total of two and a half man-hours. If the bricks were to be unloaded manually by a team of labourers, stacked on the ground, loaded on to pallets from the stacks, and hoisted to position in a cage lifter, the total time required would amount to approximately ten hours.

(b) a small mobile crane with an internal hire charge of approximately 88p per hour can lift a half-ton load to a height of 50 ft (15·24 m) at a working radius of 50 ft (15·24 m) every three and a half to five minutes. This provides a hoisting capacity of approximately 7 tons (7·11 tonnes) per hour at a cost of 88p hour. The same work undertaken by a team of labourers would cost approximately £3 to £4 per hour.

Crane utilisation in relation to type and height of structure

Cranes for system building can be divided into those suited to high-rise or low-rise structures, and their operational analysis determined by maximum weight to be lifted, maximum height of lift in relation to working radius, whether or not the crane should move under load, how long it will be situated in one place, and the type of ground to be traversed by the crane in order to proceed to its next work position.

Telescopic tower cranes are suited to coordinate handling around tall structures. Floor to floor erection cycles need careful programming to provide for the delays incurred in tying back the mast to the structure at increased heights.

Short masted climbing tower cranes cost less than static tower cranes, can climb to any height subject to the length of rope that can be accommodated on the hoist drum, and are particularly suited to tall structures on sites where movement of mechanical plant is restricted. Disadvantages include incurring additional costs every time the crane is raised, and impeding the erection cycle due to the necessity for filling in openings left for their climb when installed inside a structure.

Some rail-mounted mobile tower cranes are manufactured to travel with a load under hook at a height of 268 ft (81·69 m) and lifting capacity of 4 tons (4·06 tonne) at 135 ft (41·15 m) working radius increasing to 15 tons (15·24 tonne) at 47 ft (14·33 m) radius. Such cranes have the advantage of achieving the optimum use of their hoisting capacity when travelling on straight or curved tracks. They are useful for structures up to thirty storeys high where the finished height of the building does not exceed the free-standing height of the crane. It is essential to ensure that the crane's tracks are firm and level, with adequate foundations, and that the correct weight of ballast is used.

Tower cranes of medium capacity are suited to point block multi-rise buildings up to fifteen storeys in height. Taller buildings with larger and wider plan shapes require heavier cranes capable of covering 100 ft × 60 ft (30·48 m × 18·29 m) working areas with a $4\frac{1}{2}$ ton (4·57 tonne) lift, which cost more than double.

Crawler or truck mounted mobile jib cranes are not suited for work on tall structures because their working radius is limited as building height increases, and site restrictions limit access around the structure. There are certain exceptional conditions when this type of mobile crane with a very long jib might be suitably applied, but in general, it is more suited to low-rise developments.

Portal cranes are not suited to buildings which are short in length, under three storeys or over ten to twelve storeys in height. They are economically suited to long buildings within these height limitations, and for use with extendable main beam and overhang as 'a complementary machine to tower cranes used for systems based on the site manufacture of precast concrete panel units for long medium-rise buildings.

Static and climbing telescopic tower cranes can provide a variety of uses for structures based on poured in-situ concrete construction. They can switch continuously from materials and component handling to hoisting prefabricated sections of shuttering as necessitated by the erection cycle.

A system based on the site manufacture of precast concrete panel units requires cranes capable of lifting panels into position from trailers or stacking yards and holding the units steady whilst being levelled and lined. Cranes selected must be able to erect the units furthest away from the crane on the topmost storey, and lower units gently and slowly for the last few feet unto their final positions in order to facilitate easy handling, and accurate positioning and aligning.

The height and width of a precast concrete structure, and the size, weight and number of its structural elements influence the type, size and number of cranes required on site, the size and composition of the related erection teams, and the time required to erect a given number of components each day. The free-standing height, lifting capacity and working radius of the cranes selected should be suited to the structure, component production, and stacking requirements so that they can lift the maximum total load per day, with allowance for the extra load imposed by the adhesion of any precast concrete units to the mould.

Steel framed structures are normally erected with pole or guy derricks by the steel erectors before concreting and cladding operations commence and provide support for the erection cranes and/or hoists subsequently installed for handling materials and shuttering. But static tower cranes located inside the frame may be more economic according to site conditions, structural design, and programming of erection operations.

Crane utilisation in relation to the building programme

Most building projects can be divided into substructure, superstructure internal finishings, and services phases which are partially integrated, yet programmed separately. Cranage facilities should start on site as soon as construction permits, and finish shortly after completion of the structure.

The cranes should be subordinate to the erection cycle, and normally governed by concreting operations or the placing of precast concrete units. Crane layouts require careful planning in relation to their work areas, as these are governed by the effective radius at which loads can be safely lifted, and space allocated may not be available at completion of the works to enable the crane to be readily dismantled and removed.

A radial type crane is restricted as regards maximum load and area coverage by the length of its jib. A derrick type, which is essential for effective operation on sites surrounded by tall buildings, is limited to a 270° sweep for its operating area, but has the advantage of gaining a high lifting capacity from its anchorage.

Mobile cranes with a vertical boom and fly jib for convenient self-erection, and a load radius of 5 to 6 tons (5·08 to 6·10 tonnes) lifting capacity can provide versatility of operation suited to the building programme of low-rise developments, as the base machine is able to enter a site before access roads have been laid out; travel up inclines of 1:4 gradient; operate long boom drag line or grab crane excavating equipment; and travel on roads or virgin site on inclines of 1:20 with complete mobility around buildings, acting as a standard jib crane for heavy lifting of plant and structural units delivered to site.

On smaller low-rise developments, a truck mounted telescopic jib crane with lifting capacity of 8 tons (8·13 tonnes) at 65 ft (19·81 m) height and working range of 20 ft (6·10 m) reducing to $1\frac{1}{4}$ tons (1·27 tonnes) at 55 ft (16·76 m) may provide versatile use. The crane can be erected within a few minutes, and is able to alter the length of its jib to reach across the width of a building. Lifting capacity can be changed by telescopic action in a matter of seconds, thus obviating the dismantling time for a mast crane used for similar operations. The crane can move rapidly and safely on sloping sites by reducing the length of its jib. When the crane has finished operations for the day on a particular site, it can be rapidly transferred to other sites at a travelling speed on roads of 35 m.p.h.

Crane costs

Tower cranes are the most expensive kinds of cranes used in system building. Their basic costs relate to type, jib length, height of mast, hoisting capacity and working radius, speed of lift, type of control and chassis, erection and dismantling costs, foundation costs, extra costs of tying back static cranes to the structure to gain increased heights, and the extra costs of rails and foundations for travelling cranes.

Approximate costs of heavy static tower cranes vary considerably, from approximately £11,000 with 130 ft (39·62 m) mast height and 6 tons (6·10 tonnes) basic lifting capacity to approximately £25,000 with 210 ft (64·00 m) mast height and 15 tons (15·24 tonnes) lifting capacity, and up to £60,000 and over for heavier cranes.

A tower crane capable of lifting a load of 10 tons (10·16 tonnes) at a realistic working radius costs at least double that of a comparable portal crane, plus much higher erection costs.

The optimum life of a crane varies according to its purpose and degree of maintenance and repair. Slow-moving infrequently dismantled and re-erected portal cranes have a longer potential working life than faster operating and more lightly constructed and frequently used tower cranes. But unless a mobile jib or portal crane can be operated over a sufficiently long period to justify its purchase (i.e. at least 45 per cent utilisation of a normal potential of 1800 to 2000 hours per annum throughout a working life of five years), it will usually be more economical to hire rather than purchase.

The cost of efficient crane utilisation on low-rise projects for housing depends on the speed of the erection cycle, but normally should not exceed £30 (approx) per dwelling. This cost will be increased out of all proportion by inefficient planning of crane operations, inconsistent flow of components to site, and complicated jointing details which entail long waiting periods when the crane has to hold the units in position whilst they are being fixed.

Restrictions on contract time may necessitate a crane working over-time and thus help to reduce site on-costs. But if subjected to excessive travel, and unskilfully operated, the wheels, gears and motors of rail-mounted tower cranes, which are only intended for short occasional travel, will wear in a similar manner to the plates, pins and gears of crawler cranes. And when mobile cranes are used for travel on uneven, rocky or waterlogged ground, the replacement or rebuilding of their running gear can become necessary with one-half or one-third of their normal working life.

THE APPLICATION OF WORK STUDY TECHNIQUES TO PLANT OPERATIONS

Work study techniques can provide a valuable planning tool by deter-mining methods of operating plant continuously at optimum capacity, enabling contract works to be controlled more closely by improved plant selection and position on site, and determining plant outputs for more accurate estimates of plant costs on the basis of a systematic collection of plant data.

The work study of plant includes selecting the correct type and capacity plant for each task to be undertaken, matching related equipment, positioning plant on site, determining routes for plant movements, establishing potential outputs under varying site conditions, assessing unit costs, and comparing available alternative methods on the basis of a systematic collection of plant data.

Production studies can be undertaken at daily or weekly periods over each minute of the day to establish and find the explanation and reason for every delay in plant operations. Unproductive work may be found to be due to a great variety of causes—failure to provide materials at the right moment, inadequate matching of related plant, insufficient labour teams, inefficient maintenance, lack of engineers for setting out work, and other causes due to lack of efficient preplanning or supervision.

Idle time may be due to adverse weather conditions, down time, dissatisfaction of operatives with their bonus targets, non-arrival of materials or components, plant breakdowns, and other reasons too numerous to detail.

7

Simplified Tendering and Contract Procedures

Economic industrialised system building necessitates the early cooperation of designers and contractors for the efficient preplanning of a project in all its aspects in order to commence and complete construction works with a minimum of delay and variation from completed drawings and specifications. As a result, more effective methods are essential for obtaining competitive tenders to substitute present costly, time-wasting and ineffectual methods now generally adopted.

When several tenderers are selected to submit lump sum prices on the basis of substantially inaccurate drawings and 'accurate' bills of quantities, clients are unnecessarily adding to the costs of building, because every contractor has to adjust his prices to comprehend overheads incurred in unsuccessful attempts, or else take part in the organisation of a price ring, which defeats the whole object of competitive tendering. Considerable time and cost is wasted, and the commencement of works on site delayed pending the preparation of 'accurately measured' and 'fully described' bills of quantities subject to a virtual remeasurement of the billed items for 'the adjustment of variations'. Final balances of payments to contractors and nominated subcontractors and suppliers are withheld for years pending settlement of 'final accounts'. These accounts invariably inflate original 'lump sum' contract prices obtained from 'accurately measured' and 'fully described' bills of quantities based on incomplete 'contract drawings' and specifications, and substantially reduce the real value of long outstanding balances of payments due to the continually falling purchasing power of the pound, as well as rising prices and inflation.

Competitive tenders which are really competitive, and not just arrangements made between tenderers, are necessary to maintain economic costs, but they should be obtained in a form which minimises the considerable abortive costs of unsuccessful tenderers by being based on simple, concise bills of quantities adequate for tendering purposes that enable estimators to price the bills sent out with the tendering documents in a reasonably short period of time. Bills of quantities should be based on a simplified method of measurement and adequately completed drawings and specifications which obviate the need for remeasuring contract works in order to 'adjust variations', and inflate the contract sum.

The information which estimators require from a bill of quantities in order to submit keenly competitive tenders is entirely different from the information required at post-tendering stage, and cannot be included in tendering documents. Moreover, economic construction necessitates the selection of a contractor at the initial stage of a project so that he can cooperate fully with the design team preparing the working drawings, and advise on alternative techniques of construction to achieve savings. A 'professional adviser' quantity surveyor is usually unable to make such assessments because he lacks the necessary education, knowledge, and experience of mechanical plant utilisation, network analysis, programming works, site control, computerised costings of contractor's current projects, and the economics of construction.

Early selection of a contractor can be made readily by obtaining competitive rates on the basis of a budget figure based on initial sketch plans, outline specifications, and a comprehensive schedule of items covering the proposed works. The tendered schedule rates can be subsequently used for pricing bills of quantities prepared in accordance with a simple and realistic standard method of measurement from completed drawings and specifications.

The information contractors require after tendering stage cannot be prepared at tendering stage because it relates to the purchase of materials measured net in the tender bill, pre-expenditure control—which requires budget assessments for ancillary items such as site offices, small tools, welfare and safety requirements; selection of mechanical plant and outputs in relation to labour teams and manhour production for eight-hour shifts; subcontract purchases; organisation of subcontractor's work; valuation of interim certificates, and bonus targets.

Such information needs to be incorporated in several documents, one of which being a working document in the form of an analysed estimate budget to minimise wastage and facilitate pre-expenditure control. Labour should be separated from materials, and each scheduled separately, with labour requirements in a form that enables work to be planned on site. Daily tasks need planning for teams and individuals, with provision for comparison of daily and weekly outputs. Estimates of tasks require amending on experience gained from the contract. Work loads of all items of mechanical plant and equipment require scheduling and effective programming.

Experienced estimators habitually base their lump sum prices for industrialised building systems of precast panel construction on rates for the total quantities of concrete, steel, and inserts required for a project. They are able to tender for major construction works such as factory, office and housing developments on the basis of a rate per sq ft (m^2) or cu ft (m^3) and a study of the drawings and specifications. Contractors are not assisted by the innumerable items and long-winded descriptions unrelated to the economics of construction as presented to them in bills of quantities for unit items measured without relation to position as prepared in accordance with the current standard method of measuring building works.

Construction is a dynamic process, and problems of handling and hoisting materials and components to placing points represent a significant part of construction costs, which are not indicated in bill items. Instead of wasting weeks of their valuable time in attempting to price such minutiae, estimators frequently prefer to take a price from other tenderers and save their efforts for more useful and remunerative work.

The increasing trend towards larger scale developments on vast sites let on the basis of fixed lump sum 'package deals' renders even more time-wasting and costly the professional quantity surveyor's function as an adviser paid one fee for preparing 'accurately' measured and 'fully described' bills of quantities based on the current S.M.M., and a second fee for virtually remeasuring the works already measured all over again in order to determine final accounts long after completion of the contract works. The economic cost of a building project does not depend solely on obtaining an initial competitive tender figure, but also on effective critical path scheduling; pre-expenditure control based on a cost budget; resources planning to ensure the most economical use of available labour, materials and plant; and programming contract works to obtain the most effective return on the employer's capital, matters normally left as an exercise for the 'unprofessional' contractor's surveyor to perform.

To become really effective, the 'professional' quantity surveyor should carry out these functions, and be in a position to take into account all the different elements contained in the contract bill and record all results achieved on similar contracts. He should also be able to plan resources in relation to cost estimates and site programmes with the necessary flexibility for efficient minimum cost expenditure; control the critical path method of site operations; and optimise each situation as it arises during the course of construction. The feedback of information from sites can be processed and fed into a computer for consideration against actual progress, forecasting future trends, and reassembly of all previous experience. This can provide useful information for pricing, instead of the frequently worse than misleading 'historic' prices manipulated by meaningless cost indices.

Some years ago, after contractors first decided to cut down overheads by employing one man to compute their quantities for competitive tendering, they helped to evolve an increasingly complicated method of measuring to ensure payment for authorised works undertaken which were not clearly shown or described in the documents sent out for tendering purposes.

Today, great savings in time and man's mental and physical labours have resulted from the use of comptometers, computers, mechanical plant and equipment, powered tools, advanced theories of structural design, modern techniques of construction, and many other ingenious devices. Yet, despite all these developments, such savings are more than discounted by the vast daily wastage of time and labour drained away on the production of unnecessary paperwork in respect of the preparation of vague and incomplete drawings and specifications used as a basis for 'accurate' bills of quantities sent out to tenderers; the preparation of 'accurate' bills of quantities based on a complicated, inflexible and unrealistic method of measurement and incomplete data, and subject to innumerable 'adjustments for variations'; the pricing of thousands of items contained in such bills; the checking of their arithmetical computations; the more or less practical remeasurement of the bills for the adjustment of variations; the pricing and agreement of final accounts containing these adjustments; the technical audit of such final accounts; the negotiation and settlement of contractual and ex-contractual claims arising out of such documents regarding claims for delay and other matters—delays that prevent works commencing on site for months and years, hold up progress of the works, and eventually delay payment of outstanding balances due to contractors for similar periods.

Long-winded descriptions of minutiae, and innumerable differentiated items of quantities contained in current bills of quantities sent out to tenderers, despite tower cranes, mechanical plant, powered tools,

British Standard Specifications and Codes of Practice, frequently do not represent the extent of completed contract works, or all the conditions under which they are to be carried out, and usually result in very considerable and costly delays.

Civil engineers have always refused to countenance such an unsatisfactory state of affairs. They well understand the importance of mechanical plant and construction techniques in relation to site problems and costs, and the vital necessity of providing tenderers with adequately completed drawings and specifications at tendering stage, or else a bill of quantities which does not pretend to be more than a schedule of rates.

The current Standard Method of Measuring Civil Engineering Works enunciates the basic principles that 'a bill of quantities should be as simple as possible provided it adequately covers the work to be done', and 'descriptions in a bill should be as brief as possible, and only in sufficient detail to ensure identification of the work covered by the respective items with that shown on the contract drawings and described in the specification, which is required to make clear the exact nature of the work to be performed'.

No matter how great a complexity of measurement, nor however 'standardly phrased' a description may be, unless the drawings and specifications from which the bills are prepared make clear the exact nature of the work to be carried out, they are of but little value.

A bill of quantities forming part of tendering documents based on the R.I.B.A. conditions of contract is prepared for the express purpose of enabling building employers to obtain firm competitive lump sum prices which represent the actual and final cost of their proposed enterprises. Nevertheless, the extent to which such prices do so depends on the extent to which the drawings and specifications sent out to tenderers represent the actual scope of the proposed works, as well as numerous complex factors, some of which may be quite unknown at the time of tendering. As a result, employers are frequently called upon to pay much larger sums for their building projects than represented by the 'firm' lump sum prices obtained by competitive tender.

Building operations involve many different persons over considerable periods of time, are subject to changes of mind, human errors, weather conditions, economic booms and depressions, unforeseen happenings, and other uncontrollable influences which can impede continuity of the works, and thereby increase construction costs. These costs are also affected by such diverse matters as variations in price levels of other industries, credit squeezes, the sudden imposition of unforeseen tax legislation, and shortages of all kinds of labour and materials. No amount of 'accurate' measurement of 'fully described' items can adequately comprehend these factors. Neither can incomplete tendering drawings and specifications which fail to indicate the full extent and nature of the proposed works.

'Accurate' bills of quantities prepared in accordance with the current standard method of measuring building works which form part of tendering documents, contain no provision for the effect on costs of position in the works, or of the effects of repetition on labour outputs. Moreover, the R.I.B.A. conditions of contract expressly state that 'as and when from time to time it may be necessary, the architect shall, without charge to the contractor, furnish him with two copies of such drawings and details as are reasonably necessary either to explain or amplify the contract drawings, or to enable the contractor to carry out and complete the works in accordance with the contract conditions'.

Exactly what drawings and details are to be considered reasonably necessary is left undefined. But the meaning of this clause ensures that if, on signing the contract, a contractor were to ask for details of holes and chases for engineering services on the eighteenth floor of a multistorey building (the design of such services having been sublet by the architect to specialist firms or consultants), the reply permitted under the terms of the clause would enable the architect to refuse the request on the grounds that such details were not necessary at this initial stage of the proceedings, as there was plenty of other work for the contractor to undertake.

Such a lack of detailed information prevents the contractor from being able to preplan a job adequately on the basis of flowline production, and consequently increases his costs of building. If such information is not available for the contractor, it would not have been furnished to the surveyor preparing the bills of quantities. Consequently the contract quantities cannot have been accurate in respect of this work, although doubtless covered by inflated 'provisional quantities'.

Thus the very conditions of contract preclude the possibility of a really accurate premeasurement of the works, let alone all those unforeseen happenings and variations that frustrate even comparatively well planned schemes.

As developments become larger and increased amounts of capital are required for external works, garages and public utility services, mechanised handling and site factory plant and equipment, and other items which do not yield an adequate return on capital until completion of the works, a more realistic form of valuation for interim payments is essential in order to obtain a more profitable use of the employer's investment, and ensure an economic cash flow to the contractor.

The economics of building relates to both the employer's and the contractor's capital investments. Both have the same aim of obtaining the maximum yield on their investments, yet the means by which each may obtain such a result is entirely different. The employer's risk is limited to obtaining an effective economic tender from a competent contractor, whereas the contractor's risks are spread over many different sources of capital investment, overheads, labour, materials, plant, unknown circumstances. The present unrealistic standard method of measurement for building works does not provide either party to a contract with adequate assistance to achieve their aims.

Certain principles laid down in the current standard method of measurement make it unlikely that work 'accurately' measured and 'fully described' in the bills of quantities will relate factually to the works as carried out.

Rule WI(c) requires painting material applied by a particular method (e.g. from cradles) to be so described, stating the method of application. But when tenderers are not present during the design stage of the building, the use of cradles depends on the contractor's eventual decision as to whether or not it will suit him better to utilise external scaffolding according to the particular techniques of construction he may wish to adopt, and not on the quantity surveyor's imagination at the time of preparing the bills.

Various rules of measuring affect the accuracy of 'accurate' quantities by requiring non-existent excavations and concrete to be 'accurately' measured merely for the sake of complying with theoretical rules regarding working space.

The whole basis of measurement—net quantities of work fixed in position ignores the fact the construction is a *dynamic* process, and ensures the inaccuracy of the 'accurate' quantities measured. Such quantities do not represent the factual extent and construction problems of the works undertaken. They do not include any quantities for increase in bulk for the disposal of excavated materials, or to compensate for the shrinkage in volume of 'wet' materials such as concrete, or for cutting to required sizes, trampling aggregates into the ground, and the many other sources of materials wastage on site, which can be minimised by effective site management, but never entirely eliminated.

'Accurate' quantities included in the bills for formwork are measured in accordance with nearly forty different 'principles' of measurement. But they do not help estimators to price the items measured, as they have to take off all the formwork again in order to determine the number of times it can be utilised. This duplication of measuring occurs despite the formwork having been 'fully described' and 'accurately' measured in accordance with the fifth edition (revised) of the Standard Methods of Measuring Building Works.

In reality, S.M.M. 'accurate' quantities cannot be really accurate, and the 'full' descriptions required to be given in accordance with that document are not really comprehensive. Thus according to the rules of measurement, a comparatively simple item such as a precast concrete panel unit would be enumerated and described in such terms as: '6 in Precast concrete (4000 lb ($281 \cdot 23$ kgf/cm^2)–$\frac{3}{4}$ in (19 mm) max. aggregate) wall panel size X by Y, reinforced with Z rods at B centres, and bedded in cement mortar (1:3).'

Not a word is required by the S.M.M. principles of measurement to be given regarding the *height above ground level at which it is placed*—which might be 2 ft or 200 ft ($0 \cdot 61$ m or $60 \cdot 96$ m). In what sense is such a description to be considered 'full', when it is not only silent about the height to which the panel has to be hoisted, but is also mute regarding its method of production, i.e:

Strike mould for previous panel.
Clean mould.
Reassemble mould.
Apply mould oil to mould.
Cut and bend steel for mould.
Fix steel in mould.
Place concrete in mould.
Cure concrete.
Strike concrete.
Stack panel in yard.
Handle panel to position.
Hoist panel.
Line and level panel.
Strike props to panel.
Lay mortar bed to panel.
Strike off excess mortar to panel.
And so forth, and so on.

One clarification of the current S.M.M. issued recently by the Standing Joint Committee states that 'it is most important that the specific words or phrases of the S.M.M. are used'.

If this advice were to be strictly followed, even more confusion would result than at present. For instance, rule D6(e) states that 'excavating in rock shall be described as *excavating in rock*', rock being described as '*any material* met with in excavation which is of such size or position that it can only be removed by means of wedges, compressed air or other special plant, or explosives'.

And rule D13 states that 'breaking up concrete, reinforced concrete, brickwork and the like met with in excavation shall each be given as *extra over the various descriptions of excavations*'.

It can happen, and in fact sometimes *does* happen, that when excavations are proceeding for major projects in large cities, hidden concrete foundations of old buildings are encountered on site of sizes in the region of 50 ft (15·24 m) in length × 7 ft (2·13 m) wide and 9 ft (7·74 m) deep. It is quite useless attempting to remove such large concrete foundations with compressors—they merely chip the surface of the concrete and do not break it up. The use of explosives or special plant is required to fracture such concrete and fragment it into sufficient sizes for compressors to be subsequently used. How then is the categorical demand of using the specific words or phrases of the S.M.M. to be obeyed ? Is the removal of such foundations 'excavating in rock' under rule D6(e)—because it is a material that requires to be removed by explosives or special plant ?

Or is its removal to be described as 'Extra over excavations for breaking up concrete'—under rule D13, because it is concrete ? Or should it be fully described as both at once ? Clearly, a clarification of the clarification is needed here—and so *ad infinitum*.

The S.M.M. 'principle' of providing net quantities of unit items fixed in position does not relate to the actual realities of modern methods of component production and techniques of construction. It is based on outdated pre-1914 conditions, when operatives were more susceptible to control, materials costs were of greater importance than relatively stable labour costs, horses and carts were used to remove surplus excavations from sites, and there was comparatively little mechanical plant and equipment available to aid man's physical efforts.

The vastly increased replacement of human labour by machines has achieved remarkable results for many years which greatly affect construction costs, but are not reflected in the current S.M.M. of measuring building works. The unmeasurable positioning and layout of cranes on a site vitally affect construction costs and very considerably more so than do the measurable 'stop ends' on plaster cornices. The crane's travel determines the locations for unloading materials, setting up concrete batching plants, precasting concrete units, assembling sections of shuttering, and many other site operations, whereas 'stop ends' are merely trivial. Moreover, many of the S.M.M. principles of measurement are rendered entirely meaningless by construction techniques such as sliding shutters and icosdiaphragm walls.

A radical change from the Current Standard Method of Measuring Building Works is essential for economic construction for the following reasons. The principles of measuring enunciated therein include those which are contradictory, meaningless, require measurement of non-existent work, and are not related to construction costs. The majority of the 'accurate' quantities billed are meaningless, because they are based on inaccurate drawings and specifications, and have to be re-measured all over again for the 'adjustment of variations'. The standard method of measurement relates to unit rates based on manhour production, whereas in fact labour is increasingly being replaced by machines, and the only practical method of estimating labour is on shift team output related to mechanical plant. Unit rates do not take into account the effects of repetitive operations on labour output, or of position in relation to handling costs. Nor do the rates reflect the way work is carried out, and so cannot reflect the actual costs of construction. The rates do not enable designers to have any conception of the effects design detailing is having on construction costs. And even more significantly, the rates do not take into account all those factors termed 'preliminary particulars' in Section B of the S.M.M. These 'particulars' can amount to hundreds of thousands of pounds on large contracts, and cannot be scientifically or accurately related to all the innumerable 'accurately' measured and 'fully described' minutiae which inevitably follow later in the bills. Moreover, no detailed cost analysis is provided of these preliminary particulars, so that lowest tenders may be accepted which are not really economic because the tenderer has not included in his price allowance for sufficient site staff, thus ensuring trouble when work starts on site. The total contract price is based on unit rates which provide tenderers with the possibility of taking advantage in order to obtain a high final contract sum in relation to the original tender figure by pricing low those items which it is anticipated will be reduced in quantity, and pricing high those items which it is anticipated will be increased in quantity. The work billed results in an adjustable tender figure in isolation, without relating the employer's expenditure to the various capital sums involved in the most economic manner. Estimators have to base their unit rates on many unmeasured and undescribable factors not included in the bills which affect the whole of the price level for a job. These include the availability of labour and general level of skill and output; the degree of bonusing in each trade, the degree of mechanisation practical for a job, the type, nature and most effective utilisation of mechanical plant, the volume of other construction work proceeding in the area which may be causing a shortage of labour, shortages of local sources of essential materials such as ballast; and seasonal difficulties.

The claim has frequently been made that bills prepared in accordance with the current S.M.M. are the most suitable kind to assist estimators to price tenders, and employers to obtain firm competitive prices for the cost of their building enterprises. In actual fact, such prices do not represent these costs. And the bills on which they are based do not include quantities which enable contractors to order materials other than formless materials in bulk. Neither do they provide information regarding utilisation of formwork, the sequence of operations for setting bonus targets, or programming a job into teams working in sectionalised areas in order to benefit from the effects of repetition on output. Despite all the 'accurate' measuring and 'fully' describing, the contractor's estimator, manager, and bonus surveyor have to take off the quantities all over again to suit their particular purposes.

Instead of 'fully described', 'accurately' measured, unrelated-to-reality quantities, which result in a priced bill that is merely a set of random numbers, and has about as much use, tenderers require simple bills which present the basic information they require in a form which enables them to make their own breakdown of costs. This analysis usually takes the form of materials schedules, assessments of gang strengths and mechanical plant requirements in order to obtain weekly and total outputs for each relevant task; and separation of repetitive work from non-repetitive work for assessment of improved efficiency as work proceeds above first floor level. Tenderers should be provided with as many sets of the tendering drawings and specifications as they may require in order to obtain competitive prices for their subcontract trades.

Contractors who finance their own speculative development schemes would not dream of using anything more formidable than a simple form of bill to serve their purpose of building at a minimum cost, and evaluating the project cash flow in time—a criterion for good economic valuation which an 'accurate and fully described' bill of quantities fails to provide.

Government departments limit the estimated costs of their projects by the simple expedient of setting a rate per square foot of building.

Experienced surveyors who keep cost records for various types of construction over long periods and are constantly supplied with information obtained from computerised feedbacks for their current projects can readily determine wastage and errors. They are sufficiently well informed to be able to submit firm lump sum tenders for major projects on the basis of an examination of the drawings and specifications, and a rate per square foot of building. Such estimates are based on the experience of other contract works, and the average tendency produced by the variation of all relevant factors influencing costs being likely to be found within fairly narrow limits as indicated by the Central Limit Theorem of Probabilities.

In the United States of America, where building costs have remained relatively stable over the past ten years in comparison with ours, variations on contract sums are practically unknown. Firm contract prices remain firm, and tendering procedures are based on a very simple form of bill, and at least thirty sets of the tendering drawings and specifications sent out to each firm invited to submit a 'bid'.

The highly competitive American building industry is not provided with fully measured and detailed bills of quantities, and lacks price arrangements between tenderers. The architect's drawings and specifications describe some materials and components by performance specifications, and others by specifying a particular manufacture, or equal. A contractor is selected by keenly competitive tender, and is responsible for selecting all manufactured items required. His margin of profit will be small.

The contractor arrives at his final selection of manufactured items by a 'dutch auction' between alternate sources of supply. Manufacturers attempt to avoid a price war by providing special 'appeal' to the contractor that may lead to their selection for other reasons than price alone. Thus baths may be provided with thin moulded plastic inserts dropped in for protection during handling, instead of paper tape protection. However, no innovations are permitted which would restrict their ability to compete for contract works as designed; but short cuts and devices may be used that enable work shown or specified to be undertaken more effectively. For example, woodworkers' standard overalls may be redesigned so that nails can be obtained from pockets without stopping. However, no materials or components of a special kind may be introduced. Such procedures may not be suited to the British way of life, nevertheless no building industry in any country should be burdened with such time wasting and costly phenomena as 'fully described', 'accurately' measured bills of quantities prepared in accordance with the S.M.M., despite the fact that such ineffective bills permit architects to send out to tenderers incomplete specifications and drawings with the comforting assurance that they are afforded financial protection by so doing.

'Risk bearing' forms of 'lump sum' contracts during periods of boom, when the volume of work unleashed on the building industry becomes greater than it can adequately cope with, are more or less subject to the law of supply and demand, instead of that law of the jungle which operates during periods of depression. Consequently, the usefulness of bills of quantities prepared during these times for the express purposes of obtaining competitive lump sum tenders are not only related to the extent that the drawings and specifications on which they are based make clear the exact nature of the work to be performed, but also upon the extent to which tenderers are prepared to submit keenly competitive prices. The truth of this 'law' may be evidenced by comparing differences between the highest and lowest tenders obtained during a 'period of expansion' with those obtained during a 'period of recession'. Or by comparing the difference in tendered rates during the two periods for 'basement excavations not exceeding 5 ft (1·52 m) deep' and those 'exceeding 5 ft (1·52 m) and not exceeding 10 ft (3·05 m) deep'—a remarkable difference made in times of boom, despite the fact that mechanical excavators in operation do not usually discriminate between such niceness of measurement.

Quantities are but one facet of the diverse information required for keenly pricing tenders for risk bearing lump sum contracts—there are many other vital factors bearing on costs that require assessment which by their very nature are unmeasurable. And not only all those 'preliminary particulars' and the like which are set out in Section B of the current S.M.M. Building Works. Or those contingent and potential causes of expenditure classified as 'contractor's risks' in the current S.M.M. or Civil Engineering Works.

Some of these factors involve considerable costs, which estimators are left to assess without the guidance of any quantities, and relate to the most advantageous and economic use of mechanical plant and techniques of construction; the economic implications of varying site conditions such as ground and water levels; the comparative advantages and disadvantages of transporting men daily to and from a site instead of erecting a hutted camp; site restrictions limiting the movement of mechanical plant and the storage of materials; and police regulations limiting the period for unloading materials at site or imposing the operation of one-way streets.

Other unmeasured factors relate to the economic implications of design such as the height and shape of the proposed building, the amount of prefabrication possible, the amount of repetitive work at each floor level, and the like. And other factors relate to general circumstances prevailing at the period of tendering, the availability or otherwise of labour in the district, national shortages of materials, impending change of government or rate of bank interest, inclement weather, the international situation, and many other unmeasured and unmeasurable considerations.

No matter how complex a method of measurement may be, it cannot adequately take into account such factors, and its inflexibility may well prevent estimators from exercising their skill to achieve economies when tendering by adopting alternative methods of construction to obtain savings that could be passed on to the building employer.

Considerable savings in construction time and costs could be achieved by establishing on a National basis a simple standard method of measuring construction works related to the comparatively few major items in which the greater part of costs are concentrated, and the use of one effective standard form of contract to replace the standard forms of contract of the Royal Institute of British Architects, the Institute of Civil Engineers, the Institute of Structural Engineers, and the General Conditions of Government Contracts for Building and Civil Engineering Works Form CCC/Wks/1, in order to achieve a simple contract procedure that enabled construction costs to be controlled, and a contractor to be selected during initial stages to form part of the design team.

The selected contractor's expertise and experience would help architects to investigate site conditions and finalise drawings and specifications so that a project could be adequately preplanned and later costly variations eliminated. By this method, one measurement of the works to be executed would suffice to compute the final contract sum. In order to estimate net costs, and required overhead and profit margins in accordance with assessments of risks and company policy, tenderers should be provided with quantities of the comparatively few major items contained in S.M.M. bills that include the majority of costs; a detailed analysis of preliminary items; schedules of resources, with key dates for ordering materials and requisitioning plant; and a proposed overall construction programme and method statement indicating the most effective construction techniques to be adopted for the tenderer's agreement or amendment.

A simple, flexible and effective method of measurement for both building and civil engineering works related to drawings and specifications that made clear the exact nature of the work to be performed would provide estimators with the bulk 'all-in' quantities of the main elements of construction, and enable bills of quantities for risk-bearing lump sum contracts to be more readily, economically and usefully prepared.

When for one reason or another, only incomplete drawings and specifications were available at the time of tendering, such a method of measurement would enable schedules of rates to be prepared readily as a basis for competitive tendering and the assessment of a final contract sum based on a single measurement of the works as executed.

'All-in' quantities are those which are deemed to include in the measurement of work undertaken all contingent and temporary works, expenses, liabilities, risks, and everything else necessary for the proper execution and completion of the work measured, in accordance with the contract documents.

The measurement of excavations and earthworks and some of the factors influencing their pricing is influenced by the moisture content and nature of the soil, and the wide variety of excavating and earth-moving plant and equipment available in the open market. The type, nature and extent of timbering or sheet steel required to uphold the sides of excavations is affected by such factors as the nature of soil, site water level, weather conditions, and the comparative economies of battering the sides of excavation rather than upholding them. A total 'all-in' measurement of the net cubic contents of the voids to be formed, classified according to the nature of soil (soft, hard, or rock as defined in the Conditions of Contract), and the type of excavation (shallow surface, bulk in open, cuttings, trenches, pits, etc.), would suffice to enable estimators to exercise their skill. All such incidental items as increase in bulk, allowances for working space, disposal of soil, multiple handling, differing depths (in most cases), planking and strutting, grading, levelling and ramming bottoms, keeping site free from water, etc., would be deemed to be included in the rates for the 'all-in' unit items of excavations, billed in cubic yards.

Such inclusions would suit experienced estimators, who are used to assessing such unmeasurable items as the economic impact of complying with all the limitations, restrictions and difficulties of working on a confined site located in the centre of a busy city thoroughfare, and are able and willing to tender competitive rates per superficial foot (m²) as the basis for lump sum contract prices based only on drawings and specifications for projects of over £1 million.

Items such as stripping turf, breaking up pavings and foundations, and the like, would be measured as 'extra over' items, and exceptional depths of certain types of excavations given separately in cubic yards (m³).

As regards brickwork, there is no point in the current S.M.M. requiring 'facework to returns 9 in (0·23 m) wide to be given in superficial yards' as opposed to 'fair ends to one brick wall faced both sides in linear yards (m)' whilst at the same time making no distinction whatsoever between walls built between cill level and window head over, and those built between window head and cill level above. Or for that matter, between walls built at first floor level and those built at twenty-first floor level.

Contractors who have sublet brickwork to piecework teams, and paid them liberally for building the perimeter walls of a building from footings up to ground floor cill level, are well aware of such undifferentiated variations in cost when they discover that the team has not arrived for work on the following and successive days, and cannot be traced.

Instead of stuffing bills full of innumerable items of measured brick minutiae without separating items according to location as regards openings and position as regards heights, tenderers should be provided with bills of quantities based on drawings and specifications which make clear the exact nature of the work to be performed, and include 'all-in' quantities of the main elements of construction.

Such simplified bills would avoid holding up works starting on site, disorganising building programmes due to variations, and delaying payments of final balances of accounts, and also enable estimators to use time wasted in pricing thousands of minutely measured details by the more useful thorough study of the tendering drawings, specifications, and site conditions with a view to achieving economies, an essential task which in times of boom is practically eliminated.

Moreover, building employers would be saved the expense of innumerable costly variations necessitated by a method of measurement which requires the raising of a variation order every time the architect

15

changes his mind over the merest trifle. Claims for delays, disorganisation of programmed works, and other contractual and ex-contractual claims would be reduced, and employers could gain possession of their completed buildings more speedily, and at far less expense.

Concrete operations are now increasingly expedited by the use of batching plant, pumps, conveyors, vibrators, truck mixed deliveries, sliding forms, new methods of precasting and prestressing, tower cranes, and many other innovations.

Stonework, no matter how minutely classified, nor how many separate labours be measured on it, is invariably lumped together as one total foot cubage for the job, and priced at one and the same unit rate on the basis of the estimator's experience and examination of the drawings. The current S.M.M. for Building Works unwittingly recognises this fact at times, despite its voluminous principles of measuring natural stonework, by giving up the attempt to measure labours separately on tracery. And after requiring labours on superficial items of stonework, such as rebates, sinkings, chamfered angles and the like to be given separately in linear feet with the further separate measurement of their stops and mitres, the S.M.M. permits these very same labours *not* to be measured separately on superficial items of stonework, provided they are included in the description with the word 'rustications'.

A simplified bill would include general clauses such as the following to assist tenderers:

In submitting a tender the contractor will be deemed to accept the method of measurement and description adopted and used in this Bill of Quantities.

The lump sum price submitted by the contractor is to allow for all elements of cost in completing the works, as the rates, prices and total amounts of the items and net quantities included in this Bill shall be deemed to include everything set in place and fixed complete, including all expenses and liabilities set forth in the General Conditions of Contract, Specification and drawings, as well as for everything necessary to be used during the execution of the works and for the proper completion in a sound and watertight condition and maintenance thereof for the period stated in the Appendix and in accordance with the General Conditions of Contract.

The volume of the building is . . . feet cube (m^3) and the total floor area (measured between inside faces of external walls) is . . . feet super (m^2).

The descriptions of materials and workmanship, general trade preambles, preliminary particulars and insurances contained in the specification on pages x to y shall apply to the works as a whole, and the contractor is to allow hereunder, the separate sum or sums he may require for compliance with their provisions as listed below.

The draft for a simplified National Standard Method of Measuring Construction works for either building or civil engineering contracts could be prepared for circulation and eventual agreement by all relevant parties along the following lines:

Demolitions and alterations

The responsibility for the safety of the existing and adjoining structures shall be the sole responsibility of the contractor during the entire contract period.

The contractor is to visit the site, take all necessary dimensions and particulars, and allow, where listed below, for executing and completing the whole of the demolitions and alterations as indicated on drawings nos. x and y and described in the specification on page z.

Excavation and earth works

The total 'all-in' quantities of excavations and earthworks shall be given in yards cube (m³) and classified according to the nature of soil as in soft ground, hard ground, or rock as defined in the conditions of contract, and subdivided into the following categories: shallow surface excavation; excavation in bulk or in dumplings between trenches; cuttings for roads; pits and pier holes in stages of 10 ft (3·05 m) depths; trenches in stages of 5 ft (1·52 m) depths.

Planking and strutting, disposal of spoil, grading, levelling and ramming bottoms of excavations and all other incidental expenses, including keeping the site free from water, shall be deemed to be included in the rates for excavation, with the sole exceptions of the following items, to be measured as 'extra over' excavations for: stripping turf (in yards super) (m²); breaking up pavings (in yards super) (m²); breaking up brick and concrete foundations, or similar obstructions (in yards cube) (m³). *Hardcore.* The total 'all-in' quantity of all hardcore filling and beds of over 12 in (305 mm) consolidated thickness to be given in yards cube (m³). Beds under 12 in consolidated thickness shall be given in square yards (m²); blinding the surface of hardcore to receive concrete as an 'extra over' item in yards super (m²).

15*

Piling

The total feet run (m) of all precast and bored piles and driving shall be given, with a description of the superimposed load per foot super, (m²) and average length of pile.

The total yards super (m²) of all sheet steel piling and driving shall be given, with a description of the thickness, average depth, and type of pile.

Concrete work

Concrete work shall be generally classified according to type, quality or mix, and position as regards in foundations or superstructure, subdivided according to location in the structure. The total 'all-in' quantity of the various types of concrete shall be given in yards cube (m³), all concrete not exceeding 12 in (305 mm) thick being kept separate.

Bush hammered and other types of special finish to concrete surfaces shall be given in yards super (m²).

Expansion joints and similar items shall be given in yards (m) run.

Where the cross section of in-situ concrete is reasonably uniform throughout its length, shuttering shall be included in the rate for the concrete. Alternatively, shuttering for in-situ concrete may be measured separately and classified as wrought or sawn and subdivided into shuttering to: soffits, with lengths of strutting over 15 ft (4·57 m) kept separate in stages of 15 ft (4·57 m) (in yards super) (m²); walls and vertical surfaces of foundations, etc. separated into walls not exceeding 12 in (305 mm) thick, walls 12 in (305 mm) to 2 ft (0·61 m) thick and walls over 2 ft (0·61 m) thick (in yards super; m²); beams and columns stating the girth and beam section (in linear yards; m).

Reinforcement for all types of concrete shall be given separately according to type (bar, square twisted, mesh fabric, etc.) and size, and the total 'all-in' quantities of each type shall be given separately in tons or cwt (tonnes).

Components of industrialised buildings

The total 'all-in' quantities of components fabricated in factories shall be given as numbered items according to description, or by reference to manufacturer's catalogue.

Hollow block and hollow beam construction

The total 'all-in' quantities of slabs and beams shall be given in yards cube according to description.

Brickwork and Blockwork

The total number of each kind of brick shall be given in thousands, separated only according to different mortars, whether in substructure or superstructure, position in work, and shape and contour, e.g. general brickwork, walls with battered face, circular on plan, chimney shafts, manholes, arches.

The total 'all-in' area of brick face work and fair face shall be given in yards super (m^2).

The total 'all-in' quantities of all blockwork shall be given in yards super (m^2) according to thickness, manufacture, and mortar. Damp proof courses and similar items shall be given in yards super (m^2). Cills, brick reinforcement and similar items shall be given in yards run (m). Fireplace surrounds, chimney pots and similar items shall be enumerated.

Underpinning

The total 'all-in' quantities of all underpinning shall be given in yards run (m) according to description, and shall be referred to the detailed sections and lengths shown on the architect's drawings.

Masonry and rubble walls

The total 'all-in' quantities of all stonework other than cills, curbs and similar items of small cross-section shall be given in yards cube according to material and mortar. Cills, curbs and similar items shall be given in yards run (m).

Asphalt work

Generally, asphalt work shall be separated into damp proofing and tanking, paving, and roofing; and the total 'all-in' quantities of each shall be given in yards super (m^2) according to thickness.

The total 'all-in' quantities of skirtings and the like shall be given in yards run according to heights in stages of 6 in (152 mm) measured to the nearest 6 in (152 mm).

Roofing

The total 'all-in' quantities of the areas of roofing shall be given in yards super (m^2) according to material and description. Individual items such as eaves, verges, valleys, hips and the like shall be given in yards run (m). Metal aprons and flashings shall be given in yards super (m^2) according to type and weight.

Carpentry

Generally, carpentry shall be separated into wrought and sawn timber according to material, framed and unframed timber, and sections above 4 sq in (cm²) and sections below 4 sq in (cm²). The total 'all-in' quantities of all timber shall be given in foot cube (m³) according to location and the categories of roofs, floors, etc.; all boarding shall be given in yards super (m²) according to thickness and description; and all grounds, fillets, battens, etc. shall either be given in feet run (m) per sectional inch (cm²) or alternatively shall be reduced to a total feet cube (m³).

The plugging of timber to any type of surface shall be measured in feet run (m).

Joinery

Generally, joinery shall be separated according to material into flooring, linings, casings, partitions and the like; doors and windows, including frames and architraves, and related to the architect's door and window schedules; skirtings, cornices, mouldings and the like; fittings, staircases and similar items.

The total 'all-in' quantities of flooring shall be given in yards super (m²) according to thickness and description; linings, casings, and partitions, etc., shall be similarly given; framed partitions, borrowed lights etc., including frames and architraves shall be given in feet super (m²); skirtings, cornices, mouldings etc., shall be given in feet run (m) per sectional inch (cm²); fittings, staircases and the like shall be enumerated.

Ironmongery

The total quantities of ironmongery shall be listed in accordance with the architect's schedule of ironmongery.

Structural steelwork

Generally, structural steelwork shall be separated according to method of fabrication into the following categories: grillages and girders; stanchions, columns and portal frames; roof members, braces, struts and rails; bolts and sundry items; and the total 'all-in' quantities of each category shall be given in tons and hundredweights (tonnes).

Metalwork

The total 'all-in' areas of plates, duct covers and the like shall be given in feet super according to description or manufacturer's catalogue;

frames, bars, handrails, etc., shall be given in feet run (m) according to section; sheet metalwork shall be given in feet super (m²) according to description; metal windows and doors, etc., shall be enumerated according to type and size; curtain walling shall be given in yards super (m²) according to description; balustrades, railings, gates, ladders, etc. shall be similarly given in feet run (m).

Plumbing installations

Total 'all-in' quantities shall be given for plumbing installations according to the following categories: Gutters, rainwater, soil and plastic pipes shall be given in feet run (m) according to description and size. Copper, lead, mild steel and cast iron pipework shall be given separately in tons and hundredweights (tonnes). Bends and other fittings shall be enumerated and described. Hopper heads, valves, connections to mains and the like shall be enumerated and described. Sanitary fittings shall be similarly enumerated and described according to manufacturer's catalogues.

Insulation

The total 'all-in' quantities of insulation to pipework shall be given in yards run (m) according to material and size of pipe; boilers, etc., shall be enumerated and described.

Engineering installations

Each individual installation, such as heating, hot water, ventilation, gas, electrical, lifts, compressed air etc., should be adequately shown on the architect's drawings and described in his specifications, and the contractor referred to these tender documents and instructed to obtain competitive lump sum estimates with priced quantified schedules of items from a list of approved firms nominated by the architect, and prepared on the following basis of measurement: items forming the supply source and user end shall be numbered and described; transmission circuits shall be measured in lin ft (m); and circuit valves shall be numbered.

Builder's work in connection with plumbing and engineering installations

The total 'all-in' quantities of holes shall be given in numbered items according to description. Floor chases, wall chases, duct covers and casings, etc., shall be given in feet run (m) according to description. All other sundry items of builder's work shall be included for by the tenderer in accordance with his knowledge and experience as a percentage of the cost of the particular engineering, etc., installation.

Plasterwork and other floor, wall and ceiling finishes

Total 'all-in' quantities shall be given according to the following categories: Floor finishings and beds shall be given in yards super (m²) according to thickness and material. Wall finishings and screeds shall be similarly given, including keying. Ceiling finishings shall be similarly given, including keying, Skirtings, cornices and similar items shall be given in yards run (m) according to materials and description. Finishings to staircases shall be enumerated according to materials and description.

Only the quantities of such labours as arises; quirks, etc., considered by the surveyor to be of sufficient value to be measured separately shall be so measured.

Glazing

The total 'all-in' quantities of glass and patent glazing shall be given according to kind, quality and description. Velvet or wash-leather strip shall be given in yards run (m).

Painting and decorating

The total 'all-in' quantities of painting, polishing, etc., shall be given in yards super (m²) according to preparation, material, and number of coats (measured overall windows and doors).

External works and drainage

Generally, external works shall be measured in accordance with the principles given in the foregoing sections. Drainage shall be measured and total 'all-in' quantities given in accordance with the following categories: trench excavation for pipes in yards run (m) in stages of 1 ft (0·305 m) depths; concrete beds in yards run according to width of trench and thickness; pipes in yards run (m) according to material and size; pipe fittings, manholes, sewer connections shall be enumerated and described.

The total 'all-in' quantities of fencing shall be given in yards run (m) according to description, and shall include excavation and filling or concreting post holes. Gates shall be described and enumerated as 'extra over' items.

Simplified bills of quantities based on completed drawings and specifications and the foregoing suggested outlined methods of measurement would enable competitive tenders to be obtained with no less 'firmness', but with very much less expenditure of time and money than those obtained by present outmoded procedures.

By providing basic data in a simple form estimators could assess their total materials costs, labour, and plant outputs for a job in order to agree, or amend, the proposed construction programme and method statement sent with the bills.

The rates for items in simplified bills prepared for tendering purposes would not apply to variations. Any essential variations that arose later would be priced individually on their merits, bearing in mind any disorganisation caused to the construction programme.

Simplified bills would be divided into 'substructure', 'superstructure', and 'non-structural' sections, with 'repetitive' works on multistorey buildings defined and kept separate from non-repetitive work in trade subdivisions. Carpenter and joiners' work would be separated into first and second fixings. The final summary would comprise substructure, superstructure (non-repetitive work), superstructure (repetitive work), non-structural works, external works, and a percentage addition to be filled in for preliminaries.

One master of the nineteenth century, whose rational theory of architecture revolutionised design at a time when the permutations of the Romantic movement were deteriorating under their own complexity, describes his method of estimating a large building in the following terms:

The surface covered by the main building comprising the vestibule, which has only a ground floor, is approximately 1,060 sq yd (886·29 m²). Reckoning the cost of the building at £37 per sq yd (m²), as the building has only one floor of cellars, a ground floor and a first storey below the attics, we should be well within this rate. The principal building will therefore require a sum of about £39,200.

The outbuildings cover a surface of 800 sq yd (668·90 m²). These buildings have cellars under part of the ground floor, and one storey in the roof. Their average cost would be £14 per sq yd (m²) at most, which comes to about £11,200.

Adding for drains, paving, water, lighting and accessories £10,000, this gives a total sum of £60,040.[1]

1 Eugene Emmanuel Viollet-le-Duc, in his *Discourses on Architecture*, 1860, lecture XVII.

Experienced surveyors still adopt this principle for assessing approximate costs from preliminary drawings, but require the use of simplified bills of quantities to obtain competitive estimates from fully detailed drawings and specifications in order to submit firm tenders which will represent factually the final cost of proposed works.

8

Future Trends, Suggestions and Conclusions

FUTURE TRENDS

Present research into structural and metallicised plastics; adhesives to replace cement for binding aggregates; synthetic aggregates; load-bearing steel sandwich panels; processed volcanic earths and waste products; and the development of prestressed concrete and other materials may introduce a new scale of dimensions and structures by greatly increasing flexible spans. This could eventually lead to new types of larger and lighter structural elements that would revolutionise present industrialised building techniques.

The development of economic systems for district heating with computer control of temperature based on a large central heat source from which heat in the form of hot water or steam can be piped to dwellings over vast areas, may lead to the provision of physiologically correct adjustment of heat radiation and movement according to location and time of day, and electrical action upon the ventilated air to enhance it with a real and natural impression of freshness.

The increased use of automated methods of factory production, with consequent reduction of employees will tend to replace present standard north light structures with windowless buildings entirely lighted and ventilated by artificial means.

The development of suitable mass production methods such as the following for vast outputs of selected standardised interchangeable components in relation to an organised national volume of demand could achieve substantial economies of construction costs by the development of manufacturing methods for semi-automatic operations and short cycle times which involve such processes as ultrasonic techniques for bonding; photo-electric guards for the arrestor mechanisms of machinery; electro magnetic devices such as tape-controlled processes to eliminate hand fitting and reduce assembly time, and other ingenious devices.

The creation of new process dependent industries leading to reductions in labour requirements similar to those achieved in the production of aircraft would eventually achieve substantial cost reductions.

Advanced mechanised construction techniques may be developed in order to reduce site labour requirements, and speed erection. For example: the development and greater use of light conveyors for handling materials and components to required positions at successive floor levels; the development of road/rail vehicles for transporting heavy structural elements to sites distant from factories; the improved design of soil cutting tools and use of vibratory techniques to reduce the resistance of soil in front of prime movers; the use of hovercraft principle to reduce ground pressure under the wheels of haulage plant to allow earth moving machines to operate effectively over a wider range of soil and weather conditions; the economy of crane design due to more uniform techniques of construction and revision of current design assumptions in relation to crane fatigue; the development of an excavating machine which concentrates a high proportion of its power into a high-speed rotary cutting tool operating on a small excavating face.

The modernisation of construction, and increase of the whole level of building productivity depends on integrating the currently divided professions, management, technicians, craftsmen, and manual workers into a team supported by the economic mass production of a sufficient number of suitable standardised interchangeable 'open' components manufactured by semi-automated production methods in relation to a planned national volume of demand for delivery to sites as and when required for rapid erection in buildings of all types.

At present, manufacturing industries tend to compete with one another when they could more economically operate in combination, and too many different types of system and components have been designed in relation to a comparatively small, discontinuous, and unorganised volume of demand. This prevents the full benefits of industrialised system building to be obtained. Economic component production depends on long term national planning in relation to the vast scale manufacture of effectively designed and suitably selected standardised open interchangeable components with a minimum of essential variations related to available supplies of materials, labour, suitable mass production methods, and simple jointing techniques. More effective combinations of the characteristic properties of steel and concrete are required for structural elements than provided by current methods of reinforced concrete.

The economy of the site assembly and erection of standardised interchangeable components suited to a variety of building types is strongly influenced by jointing techniques, efficient programming and site control, and satisfactory bonus incentive schemes related to increased outputs which benefit both labour and management. The main problems include the following. Many existing 'closed' systems which are similar in type, but not economically viable should be eliminated. The increased simplification and more severely restricted standardisation of ranges of selected 'open' interchangeable components with jointing techniques suited to the performance and user requirements, and flexible design of each particular building type, need to be developed. The further development of selected components is essential for interchangeability to other building types such as cladding units suited to both hospitals and dwellings. The development and increased use of light-weight materials would achieve taller buildings with savings in foundation costs where building land is scarce and density ratios high. The more open planning of 'multitype' buildings capable of extension in height and facile remodelling is required to suit future improvements in living standards and changed user demands. The preparation and completion of fully detailed drawings and specifications before contract stage is essential to facilitate tendering and the efficient preplanning of projects; gear materials and component deliveries to erection requirements; and minimise double handling and non-productive time on site. Once such documents have been prepared for standardised buildings, drawing office costs can be substantially reduced. The simplification of tendering and contract procedures is required to enable a contractor to be selected at preliminary planning stage and competitive tender prices to be obtained at contract stage which factually represent the final cost of preplanned projects.

The building industry is moving from a craft industry towards a more intensively mechanised industry based on the substitution of machinery, factory labour, and semiskilled labour for craft trades. It is passing through a transitional stage of 'system building' before entering a final stage based on the site assembly of factory produced standardised interchangeable components mass produced in vast series for a variety of building types. The efficient reorganisation of the industry will necessitate increased standardisation of component production and construction techniques; modular coordination on a national basis; improved communications and management; integration of demand and production; and the re-education of all concerned. It will be necessary to create new

16

manufacturing, assembly and testing techniques for radically new types of components, as well as new ways of analysing and defining problems that arise.

SUGGESTIONS

The simplification of present uncoordinated and complex designs and conditions affecting system building is long overdue and essential for economy, and relates to: the standardisation of a comparatively few structural elements of high strength/weight ratio and light non-structural components suited to interchangeable assembly for a variety of building types; standardisation of simple jointing and erection techniques to simplify the design of mechanical plant and equipment; and central and regional government long-term planning of building related to national and local needs and capacities. The preparation of fully detailed and completed drawings and specifications before contract stage could be based on standardised structural elements and components, and related to annually priced national Schedules of Components. A National simplified standard method of measuring building and civil engineering works would greatly reduce tendering costs. The amendment of building regulations, bye-laws, fire regulations, codes of practice, design codes, and standard specifications to obtain unified procedures and performance requirements needs to be based on reality, and present day needs. The integration and gradual coordination of the many separate, competing, conflicting, and duplicating industries, organisations, and professions should be aimed to form more coherent and efficient units organised for effective economic production and service. New industries and factories should be sited strategically in relation to planned national and regional development and transportation. For example, sufficient space could be made centrally available for siting temporary factories mass producing precast concrete structural elements used on Ministry and Council developments in London.

Precast concrete panel and frame systems are unadaptable to future changes of user and living conditions. Many new office buildings recently erected in crowded urban areas based on these forms of construction will become obsolete in the comparatively near future due to lack of requisite floor space, improved standards of air conditioning, sound insulation, and other technological improvements. We are building now for a forty to sixty years unchanged environment, but instead should base our thinking on designs that will provide structural stability to take increased loading from future user requirements; bigger spans to enable removable non-structural units forming rooms to be utilised for increasing living and working space within the building, and enable curtain walling and other forms of cladding to be readily altered to suit changed user requirements.

Population increases expected to take place within the century will inevitably affect design requirements, so that the present scarcity of land will tend to increase, thus necessitating higher buildings; and sewage problems may arise in densely populated urban areas.

Advances in building technology will also affect design solutions in view of the psychological needs of mankind for larger living, working, and recreational areas; the utilisation of North Sea gas, which may render uneconomic the use of electricity for domestic purposes; the more general use of new lightweight materials for non-load-bearing walls in place of brickwork and concrete.

Current tendencies to seek quantity and speed of erection at the expense of quality that must result from the advances of technology, if unchecked will eventually lead to the creation of more slums, and the unnecessary and costly demolition of dense reinforced concrete structures capable of lasting hundreds of years, yet too confined in area and lacking current living standards to justify their continued existence on valuable land.

Design requirements should attempt to solve such problems by providing multipurpose buildings with sufficient foundations to take future increases of loading from increased storey heights, and additional floor loading due to change in user requirements. Some form of frame construction could be developed to achieve more open planning to provide for changes of building type and user requirements by using new and lighter materials to facilitate replanning of internal rooms and alterations to façades. Pipework should be provided in service ducts for future installations using cheap gas, and ducting installed in substructures to accommodate future sewers.

Reinforced concrete does not provide the most effective and economic use of the best characteristic properties of steel and concrete for system building because of the low strength/weight ratio of concrete, the need for tolerances in joints instead of precise connections; hidden deficiencies, dependence upon ancillary works such as shuttering, moulds and scaffolding, and requirements for quality control of mixes and finishes produced by unskilled labour.

More economical design of standardised interchangeable structural elements and cladding units for flexible assembly into a variety of multipurpose tall buildings that provide ready adaptation to future changes in user requirements or improved living standards necessitates the maximum repetition of comparatively few light structural elements which satisfy performance requirements, and combine requisite strength, stiffness, lightness, fire protection, heat and sound insulation, and a variety of pleasing external and internal finishings with precise joints; and standardised cladding units of light materials prefabricated in vast series for rapid erection in multistorey units, incorporating plastic, aluminium or other lightweight material windows to reduce loading and minimise maintenance requirements. In this connection it should be noted that the recently built Greenwich District Hospital was constructed from four standard components but cost £2,138,070, of which £1,118,600 related to mechanical services.

The development of steel frames with central access and service cores, prestressed light-weight aggregate precast concrete floors, and plastic or other light weight materials which eliminate maintenance painting of façades simplifies stress problems by utilising floors to provide stability through acting as beams to bring loads to a central stiffening core. A light steel frame designed to act both as a reinforcement and template for setting out the final construction, provide rapid under cover working for all trades, and lighten loading on foundations, can enable a faster erection cycle to be worked with less ancillary works based on three-storey lifts and simple precision jointing techniques for building types with limited spans.

A suggested system of standardised steel girders and pre-fabricated dropped shuttering for tall composite steel and concrete structures

Reduction in the weight of the steel frame is achieved by standardising light steel sections (e.g. 6 in × 3 in (152 mm × 76 mm) steel tees) for all girders, and encasing them in light weight aggregate concrete of standard profiles with a variety of finishings or facings obtained in the shutters.

Increased loading and spans is readily achieved by additional steel reinforcement, enlarging the concrete casing, prestressing the reinforcement to the concrete casing.

The joints of tee girders to steel columns of the frame are formed by welding on steel plates to the ends of the tees for bolting to the columns.

Standardised prefabricated shutters of steel designed as indicated in Fig. 8.1 page 223 support loads, avoid propping and hoisting to floor levels, and provide many uses. Pulley blocks and chains enable shutters to be lowered down inside the building from the roof steelwork to

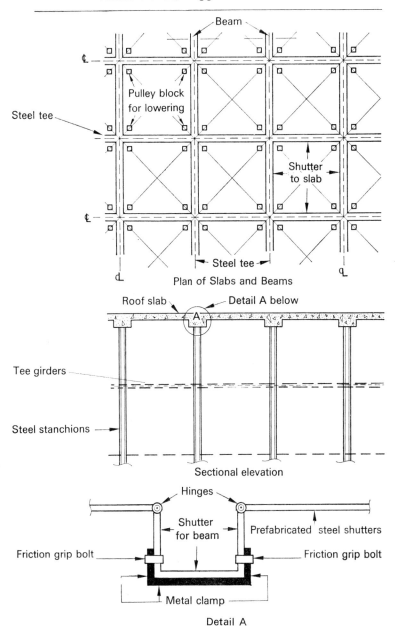

FIG. 8.1. Prefabricated dropped shuttering for in-situ concrete slabs and beams.

provide clear working areas, and use on all successive floors without cranage.

For precast concrete floor and roof construction, the standardised prefabricated shutters to the steel girders are designed to support the ends of the precast units as indicated in Fig. 8.2.

The erection cycle for the structure is based on three-storey lifts, with the central services and access core proceeding three storeys in advance of the main construction to stabilise the frame during erection, and act as a temporary hoist for materials and operatives. The tee girders are

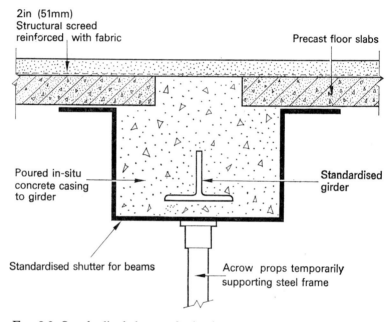

FIG. 8.2. Standardised shutters for in-situ concrete casing to girders.

temporarily supported for the full height of the structure on 'Acrow' props left in until the concrete roof slab is cast as indicated in Fig. 8.3, page 225.

Concreting operations start at roof level, so that the standardised prefabricated shutters can be lowered to the next floor thirty-six hours after pouring, or in less time with accelerated methods of concrete curing. At the third floor below roof level props are inserted, and the suspension device for the shutters is repositioned on the floor underneath

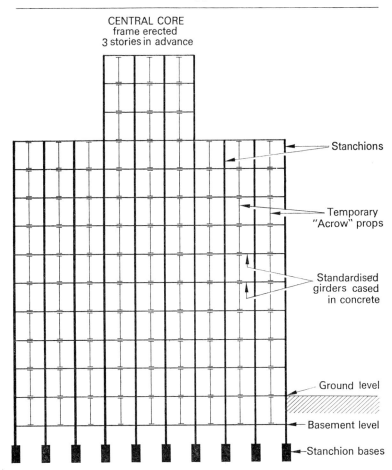

FIG. 8.3. Method of erecting frame.

to enable the roof and two successive floors below to be released for finishing trades.

The cycle of erection operations is planned to take four days per floor so that by the end of four weeks four floors would be concreted, and two floors finished complete ready for handing over to the employer a few months after commencing work on site.

CONCLUSIONS

Force of habit chains us down to a trivial state of thought, from which men like Galileo, Kepler, and Newton could escape by thinking differently, and by so doing penetrate more deeply into the hidden reality behind visible appearances.

Kepler could look at a melting snow crystal and see in it the 'harmony of the spheres'. Newton was able to notice an apple fall from a tree and deduce from the happening that the force causing it to fall was the same force that held the moon in orbit. Many men before Galileo had seen a suspended weight swing in front of their eyes with a measured beat, but he was the first to conceive the notion of applying this to the measurement of time. Samuel Brown, when walking in his garden one day, noticed a tiny spider's web suspended across his path, and the result was the invention of the suspension bridge. The Marquess of Worcester, when confined in prison saw the tight cover of a vessel containing hot water blow off before his eyes, and published the result of this observation in his *Century of Inventions*, which led Savary, Newcomen and Watt to perfect the steam engine.

We forget that we live in a *mysterious* universe, and that the art of living in it is not a mere semi-automated computerised process. Clark-Maxwell's earliest memory was of looking at the sun and *wondering*. Einstein tells us that he 'developed so slowly that he only began to understand about time and space when he was grown up, and in consequence probed deeper into the problem than most men'. Newton, when asked how he came to make his remarkable discoveries replied: 'By thinking deeply upon the problems involved.' There have been remarkable occasions when a scholar working alone without any contact with laboratories has foreseen the existence of quite original and unexpected discoveries in the world of nature, as Hamilton did with his discovery of conical refraction.

Today we can afford no longer to build 'one-off' tailormade schools, dwellings, hospitals, offices and other types of buildings with similar basic requirements. It is essential for the national economy that vast numbers of standardised components are mass produced in factories for open assembly into a variety of different building types, so that the cost of building is reduced to a mere fraction of present-day costs.

Architecture is related to the phenomenal world of appearances, and not to the vaporised world of modern physics, where in any object that appears to the eye as solid and at rest, the smallest particles of which it is constructed are said to be in a violent state of irregular agitation.

If we are to achieve a modern architecture of lasting value and beauty based on programmed system construction, we need to reformulate and develop certain forgotten ideas about 'harmony' and 'proportion' and apply them with discrimination to the correct 'symmetry' of mass produced standardised component parts of buildings that can be rapidly assembled with mechanised erection techniques, and easily jointed. But before this becomes a possibility, we need to acquire a better sense of values, and learn how to see the wood in the trees.

Index

DIS

JUN